MINISTRY NOTICE No. U.S. OF KOREA

T.C. İSTANBUL
ÇIKIŞ
10 11 90 03
3
ATATÜRK HAVA HUDUT KAPISI

DEPARTMENT OF IMMIGRATION
PERMITTED TO ENTER
AUSTRALIA.
24 APR 1986
on
For stay of 12 Month
SYDNEY AIRPORT 54

IMMIGRATION DIVISION BANGKOK THAILAND
A 72 DEPARTED
– 6 FEB 1988
SIGNED

THE INSIDER'S GUIDE TO

TURKEY

IMMIGRATION & ETHNIC AFFAIRS
...........Person
30 OCT 1989
DEPARTED
AUSTRALIA
SYDNEY 32

中华人民共和国
广东省公安厅

上陸許可
ADMITTED
15. FEB. 1986
Status: 4-1-4
Duration: 90 days
NARITA(N)
Immigration Inspector

ADMITTED
20 OCT. 1988
Status: 4-1-16
Duration: 180 days
Port: HANEDA
Signature

No. 011278

日本国

THE UNITED STATES
OF AMERICA
NONIMMIGRANT VISA
ISSUED AT
SSED
Air Port

U.S. IMMIGRATION
170 HHW 1710
JUL 20 1988

HONG KONG
(1038)
– 7 JUN 1987
IMMIGRATION
OFFICER

THE INSIDER'S GUIDES
JAPAN • CHINA • KOREA • HONG KONG • BALI • THAILAND • INDIA • NEPAL • AUSTRALIA
HAWAII • CALIFORNIA • NEW ENGLAND • FLORIDA • MEXICO
THE SOVIET UNION • SPAIN • TURKEY • GREECE
KENYA

The Insider's Guide to Turkey
First Published 1991
Moorland Publishing Co Ltd
Moor Farm Rd., Airfield Estate, Ashbourne, DE61HD, England
By arrangement with CFW Publications Ltd

©1991 CFW Publications Ltd

ISBN: 0 86190 283 1

Created, edited and produced by CFW Publications Ltd
Fax (852) 5438 007
Editor in Chief: Allan Amsel
Original design concept: Hon Bing-wah
Picture editor and designer: Michelle Chan
Text and artwork composed and information updated
using Xerox Ventura software

ACKNOWLEDGMENTS
The Author would like to acknowledge the kind assistance given him by many people,
but particularly by Mrs. Gülsen Kahraman of
the Turkish Ministry of Culture and Tourism.

DEDICATION
For Tim and for Bernard

Printed by Samhwa Printing Co Ltd, Seoul, Korea

THE INSIDER'S GUIDE TO
TURKEY

by Donald Carroll

Photographed by Nik Wheeler

MPC

Contents

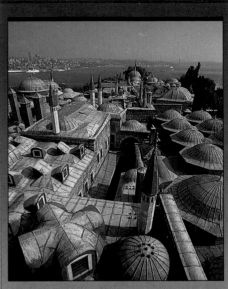

The Neolithic Age • The Bronze Age •
The Dark Age • The Persians and
Greeks • The Romans • The
Byzantine Empire • The Rise of
Islam • The Arrival of the Turks •
The Ottoman Empire • Atatürk
and the Turkish Republic •
Contemporary Turkey

TURKEY

EUROPE

BLACK SEA

BULGARIA

Sinop

Amasra

Kastamonu

Demirköy
Kırklareli
Edirne
Zonguldak
Karabük
Mer

Didymotejchon
Bahaeski
Saray
Çerkezkö
İstanbul Boğazı
Şile
Kandıra
Akçakoca
Ereğli

Lüleburgaz
Ereğli

GREECE
Uzunköprü
Hayrabolu
Çorlu
İSTANBUL
Kartal
İzmit

İpsala
Keşan
MARMARA SEA
Yalova
Gölcük
Adapaza
Ankara
Kırıkkale

Malkara
MARMARA ADASI
Erdek
KAPIDAĞ
Gemlik
İznik Gölü
İznik
Bilecik

Erdek
Erdek Körfezi
YARIMADASI
Bandırma
Mudanya

Saros Körfezi
GELIBOLU
Gelibolu (Gallipoli)
Manyas Gölü
Apolyont Gölü
Bursa
İnegöl
Eskişehir
Polatlı
Hirfanlı Barajı
Kırşehir

YARIMADASI
Biga
Gönen

Çanakkale Boğazı
Çanakkale
Çan

Kulu
Şereflikoçhisar

AEGEAN SEA
Troy (Troia)
Balıkesir
Tuzgölü
Nevşehir

Ezine
Edremit
Niğ

Edremit Körfezi
Burhaniye
Pergamon (Bergama)
Soma
Kırkağaç
Uşak
Afyon
Akşehir
Konya

Ayvalık
LESVOS
Çandarlı Körfezi
Kınık
Akhisar

Aliağa
Manisa

İzmir Körfezi
Menemen
Balçova
Turgutlu
Sarıgöl
Dinar

Çeşme
İzmir
Buca
Karaman

Urla
Gaziemir
Selçuk
Tire
Nazilli
Buldan
Pamukkale

Ephesus
Kuşadası
Aydın
Aphrodisias
Denizli
Karaman
Mit

Kuşadası Körfezi
Söke
Çine
Karacasu
Tavas
Erdemii

Didyma
Milet
Yoran
Güllük
Milâs
Yatağan
Muğla
Kale
Termessos
Perge
Aspendos
Manavgat
Silifke

Güllük Körfezi
Yalikavak
Bodrum
Köyceğiz
Antalya
Side
Alanya

Gökova Körfezi
Reşadiye
YARIMADASI
Marmaris
Fathiye
Elmalı
Anamur

Datça
Fathiye Körfezi
Kalkan
Finike
Antalya Körfezi

Patara
Kaş
Myra

MEDITERRANEAN SEA

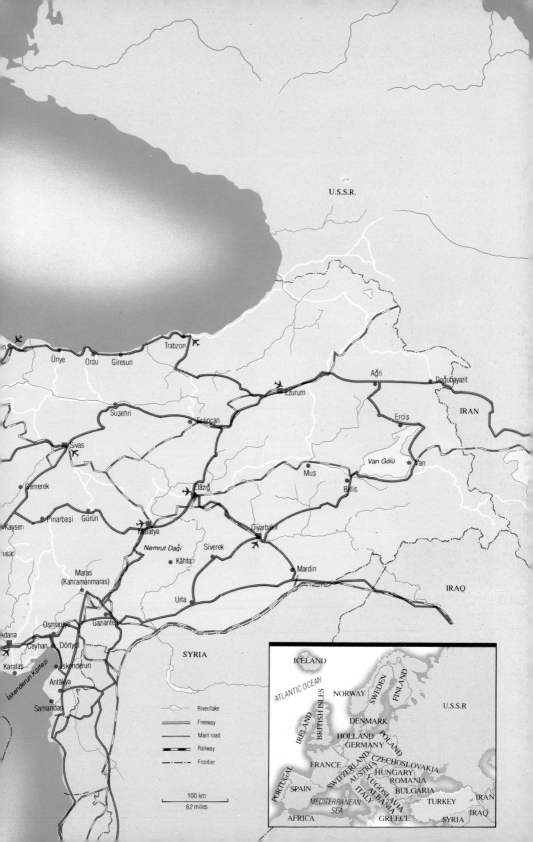

Welcome to Turkey

JUST as one of the first things you will be required to do on entering Turkey is make a Customs declaration, I think it only proper that I should begin this book by declaring what I brought to the writing of it. At the top of the list is a profound fondness for the the country and its people. As this will soon become obvious to even the most inattentive reader, there is no point in trying to smuggle it past you disguised as objectivity. Next is the fact that I have indulged my prejudices rather than tried to compensate for them: if I think one place is twice as interesting as another place, I have devoted twice as much space to it.

I have also in my travels deliberately forsworn the moth-inside-a-lampshade approach, whereby one's efforts are prized according to the amount of territory one covers and the number of boundaries one bumps into. Although I have traveled in every part of the country, and in some parts quite extensively, I haven't attempted to explore every nook and cranny just so I could say that, like Kilroy, "I was here."

I first set foot in Turkey in late February 1985. I had spent the previous autumn and winter in Lindos, on the Greek island of Rhodes, and before returning to London I thought I'd take the opportunity to have a closer look at those shadowy lumps to the east called Turkey. Tellingly, the captain of the little ferry that rolled and splashed its way the 19 km (12 miles) from Rhodes to Marmaris on the Turkish coast had barely finished changing the flag on his mast, replacing the white-on-blue cross of Greece with the white-on-red crescent and star of Turkey, when I found myself already beginning to jettison some of the preconceptions I had about Turkey. One was the assumption that offshore islands like Rhodes were, topographically, merely condensed examples of the mainland: footnotes in the water. In fact, there could hardly have been a sharper contrast between the jagged, rocky landscape we had just left behind and the pine-forested mountains that rose steeply on either side of the deep fjord leading to Marmaris.

The second revelation concerned the Turks themselves. Like most Westerners, I had grown up with the vague conviction that the Turks were bad news. Which is not surprising, considering the bad press they have received in the West. The medieval Church, in its catalogue of the dire consequences of sin, included plagues, floods, comets, earthquakes, and Turks. And in the sixteenth century Martin Luther prayed to be delivered from "the world, the flesh, the Turk and the Devil." This sort of thing can cause a severe image problem. Needless to say, then, I was overjoyed to discover that the image and the reality were not even distantly related. Indeed, I had never come across a friendlier, more hospitable people. I still haven't.

The third revelation was the food. It was, in a word, delicious. I had always been fond of most of the Greek and Middle Eastern dishes with which I was familiar, but it had never occurred to me that they were merely inferior provincial variations on the great theme of Turkish cuisine.

After a couple of days of enjoying the warmth of one's welcome and the irresistibility of one's meals, I rented a car with the intention of driving, in leisurely stages, to Istanbul. My first stop was Bodrum, 165 km (102 miles) up the coast. Best known as a holiday resort, with its forest of yacht masts tilting in the harbor below the magnificent Crusader castle, it turned out to be, even in the blustery February chill, a town of unsuspected charm as well as the gateway to a peninsula of infinite and seductive beauty. Two months later I was still there — while 25 km (16 miles) away, near the fishing village of Yalıkavak, tractors and camels were carrying building materials up a mountainside to an olive grove overlooking the Aegean where I had decided to build a house. In the end it took 15 months and almost as many crises to complete and furnish the house, but it was well worth it. Today I spend at least four months of the year there — and they are always the happiest four.

In the years since I first stepped off the ferry in Marmaris I have learned much about the Turkish character, some of it quite surprising. What is not at all surprising, after only a short time in the country, is the friendliness of the people. And it is absolutely genuine. Tourists are naturally inclined to sus-

The surreal "fairy chimneys" near Göreme in Cappadocia. These strange shapes, formed by volcanic lava, were homes to the area's earliest inhabitants.

pect that when they are plied with little glasses of tea in shops, or when shopkeepers insist on chatting to them, or when waiters are eager to know where they are from, they are being wooed as customers. But in fact I can honestly say that I don't know one Turk who wouldn't rather make friends than make money. Friendship is very important to the Turks.

So is sincerity. With rare exceptions, the Turks are utterly without artifice, though they are quick to spot insincerity in others. Indeed, their lack of false emotion can be unsettling at first. I will give an example.

During the building of my house I was introduced to the wife of one of the workers, and when I enquired about her children she explained that she had once had three but now had only two because she had boiled her baby to death. It seems that she had been boiling milk to make yogurt, and when she nipped outside for a brief moment to check on her other two children the infant somehow managed to tumble into the vat of scalding milk. The child took nine agonizing days to die. The point of this horrific story is that it was told to me matter-of-factly, almost offhandedly. I found this difficult to comprehend until, later, I realized that the poor in Turkey simply cannot afford the luxury of useless emotions, such as, in this instance, prolonged grief. Life is hard enough without carrying an added burden of one's own making, and they are too honest to pretend that they *are* thus burdened.

Such stoicism might give the impression that the Turks are a dour lot. Nothing could be more mistaken. They have a deliciously subtle sense of humor. I remember on my

first visit to Istanbul I decided to telephone a shipping executive whose business card I had with me as a souvenir of a most convivial evening in Bodrum. After agreeing to meet for dinner, I tried to determine how far his office was from my hotel. He said his office was in Karaköy. "Oh," I said, looking at my map, "you're on the other side of the bridge." "No," he deadpanned, "I'm in Karaköy. *You* are on the other side of the bridge."

It is no accident that the most popular figure in Turkish folklore is the Hoca, a mythical comic hero in whose jokes one finds distilled the Turkish sense of the absurd mixed in with some shrewd observations on human behavior. In one such joke a man asks to borrow a saucepan from his neighbor. The neighbor grumbles, but grudgingly agrees to lend it on condition that it is returned promptly. The next day it is returned together with another, smaller saucepan. "What's this?" asks the neighbor. "Your saucepan had a baby," the man smilingly tells him. The neighbor is delighted, and thus only too happy to lend the saucepan the next time the man asks to borrow it. This time, however, it is not returned. Many days pass, until the neighbor is forced to ask for it back. Mournfully, the man tells him that the saucepan has died. "What do you mean?" demands the neighbor. "A saucepan can't die." The man shrugs. "You were prepared to believe that it could have a baby, so you must believe it could die."

In another typical Hoca joke a neighbor who is widely disliked for his tendency to borrow things and not return them asks the man next door if he will lend him his rope. "I can't," says the man, "my wife is busy spreading flour on it." "You must be joking!" exclaims the importunate neighbor. "No," the man says, "I'm perfectly serious." Whereupon the neighbor demands to know how it's possible to spread flour on a rope. "If I don't want to lend someone my rope," the man explains, "flour can very easily be spread on it."

Fittingly, the tomb of the Hoca at Akşehir is "protected" by an iron gate secured with a large padlock. But as the gate isn't attached to anything one can walk right in.

What is perhaps most striking, though, about the Turkish character is the bundle of contradictions of which it is made. On the one hand, for instance, the Turks have a well-earned reputation as fearsome warriors and as a people ferociously dedicated to their independence. On the other hand, there is a curious passivity in their nature, a meek willingness to submit to authority. T.E. Lawrence — admittedly a biased witness — once said that if you went into a crowded railway station in Turkey and shouted "Sit down!" loudly enough, everybody would do so and nobody would ask why. Likewise, the Turks manage to combine extravagant and heartfelt hospitality with a strain of xenophobia that makes them suspicious of and resistant to outside influences. (An otherwise cosmopolitan friend once declined to join me for a Chinese meal on the grounds that "a Turkish man doesn't eat with sticks.") And the same country that has produced millions of emigrant laborers who are acknowledged to be the hardest workers in Europe has also produced legions of men who will do nothing more strenuous in life than throw a pair of dice or hold a few playing cards.

And more contradictions… Turks are defiantly proud of their Turkishness, and yet at the same time nurse an inferiority complex about their place in the world. Turks are individually the most helpful people in the world, and collectively the most unhelpful. To illustrate: on three occasions, in different parts of Turkey, my car has broken down. On each occasion, the very first motorist (or, in one case, cyclist) who came upon me stopped to help — and, when needed, went to summon more help. Similarly, some visiting Americans had a flat tire late one night on their way back to Bodrum from my house, only to discover that the car had no jack in it. Once again, the first person to notice their predicament stopped, sized up the situation, and then went off and rounded up enough men to hold up the car long enough for the tire to be changed!

By contrast, however, when I wanted to leave Turkey without the car, which I had driven there from London, I was not permitted to go unless I took the car with me. When I offered to donate it to a hospital for use as an emergency vehicle, or to give it to a village as transport for the elderly, or simply to hand it over to any municipal government that could find a use for it, I was forced to run the gauntlet of an endless phalanx of

Sheep near the Zigana Pass, where Xenophon's soldiers are reputed to have cried "The sea! The sea!" Given the creatures' tendency to occupy the roads, it is quite possible that the Greeks were shouting "The sheep! The sheep!" OPPOSITE: Welcome to the world of *simit*, a snack on the run.

petty officials whose sole purpose in life, or so it seemed, was to generate vast quantities of paperwork for each other to sign or initial and then pass on so that other papers could be attached requiring further signatures and initials before being forwarded for review to other authorities who would have some forms of their own to be filled out and then approved and initialed and so on and on and on. Eventually I was defeated by what Philip Glazebrook has called the Turkish bureaucratic conspiracy "to extinguish, rather than to forbid, the individual's wish to do something awkward."

So, in the final analysis, what emerges from this mixture of hospitality and nationalism, gentleness and militarism, piety and mischievousness, playful wit and silent suffering, warmth and skepticism, industry and idleness, kindness and inefficiency? What emerges is a people who are in many respects uncannily like the Irish. If you like the Irish — as I do — you'll love the Turks. And, as in Ireland, you will be made to feel specially welcome. Indeed, the Turkish language, like Gaelic, has built into it a special way of saying "Welcome!"

Among the first things you will notice in this welcoming land are the large numbers of soldiers and schoolchildren. They are both around for the same reason: they have no choice. Both male military service and primary education are compulsory in Turkey, and with the country's high birth rate this means there are a lot of Turks either in the olive green uniform of the army or the black

The Country and Its People

THE HISTORICAL BACKGROUND

Unfortunately for anyone who would attempt to summarize it, the history of Turkey is as complex as it is long. And it is very long indeed. Whether you choose to believe the mythologists or the archaeologists, Anatolia — Asian Turkey — has always been at the center of human history. The Garden of Eden is meant to have been between the Tigris and Euphrates rivers, both of which rise in the highlands of eastern Anatolia, and after the

Flood Noah's Ark is said to have come to rest on Mt. Ararat, also in the east. In the west, not far from Istanbul, the earliest human remains ever found outside Africa — over one million years old — were discovered by archaeologists in 1986. And in the south, below Konya, is Çatal Höyük, the site of the world's oldest known human community, a Stone Age "city" dating back to about 7500 BC. Yes, a long history.

ABOVE: Collections at the Ankara Museum. OPPOSITE LEFT: One of the statues of the multi-breasted Artemis in the splendid little Ephesu· Museum. RIGHT: The statue of King Heykele of Aslantepe in Ankara's Museum of Anatolian Civilizations.

THE NEOLITHIC AGE

The people of Çatal Höyük derived their livelihood from agriculture, for which they invented an urban irrigation system, and from trading in obsidian, a dark, glassy volcanic rock found locally which was ideal for primitive tool-making. Excavations have revealed that the city covered about 13 hectares (32 acres), and may have been home to as many as 5,000 people, who somehow found the time to produce some quite

remarkable religious shrines, frescoes, pottery, and statuettes, many of which are on exhibit in Ankara's Museum of Anatolian Civilizations.

The city seems to have survived intact for about 2,000 years and then, for reasons we will probably never know, was abandoned by its inhabitants. At about the same time, around 5500 BC, the neolithic city of Hacılar sprang up near Burdur, to the west of Çatal Höyük. Hacılar is noteworthy not only because it produced some splendid painted pottery, and because here implements of copper began to replace those made of stone, but also because it is the first city known to have had houses arranged along "streets", as well as having the first houses with doors.

THE BRONZE AGE

For the next three millennia Anatolian civilization went through a long night of hibernation, until jolted awake around 2500 BC by the Hatti people, who built major cities at Kültepe, near Kayseri, and in the Kızılırmak valley northeast of Ankara. For the next 500 years the Hattian culture flourished, producing some of the loveliest works of art of the Bronze Age.

Around 2000 BC the Hatti were overwhelmed by an invading force of Thracian

cousins: the Trojan War. This was followed by a devastating invasion by waves of warriors from the islands in the Aegean. The invasion succeeded in obliterating Hittite civilization so thoroughly that it is only within the last hundred years or so that scholars have been able to confirm that these extremely civilized and advanced people ever existed at all.

THE DARK AGE

With the fall of Hattuşaş around 1200 BC Anatolia entered a dark age lasting for over

warriors known as Hittites. The Hittites built themselves a great capital at Hattuşaş, about 200 km (125 miles) east of Ankara, and for the next eight centuries developed a culture of enormous political and artistic sophistication. In addition, they became an imperial power, perennially jousting with Egypt for control of the Middle East. Finally, after wresting Syria from the Egyptians and then crushing the armies of the great pharaoh Rameses II, a peace treaty was concluded by the Hittites and the Egyptians in 1259 BC — the first recorded peace treaty in history.

Alas for the Hittite empire, the peace that it heralded did not last long. In the west, the Greeks in Troy and elsewhere along the coast came under attack from their Mycenaean

five centuries. The social and cultural cohesion that had existed under the Hittites disintegrated as new arrivals from every direction either overwhelmed or joined forces with native peoples to create a vast jigsaw puzzle of smaller states stretching across Asia Minor. In the east were the Urartians, who established a kingdom around Lake Van which by 750 BC extended all the way to the Caspian Sea. Weakened by repeated assaults from the Assyrians, they were finally overrun by the Scythians in 612 BC. In the west, the Phrygians swept in from Thrace and established a kingdom with its capital at Gordium, southwest of Ankara. The Phrygians were an exceptionally artistic people, and in the ruins near Gordium one can see the world's earliest known mosaic. After a series of defeats at the hands of aggressive neighboring states — leading to the suicide in 695 BC of their legendary King Midas — the Phrygians were finally conquered by the Lydians in 650 BC.

The Lydians, whose capital was at Sardis, east of Izmir, were as good at commerce as they were at conquest. Not only did they invent money as we know it — the idea of minting coins came from the Lydians — but they produced someone spectacularly gifted at producing it — their King Croesus. South of Lydia was Caria, which had as its capital Halicarnassus (modern Bodrum). Very much influenced by the Dorian Greeks, the Carians were to give the world the man every schoolchild knows as "the father of history," Herodotus. Southeast of Caria was the kingdom of Lycia, which occupied the southwest corner of Anatolia and left behind little of interest apart from the stunning rock tombs carved into the cliffs along the coast.

With so many small kingdoms jostling for space and power across Anatolia, and with various predatory armies from abroad making forays across the land, it is hardly surprising that the 500 years following the fall of the Hittites were distinguished by little more than constant turmoil. The exception to this generally bleak period in Anatolian life occurred in the Greek settlements along the Aegean coast. There, in the Ionian cities of Smyrna (modern Izmir), Phocaea, Ephesus, Priene, Miletus, in Aeolia, and to a lesser extent in the Dorian cities further south, Hellenic culture took root and flourished in a way that it never did in Greece itself until after 546 BC, when the Persians under Cyrus the Great stormed across Anatolia and subdued all its peoples.

THE PERSIANS AND GREEKS

For the next two centuries all of Anatolia was a part of the Persian Empire, although the Ionian cities were to prove a constant thorn in the imperial side, frequently rising up against their new masters. Nevertheless, the Persians proved to be remarkably enlightened rulers and the light of classical Greek civilization in Ionia was hardly dimmed. Then in 334 BC Alexander the Great crossed the Dardanelles and rolled back the tide of Persian domination, replacing it with an empire of his own that made Anatolia one of the heartlands of Hellenistic (and therefore Western) civilization.

Upon Alexander's death in 323 BC in Babylon, at the age of 33, his empire quickly became fragmented as his generals fought among themselves for power and territory. Yet despite the wars that raged back and forth across the vast territory that the young Macedonian had conquered, the seeds of Greek culture that he had sown continued to sprout, ensuring that even after his death the Hellenization of Anatolia proceeded uninterrupted.

The peace, on the other hand, continued to be interrupted by civil wars and invasions, the most notable of the latter being the invasion in 275 BC of the Galatians, a Celtic people who established their capital at Ankara and went on to rule most of western Anatolia. Their contribution to Turkish history is most evident today in the startling number of Turks with red hair, green eyes, and freckles. Of the number of other kingdoms dotted around Anatolia at this time, by far the most interesting was that of Pergamon, which was both powerful and committed to the encouragement of the arts and learning. The kings of Pergamon also made the wise strategic move of co-operating with the Romans, who were beginning to extend their empire, little by little, east of the Aegean. Finally, in 133 BC, the last king of Pergamon, the eccentric Attalus III, to the dismay of his subjects bequeathed his kingdom to Rome. The Romans called it the Province of Asia, and made Ephesus its capital.

THE ROMANS

For the next four centuries the spreading Roman hegemony in Anatolia brought unprecedented prosperity to the area as a whole and a special grandeur to the great cities like Ephesus, Smyrna, and Antioch (modern Antakya), where Antony and Cleopatra were married in 40 BC. Coincidentally, the two lovers had met in Tarsus, near the south coast, where a few decades later St. Paul was born — the man whose travels and preaching through Anatolia were to become a major nuisance to Rome, and *the* major contribution to the spread of Christianity.

In the two centuries that followed St. Paul's tireless evangelism, the new religion grew from being a nuisance to being a threat, at a time when Rome was already under threat from the waves of barbarians from northern Europe as well as from the newly militant Persian Empire to the east. In 268 AD tribes of Goths rampaged into Anatolia, laying waste to Ankara and other cities. The Roman Empire began to crumble, and towards the end of the third century split in half. The emperor Diocletian made Byzantium the capital of the eastern empire, reorganized

under the emperor Justinian (527–565), who extended its dominion to include Spain, Italy, the Balkans, and all of North Africa. He also codified Roman law and presided over a building program in Constantinople that culminated in the magnificent cathedral of Aya Sofia, which for 900 years was the undisputed jewel in the crown of Christendom and remains today one of the most awesome edifices ever erected.

Inwardly, however, the empire was showing signs of dry rot as early as Justinian's reign. Once the empire had been

the whole system of government, and then in 303 made one last savage effort to stamp out Christianity. It didn't work. Within two years he had abdicated. His successor, Constantine the Great, reunited the empire, accepted Christianity, convened the historic Council of Nicaea (modern Iznik) in 325, and rebuilt Byzantium into a great capital city which in 330 was dedicated as New Rome. It soon came to be known as Constantinople, and as such was to be the center of the Byzantine Empire for over a thousand years.

THE BYZANTINE EMPIRE

Outwardly, the Byzantine Empire went from strength to strength, reaching its zenith

stretched around the entire Mediterranean, its resources became overstretched and its people, especially in Anatolia, overtaxed. Then the empire's population was decimated by a terrible plague, and soon afterwards the Lombards overran Italy while the province along the Danube came under attack from the Avars. Thus weakened from without and within, Byzantine Anatolia was in no condition to fend off the Persians who swarmed in and destroyed Ankara, as well as other cities, in 622.

The partially-reconstructed Temple of Hadrian in Ephesus, which was completed in 138 AD. The archway friezes have been reconstructed from the originals now in the Ephesus Museum.

THE RISE OF ISLAM

The year 622 was a fateful one for the Byzantine Empire, and indeed the world, for yet another reason: that was the year the prophet Mohammed fled from Mecca to Medina, where he established the third great religion to come out of this part of the world, Islam. Actually, it would be more accurate to say that Islam *erupted* out of this part of the world, for by 636 fierce armies of Muslim Arabs were storming out of the desert and biting off huge chunks of the Byzantine Empire. By 654 most of Anatolia had been put to the sword by the invaders, and within two decades Constantinople itself was under siege from the Arabs. The attack was finally beaten off, as was a second one 40 years later, but by the middle of the eighth century Muslim rule was firmly entrenched in eastern Anatolia. Two strikingly dissimilar cultures — one Byzantine and Christian, the other Arab and Muslim — now inhabited the same peninsula.

Still, despite all the centuries of attacking and defending, expanding and contracting, the Byzantines were not yet a spent force. Beginning in 867, with the accession to the throne (via assassination) of the emperor Basil I, Byzantium entered a golden age of cultural revival, political stability, and military conquest. But the end of this amazingly durable empire was nonetheless approaching.

THE ARRIVAL OF THE TURKS

The beginning of the end can be dated precisely. It happened on August 19, 1071, at Manzíkert, north of Lake Van, where a mounted army of central Asian nomads known as Seljuk Turks — from the Chinese *Tu-kueh* — annihilated a Byzantine force 10 times their size, and, to add insult to injury, captured the Byzantine emperor and held him for ransom. By the time the ransom was paid the emperor had been deposed, and the Turks were pouring into Asia Minor. They quickly established control over most of Anatolia,

making their headquarters first at Nicaea and then at Konya, where they ruled their newly-conquered territories with a mixture of strength and enlightenment that rapidly turned their new state into a model of good government and often great art, much of which can still be seen in and around Konya.

However, because the Seljuks were not only powerful but Muslim, having been converted to Islam in the tenth century, the Crusades were launched in 1096 by European Christians to rescue the Holy Land from these marauders. The Crusaders had only very limited success against the Seljuks, so in 1204 the Crusaders of the Fourth Crusade decided to sack Christian Constantinople, where the Byzantines still continued to hang on to the remnants of their empire. And they hung on for another 250 years. The Seljuks, alas, remained a force for only another 40 years, until in 1243 they were destroyed by the Mongol hordes at the Battle of Kösedağ. But the seeds had been planted: thanks to the Seljuks there was now in Anatolia truly Turkish art and architecture, Turkish literature and music.

In other words, there was now the distinctive foundation of what would later be called Turkey.

THE OTTOMAN EMPIRE

The end of the thirteenth century saw the appearance of a new Turkish tribe, the Ottomans. In 1326 they took Bursa, south of Constantinople, and made it their capital; in 1354 they made their first, successful drive into Europe. A century later, in 1453, with all of the Balkans under their control, the Ottomans under Mehmet the Conqueror took Constantinople. The city that had survived for more than a thousand years as the heart of the Roman and Byzantine empires, as the great citadel of eastern Christendom, finally disappeared into history. Among Mehmet's first acts was a visit to Aya Sofia, where he knelt in prayer after declaring it a mosque; a few days later he declared that the city should be known as Islamboul, the "city of Islam".

The age of Constantinople was over, the age of Istanbul was about to begin.

The Ottoman Empire experienced its greatest glory during the reign of Süleyman

The elaborately tiled entrance to a mosque in Divriği, near Nemrut Daği.

the Magnificent from 1520 to 1566. It was a time when imperial expansion abroad was mirrored by social and cultural advancement at home. After Süleyman's death the empire continued to expand until it blanketed the map from Vienna to Mecca, but the decadence and incompetence of the sultans who followed Süleyman guaranteed the inexorable decline and ultimate fall of the empire. By the middle of the nineteenth century the Ottomans were exhausted by their frequent wars with the Russians, who coveted the Bosphorus with its access to the Mediter-

ranean. Moreover, their territory had shrunk as a result of the successful wars waged by the Greeks, who gained their independence in 1829, and by the Serbians, Bulgarians, and Egyptians.

In 1830 a campaign of reform was instituted to try to halt the empire's disintegration, but by now it was too late.

Besides, the reform process was interrupted by the Crimean War (1853–1856), in which Britain and France rushed to help the Ottomans repulse yet another Russian onslaught. Although the war was won, and the reforms reinstated, the empire continued to crumble as more pieces fell off in the wake of nationalist rebellions. As the situation became more desperate, an underground group of intellectuals calling itself the Committee for Union and Progress was formed to promote — by whatever means — a radical restructuring of what was left of the Ot-

Equestrian statues of Atatürk, the father of modern Turkey, can be seen throughout the country. This one is in Izmir.

toman Empire. Known in the Western press as the "Young Turks", they finally succeeded in deposing the deranged and despised Sultan Abdul Hamid in 1909, but before they could accomplish anything they were embroiled in the Balkan Wars of 1912–1913, during which Macedonia and western Thrace were lost. Then, of course, came World War I.

Thanks in part to a massive diplomatic blunder by the British, and a correspondingly brilliant maneuver by the Germans, Turkey entered the war on the side of Germany and the Central powers. With the Allied victory in 1918, the Ottoman Empire ceased to exist.

ATATÜRK AND THE TURKISH REPUBLIC

The question then was who would get the leftovers. There was no shortage of hungry claimants, and they all came to the table with their knives sharpened. The British and French carved off the bits they wanted, and then invited others to help themselves. The Greeks were the first to accept, eagerly occupying Smyrna (Izmir) in May, 1919, and then striking into the Turkish interior. But they came up against a problem. It was the same problem the Allies had come up against when they invaded Gallipoli in 1915. The problem was called Mustafa Kemal.

Mustafa Kemal was born in Macedonia in 1881, and as a young infantry colonel masterminded the brilliant defense of Gallipoli against the overwhelming numerical superiority of the the invading Allied armies. An ardent nationalist, he was dismayed after the war to see foreigners dividing up his country while the superannuated Ottoman authorities yawned and looked the other way. He traveled the country setting up nationalist congresses and generally rallying people to the cause of republican revolution. With the Greeks entrenched on the Aegean coast and other occupying forces nibbling away at Anatolia, he established his headquarters at Ankara and in 1920 convened the first Turkish National Assembly. Apart from setting up a provisional government, Kemal also created a new army to defend Ankara against the advancing Greeks. In August 1921, in what is said to have been the longest pitched battle in history, Kemal's army defeated the Greeks at Sakarya. The Greeks then began a retreat that ended in Izmir in September 1922. With the city in flames, what was left of the Greek invading force fled back across the sea. A year later the Turkish Republic was proclaimed, with Mustafa Kemal as its first president. Later, grateful citizens of the nation that was born under Mustafa Kemal gave him the name Atatürk, "Father of the Turks."

By any measure, Kemal Atatürk must be reckoned one of the greatest leaders of modern times; by any measure I would apply, he is easily *the* foremost leader of the twentieth century. Consider: in the short span of 15 years, from the founding of the republic in 1923 to his tragically early death in 1938, Atatürk single-handedly transformed the ravaged remains of a backward, corrupt, militaristic, Islamic empire into a modern, democratic, secular state living in peace with its neighbors.

Even that triumphal summary scarcely does justice to his achievement. To appreciate better the scope of Atatürk's impact on the history of his nation one needs to inventory — however incompletely — the individual changes he wrought in the life of his people. I will take only the most salient examples. At Atatürk's behest:

— the sultanate was abolished, ending a 641-year-old dynasty;

— the capital was moved from Istanbul to Ankara;

— Islam ceased to be the state religion;

— all religious orders and foundations were closed, and civil weddings were required in place of religious ones;

— polygamy was abolished and equal rights for women were written into the law;

— the wearing of the fez, the turban, the yashmak and other traditional Islamic and Ottoman headgear was banned;

— the Swiss Legal Code was adopted as the backbone of the Turkish system of civil justice, replacing Koranic law;

— the rapid (and expensive) modernization of agriculture, industry, and communication was begun;

— the Islamic calendar was replaced by the Christian calendar, and the day of rest was moved from Friday to Sunday;

— the international metric system of weights and measures was adopted;

— women were given the right to vote;

— the Arabic alphabet was replaced by the Roman alphabet;

— all Turks were required to take a Western-style family name in addition to their Muslim given names.

In short, the Turks were asked — no, told — to change overnight their centuries-old habits, their dress, their forms of worship, their attitudes towards women, their calendar, their alphabet, and even their names. And they did!

What's more, they thanked their leader for this unprecedented upheaval in their lives, and gave him the surname Atatürk in gratitude, and today honor his memory with statues, portraits, and ceremonial tributes all across the land. Now *that's* leadership.

Atatürk's only failure was not really his, but his liver's. Being committed to play as well as to work, he died of cirrhosis on November 10, 1938, at the age of 57. This deprived Turkey of his genius at a time when the infant republic needed all the help it could get. He was succeeded by his old friend and comrade Ismet Inönü, who kept Turkey neutral during World War II and who after the war was so scrupulous in pursuing the ideal of a truly democratic state that he made possible his own defeat in the election of 1950.

CONTEMPORARY TURKEY

Unfortunately for the fledgling democracy, the party in power for the next decade proceeded to prove that, in the wrong hands, power does indeed corrupt. Whereupon in 1960 the army stepped in and arrested Prime Minister Adnan Menderes and members of his government. After lengthy trials, all were found guilty of violating the constitution and sentenced to death, though only Menderes was actually executed. In the following year elections were held and civilian government was restored.

In 1970 the army again intervened when the government of the day showed more taste for ruling than for governing. As before, once the situation had been normalized elections were held and democracy was restored. During the seventies, however, terrorism pushed the young nation into a crisis that could have ended forever democracy's chance of taking root in Turkey. On the left there was the physical terrorism of the guerrillas who carried out murderous attacks on innocent civilians throughout the country. On the right was the ideological terrorism of the Muslim fanatics who thought they saw their chance to turn Turkey into a mullah-ridden theocracy like the Iran of the ayatollahs. And in the middle were the two principal parliamentary parties, who were so ineffectual and so paralyzed by their inability to act in concert that the entire economy, not to mention law and order, came dangerously close to collapse.

Thus, in 1980, for the third time in 20 years, the army rode to the rescue. In any context other than Turkey, that would be a facetious — if not downright sarcastic — way of characterizing a military coup. But what one must remember is that in Turkey the army is the proud legatee of Atatürk's idealism: when they move in it is for the sole purpose of underpinning, not undermining, the vision of a Western-style democracy that Atatürk left behind. Consequently, the Turkish people heaved a collective sigh of relief when the army, under General Kenan Evren, took over the government on September 12, 1980.

After restoring order to a nation on the brink of chaos and civil war, the army over-

saw the redrafting of the Turkish constitution, in order to introduce legal means of breaking up the sort of parliamentary logjams that had previously crippled the government's ability to respond in a crisis. The new constitution was submitted to the people in a plebiscite and overwhelmingly approved. General Evren subsequently resigned from the army on his election to the presidency, an office that at this writing he still occupies, and with his popularity among the people still undiminished. In 1983, the first parliamentary elections were held under the new constitution, which gave a surprise victory to the newly-formed Motherland Party under Turgut Özal, a decidedly uncharismatic economist who as Prime Minister has quietly and effectively led Turkey towards becoming the nation Atatürk envisaged by peacefully consolidating its position as a bulwark of NATO while at the same time streamlining its economy in preparation for Turkey's anticipated entry into the European Economic Community.

It would seem that, happily for everyone, Atatürk's legacy is at last in safe hands.

GEOGRAPHY AND CLIMATE

Now, having tried to give some idea of Turkey's long and fascinating past, I will try to give some idea of its vastly interesting present.

Yes, the adverb is a pun. Turkey *is* vast. It covers 780,000 sq km (over 300,000 sq miles), an area roughly equivalent to that of France and West Germany combined. Proceeding clockwise from the west, it is bordered by Greece, Bulgaria, the Soviet Union, Iran, Iraq, and Syria. And by the sea: about 75 percent of Turkey's frontier — almost 8,400 km (5,200 miles) — is coastline. From east to west the country extends almost 1,600 km (992 miles), and from north to south 650 km (404 miles). The country's highest peak is Ağri Dağ (Mt. Ararat) at 5,165 m (16,950 ft), near the Soviet border, the longest river is the Kızılırmak at 1,355 km (840 miles), which flows into the Black Sea northwest of Samsun, and the largest lake is the gigantic Lake Van at 3,738 sq km (1,443 sq miles) near the Iranian border. But the numbers tell only a small part of the story. What is so stunning about Turkey physically — and what is much more impressive than the distances involved — is the amazing topographical and climatic diversity of the country.

In the north, the Black Sea coast from Istanbul eastwards is a temperate zone with considerable year-round rainfall and high humidity. Backed up to the south by two large mountain ranges, it has lush green forests with such European trees as oak, beech, ash, and juniper, as well as orchards of cherries (for which the region is famous), apples, oranges, and pears. The coastal landscape — and economy — is also noted for its hazelnut groves, tobacco fields and, further east, its tea plantations. In the west, the Aegean coastal region has a climate that features very warm summers and, except in the north, very mild winters. Its fertile plains are dotted with fields of cotton, tobacco, corn, and sunflowers, while the hillsides are often covered with olive and fig groves. In addition, in the spring much of the region is carpeted with a dazzling variety of wildflowers; indeed, there are said to be over 8,000 different species of wildflowers in Turkey.

In the south, along the Mediterranean, the summers tend to be very hot, often rising above 38°C (100°F), while the winters are exceptionally mild, seldom dipping below 10°C (50°F). As a result, Mediterranean Turkey enjoys the longest swimming season of any stretch of coast along the entire northern Mediterranean. As with the Black Sea coast, mountains form a dramatic backdrop to the area, with the mighty Taurus range scraping the sky from behind Antalya over to the alluvial plain surrounding Adana. The vegetation is also noticeably tropical: palm trees and banana trees abound, as do fields of cotton and sugar cane. In the southeast the land is mostly flat and dry and the temperature is mostly unbearable — unbearably hot in summer and unbearably cold in winter. In the east, where it is mountainous, the thermometer rises and falls by an astonishing 150 degrees Fahrenheit, ranging from 38°C (100°F) in the summer to -45°C (-50°F) in winter, when heavy snowfalls often leave towns and villages cut off for days at a time.

Central Anatolia — that is, the rest of the country — is an immense high plateau where the altitude seldom slips below 1,000 m (3,281 ft) and which rises, unevenly but inexorably, mountain range by mountain range, up to the majestic peaks in the east. When the land isn't surging up mountainously, it mostly consists of great undulating plains either planted with wheat or sprinkled with grazing animals. And splashed down in the middle of all this are many lakes, some of them enormous. Central Anatolia is hot and dry in summer, bitterly cold in winter.

No less remarkable than the variety of flora to be found in Turkey is the variety of

fauna. Apart from being home to an estimated 25 million goats, more than in any other country, and many of which seem to spend their time in the middle of the road, Turkey has a large population of wild boars, brown bears, and wolves. There are lynxes and leopards in the Black Sea forests, hyenas in the central steppeland, gazelles in the Aegean mountains, and still many camels to be seen along the Aegean coast.

Unfortunately, what can also be seen almost everywhere in Turkey today, except in the more remote parts of the east and southeast, is a rash of new buildings. Wherever you go the country seems to be in a frenzy of construction. Now this in itself is not necessarily a bad thing; indeed, it may be a sign of a healthy economy (although it is probably also a symptom of an unhealthy inflation rate). What makes it a bad thing is the uniform

OPPOSITE: Man and donkey: a familiar sight throughout Turkey. ABOVE: Fishermen near Adana, on the Mediterranean coast, hauling in their nets.

lack of distinction of the buildings that are being built. Part of the problem is with the materials themselves. The Turkish architectural genius, which flourished for centuries, is for producing ornate masterpieces, and as such was ideally suited to expression in wood and stone and tile; with concrete it has been reduced to a talent for mass-producing cubes. To see a Turkish housing development is to be reminded of Pete Seeger's song, *Little Boxes* ("made of ticky-tacky"). Another problem is the speed with which these things are being built, especially in the big cities and

tourist areas, where the demand for housing and hotel space is greatest. This leads invariably to shoddy workmanship. I was once the guest of a wealthy Turkish friend in his holiday house in an exclusive hillside by the sea. Though the house was barely two years old, it was already in an alarming state of dilapidation, as were the houses around it. It was as if a Brazilian architect had hit on the idea of upmarket *favelas* — a kind of shanty town for the rich. It is depressing to think that in their haste to accommodate tourists who want to visit the ancient ruins, the Turks may be putting up instant ruins.

THE GOVERNMENT AND THE ECONOMY

Despite the sometimes violent growing pains suffered by the young Turkish democracy, it has emerged in remarkably good shape. It has a constitution that was overwhelmingly endorsed by the electorate; it has a 450-seat, popularly-elected parliament, the Grand National Assembly; it has an executive president elected by the Assembly who serves one seven-year term; it has a governing party which under Turgut Özal has won two consecutive general elections; abroad, it has excellent diplomatic relations with all countries; at home, it has free, compulsory education, a rapidly-improving public health service, a low crime rate, an expanding economy, a free press, and freedom of religion.

The only dark spot in all this is that the expansion of the economy has come at a high price: Turkey has a colossal foreign debt and inflation that is currently pushing 75 percent. Of course, such problems are hardly surprising when you consider that what the government is trying to do is nothing less than graft a modern, industrial state on to a medieval agrarian society. What is surprising is the degree of success with which this has been accomplished. Although it is still not uncommon to see the lone peasant squatting in the shade of a tree watching his cow and perhaps a couple of sheep grazing, Turkish agriculture as a whole has been transformed into a major earner of foreign exchange. Turkey is already the world's largest exporter of hazelnuts, figs, raisins, and Oriental tobacco, and Europe's largest supplier of wool. Cotton and citrus fruits are also big money-earners. With 40 percent of the country's total surface now under cultivation, and with a huge dam-building and irrigation program under way, Turkish agriculture should soon be making an even bigger contribution to the country's economy.

Meanwhile, the government has been moving vigorously to develop the country's industrial base. As might be expected, much of Turkish industry is devoted to the processing of agricultural products and the manufacture of agricultural machinery. The manufacture of textiles, another leading export, also plays a big part. So, increasingly, does the manufacture of automobiles. And with Turkey's abundant resources of chromium, iron, and copper, more emphasis is being placed on the metallurgical industry. The country is even beginning to export its engineering skills along with part of its labor force, and some huge construction deals have recently been signed with several OPEC countries.

Yet even with the spectacular progress the economy has made over the past few years, Turkey is still plagued by a chronic unemployment rate that hovers around 20 percent. And this in a country with one of the highest birth rates in the world, and where over half the population is under 20. The government still has its work cut out for it.

RELIGION IN TURKEY

Islam is the religion of the Turks, although

secularism is the policy of Turkey. This apparent discrepancy is compounded by the fact that while 99 percent of all Turks are avowed Muslims, only 18 percent, according to a recent poll, pray the obligatory five times a day, and only slightly over half observe the holy month of Ramazan. But one should not be misled by these figures. Turkish society is still deeply rooted in Islam, and the Prime Minister himself, Turgut Özal, is a *hacı* — someone who has made the pilgrimage to Mecca.

Sadly, thanks to the late Ayatollah Khomeini in Iran, many people in the West have come to think of Islam as a religion of bloodthirsty fanatics who enjoy executing people (a description that, lest we forget, could just

as accurately be applied to certain Christian zealots of earlier centuries). However, since a proper understanding of the Islamic faith is important to an understanding of Turkish society, I think it is worth putting the record straight regarding the true nature of Islam.

Like the other two great Middle Eastern religions, Judaism and Christianity, Islam is a monotheistic religion. There is only one God, the same one worshipped by Jews and Christians. And like Jews and Christians, who have the Talmud and the Bible, Muslims depend on Holy Scripture, in their case the Koran, for spiritual guidance. But they also nonetheless value the Bible as a sacred book, and Noah, Abraham, Moses, and Jesus are all revered as prophets. Likewise, the holy men of Judaism and Christianity are considered holy men by Muslims as well.

On the other hand, of course, Islam does not accept the divinity of Jesus, instead regarding him as one of the great prophets preceding the Great Prophet, Mohammed. This does not mean that divine status is claimed for Mohammed; he is merely the messenger of God, or Allah. And the message is a simple one. Indeed, Islam is the simplest of the world's great religions, and its simplicity is mirrored in the unadorned interiors of most mosques.

At the heart of Islam is total submission to the will of Allah (the word Islam means "submission"). This involves observing the "Five Pillars" of Islam as revealed by the prophet Mohammed, according to which Muslims must:

— profess with belief "There is no god but Allah, and Mohammed is His Prophet";

— pray five times a day, at dawn, at noon, at mid-afternoon, at dusk, and after dark;

— give alms to the poor;

— fast during the daylight hours of Ramazan;

— make a pilgrimage to Mecca at least once during one's lifetime, if possible.

Easily the most conspicuous of these pillars is the obligation to pray, as the call to prayer issued by the *müezzin* from the

OPPOSITE: Ships jockeying for position at the busy port of Izmir. ABOVE: Harvesting time in the East. This man is working a field near Mt. Ararat, long after the Flood.

balconies of the minarets five times a day is now usually amplified by loudspeakers. The prayers may be performed anywhere, even outdoors, as long as the precise ritual formula, which includes prior cleansing with running water, is followed.

Although it may come as a surprise to those whose only exposure to Islam is the sight of mobs on television waving their fists and chanting death to somebody-or-other, it is a faith that places a premium on moderation and compassion. It also emphasizes knowledge; in fact, "knowledge" is the second most common word in the Koran, after the name of Allah. And Koranic law, interpreted so sternly and inflexibly by some religious leaders, is in fact a set of moral rules designed to enable believers to improve and liberate the good that dwells in every person.

In any event, due to the secularization of Turkey by Atatürk, there is little in the Muslim traditions of the Turks that directly affects the visitor, with three exceptions: the near-impossibility of finding pork (which is forbidden to Muslims), the increasing difficulty in finding alcoholic drinks (also forbidden) the farther away you get from the coasts and the big cities, and the minor inconveniences that may result from not anticipating the two major religious festivals, Şeker Bayramı and Kurban Bayramı.

Şeker Bayramı, or "Sugar Festival", marks the end of Ramazan and lasts for three days, during which gifts are exchanged and sweets are lavished on the children. Banks and offices are closed, and most hotels and domestic travel should be booked well in advance.

Kurban Bayramı, or "Festival of Sacrifices", falls two months and 10 days later, and because it is the most important religious holiday of the year banks may be closed for five days and hotels and transportation completely booked out. The festival is based on the Biblical story of Abraham and Isaac, in which God rescinds His order to Abraham to sacrifice his son and commands him to sacrifice a ram instead. Thus, early on the morning of the day of Bayram, outside millions of homes across Turkey, a sheep is sacrificed by having its throat slit. No, it is not a pretty spectacle. But it is an oddly moving one. The sheep, which has been thoroughly washed beforehand, and even had "make-up" in the

form of dye applied to its forehead to make it more attractive in the sight of Allah, is treated with great tenderness before having its legs tied and being gently laid on its side where it is caressed until it is calm. Then the head of the household draws a knife across its throat. Whatever else it may be, it is a solemn and dignified ceremony.

It also serves a charitable purpose, because much of the meat is distributed to the poor; even the skin is given away.

Otherwise the only manifestation of religious (or quasi-religious) belief with which

the visitor is likely to come into contact is an altogether more agreeable and decorative one: the blue bead that comes in every size, either on its own with a pin attached or as part of a larger item, and appears in one form or another in every souvenir shop. Although it is a big favorite with tourists, it is even more popular with the Turks, because for them it has a very serious purpose: to ward off nazar, the "evil eye". A relic of the Turks' pre-Islamic past, belief in the malevolent power of nazar is the most widespread superstition in the country. Thus you will see the blue bead, which is supposed to have the power of sympathetic magic, being worn for protection by children all over Turkey, and even by domestic animals.

TURKISH CUISINE

Put simply, you are in for a treat. Turkish cuisine is widely, and rightly in my opinion, considered to be one of the three great cuisines of the world, along with French and Chinese. Its greatness rests on a combination of history, taste, and luck. Historically, it has benefited from the 500 years in which the Ottomans ruled much of the world and brought back to Istanbul much of the world's best cooking. It was then further refined by

the demanding, epicurean tastes of the sultans, who had as many as 1,300 chefs and helpers working in the Topkapı Palace. (Many of the world's most famous dishes were invented in the kitchens of the Topkapı.) And, finally, the Turks have had the good luck to live in a country with an endless variety of meat, fish, fruit, and vegetables. Thus, thrice blessed, it is no wonder — though it is staggering to contemplate — that the Turks have, for example, come up with 50 different kinds of kebabs and over 100 different ways of preparing eggplants.

Given this availability of raw materials and a long tradition of culinary inventiveness, Turkish cooking ought to be good. What makes it great is the painstaking care that

goes into the preparation of every dish and, above all, the freshness of the ingredients. Whatever you choose to eat in a Turkish restaurant, you can be sure that it is the freshest available — and freshly prepared. Turks do not serve yesterday's food dressed up to suit today's menu.

With so much to choose from, it's almost impossible to single out particular dishes for special mention. (For general guidelines on restaurant dining see the EATING OUT section in TRAVELERS' TIPS.) There are, however, a few things that you should not go home without

trying. Such as: every *meze* (hors d'oeuvre) you can get your hands on, but especially *börek* (paper-thin pastry filled with feta cheese or meat), *dolma* (vine leaves stuffed with minced lamb or rice and spices), *cacık* (yogurt with grated cucumber and garlic and a little splash of olive oil), *taramasalata* (red fish roe mixed into a paste with yogurt and olive oil), *patlıcan salatası* (pureed eggplant), *çoban salatası* (mixed salad of chopped tomatoes,

OPPOSITE: The Cendere Bridge, near the fabled mountain of Nemrut Daği, built at the end of the second century AD. ABOVE LEFT: Making bread the *old* old-fashioned way in Cappadocia. RIGHT: Come and get it! Turkish food appeals to the eye as well as to the palate.

cucumbers, olives, and peppers); most fish, but especially *palamut* (baby tuna), *kılıç* (swordfish), *kalkan* (turbot), *levrek* (sea bass), *lüfer* (bluefish), and *sardalya* (fresh sardines); *Cerkez tavuğu* (boiled, boned chicken in a sauce of crushed walnuts, bread crumbs, garlic, paprika, and olive oil); *Iskender kebap* or *Bursa kebap* (slices of lamb on pieces of flat bread covered in tomato sauce and topped with browned butter), and *köfte* (spicy meatballs of ground lamb); *menemen* (a concoction of baked eggs, tomatoes, and onions); and *kavun* (a sweet melon).

To wash down your meal there are a number of good Turkish wines and an excellent Turkish lager (Efes Pilsen). Plus, of course, the Turkish national drink, rakı, a powerful anise-flavored spirit similar to the Greek ouzo or the French pastis.

Perhaps the ultimate accolade that one can bestow on Turkish cuisine — I am not joking — is to say that if you were forced to live on bread and water, you would still have a delicious diet. This is because Turkish bread is irresistibly good, and plentiful, and always freshly baked, while there are so many kinds of wonderful spring water that many Turks are connoisseurs of water and order it as we would order wine.

THE PLACE OF WOMEN

The one area in which Atatürk's reforms have met the most stubborn resistance is in the Turkish attitude towards women. Traditionally, Muslim Turkish women were totally subservient to men. They had virtually no rights; a woman's role was to cook for her husband, clean his house, work in his fields, bear him sons, and keep quiet. She could not vote, or inherit property, or ask for a divorce, or even object if her husband took other wives as well. In an Islamic court the word of one man was equal in value to that of two women. Girls of thirteen and younger were bought and sold for cash as wives. And those who couldn't be sold as wives were frequently sold to wealthy families as domestic help.

Atatürk changed all that, at least in law. Female suffrage was introduced, polygamy was abolished, women were given the right to institute divorce proceedings and to have

custody of their children, inheritance rights were established as well as equal rights before a court of law, the "selling" of wives was prohibited and a minimum age for marriage was decreed.

As far-reaching as these reforms were legally, they failed to reach very far into the hearts and minds of most Turkish men — or women, for that matter. The women, by and large, still defer unquestioningly to their menfolk. The women still do all of the domestic chores — and most of the work in the fields as well. In fact, two of the most familiar images

as one travels through Turkey are of groups of women stooped over at work in the fields while, just down the road, the men sit outside a tea-house sipping tea and playing backgammon. And on those rare occasions when you see a man accompanying his wife beside the road, *he* will be the one riding the donkey while she walks. Similarly, in the cities it is most unusual to see Turkish men and women walking together; and should a man and his wife run into another couple, it

OPPOSITE: The local teahouse has for centuries been the traditional meeting place and watering hole for Turkish men. This one is in Şanlıurfa, in the southeast. ABOVE: A peasant woman shopping in the bazaar at Şanlıurfa.

will always be the men who kiss and embrace and engage in conversation, while the women stay quietly in the background.

In some parts of the country religious weddings still outnumber civil weddings (thereby denying the wife all the rights conferred by a civil marriage), and polygamy is still sufficiently widespread that the Prime Minister's wife, Semra Özal, has launched a campaign of her own against it. Likewise, in the more remote rural areas men still pay cash for young wives, and girls are still sold to wealthy families as servants.

marriages for their offspring, as a profitable marriage is one of the best ways of increasing a family's prosperity. (Even among educated, middle-class Turks, most marriages are still arranged between the prospective spouses' families.) Because a "good" marriage is particularly important to peasant families, they are more concerned than most that their daughters should marry "up". Consequently, the family of a peasant girl will resort to extreme measures if necessary to prevent her forming an alliance beneath her.

I have some personal experience of this.

Another index of the pervasiveness of male supremacy can be seen in the child-bearing function of women: not only is it their duty to bear children when they are not working, but it is their hallowed mission to bear *male* children. To a Turkish man, a son is a blessing, a daughter little better than a curse. Ask a peasant how many children he has and the chances are he will neglect to include any daughters in the total.

Not surprisingly, then, parents — and especially the parents of girls — go to considerable lengths to arrange advantageous

A couple of years ago I met and befriended a young peasant in his early twenties; he wasn't sure of his exact age, or of his birthday, although he remembered that his mother had once told him that he was born at the time the watermelons ripened. For five years he had been in love with a girl from his village, but because his family was the poorest in the village she was forbidden to see him. Once she was even sent to live with relatives, and twice her family almost had her married off to someone else. Yet despite the fact that he had to leave the village to find work, the two of them kept up a romantic and clandestine correspondence. Finally, they decided that their only hope of ever being together was to elope. It was not a decision taken

Women picking beets near Erzurum, south of the Black Sea port of Trabzon.

lightly, for an elopement in Turkey is regarded by the girl's family as a kidnaping and they will do everything in their power to get the girl back, quickly, for once the union is consummated she is worthless to them. The couple eloped nevertheless, and hid out in my house. As expected, the family came looking for them, but happily never found them. Even more happily, they are now married and reconciled with her family. But it was a close call.

This is not to say that the situation of women hasn't improved significantly in recent years. It has. Women are now entering politics and the professions in ever increasing numbers, and as more Turks travel to Europe, while more tourists from the West visit Turkey, the pace of change is bound to quicken. Still, attitudes are harder to change than behavior. One evening not long ago I went to dinner at the home of a dear Turkish friend, a man of great taste and sophistication. When I complimented his wife on how lovely she looked, my friend broke in and said, proudly, "Yes, I insist that she looks beautiful for me every evening when I get home." Whereupon the lady I was with asked him what special little efforts he made to look nice for her. He laughed awkwardly for a moment, and then glanced at me, and then smiled and shrugged, confused. He couldn't understand the question.

SPORT IN TURKEY

If a sport can be defined as a game or competitive activity that people engage in for fun, then the national sport of Turkey is easily backgammon. During the warm months the tables outside all the coffee houses and tea houses are crowded with men playing backgammon, usually at mind-boggling speed. Indeed, one of the sharpest audial memories that visitors to Turkey take back with them is the clatter of dice hurtling across backgammon boards. In the winter months the game moves indoors, and even the cafés become more backgammon halls than eating places.

If you add physical exertion to the definition, then football (soccer) is far and away the most popular sport in Turkey, for partic-

ipants and spectators alike. Almost everywhere that you see children playing you will see a ball at their feet, and in every large city you will find an impressive football stadium. Moreover, the Turks play football to a very high standard: in 1989 the Turkish champions, Galatasaray of Istanbul, reached the semifinals of the European Cup, thus making them theoretically one of the top four teams in Europe.

It is also worth mentioning, at a time when the game everywhere is disfigured by cynical and often brutal fouls, that Turkish footballers are not only skillful but sportsmanlike.

Of the sports peculiar to Turkey, the famous greased wrestling competitions are held in mid-June in Edirne, while camel wrestling matches take place along the Aegean coast south of Izmir during the months of December and January. The exciting and dangerous sport of *cirit* is a combination of classical javelin-throwing, medieval jousting, and modern polo, in which men on horseback gallop back and forth hurling wooden javelins at their opponents. *Cirit* matches are held every Saturday and Sunday from May to October in Konya, and at various times during the summer in Erzurum in the east.

In a country favored with some of the world's most beautiful coastline, it is only natural that water sports are very popular. Yachts and other sailboats can be hired, with or without crews, at many places along the southern Aegean and Mediterranean, where water-skiing, scuba-diving, snorkeling and, most recently, windsurfing can also be enjoyed from April to November.

Winter sports have never been very big in Turkey, but skiing is rapidly growing in popularity and there are now several good ski resorts. Foremost among them is Uludağ, outside Bursa, but there are also fine facilities and excellent conditions at Saklıkent in the Beydağları mountains near Antalya, at the Palandöken ski center near Erzurum, at Kartalkaya near Bolu, about midway between Istanbul and Ankara, and at Erciyes near Kayseri. No doubt many more will spring up in the near future, as the Turks learn that snow can be put to recreational use.

Istanbul
and
Environs

ISTANBUL CITY

FERİKÖY

BEŞİKTAŞ

Yahudi Mezarlığı

Feriköy Mezarlığı

Barbaros Bulvarı

Teknik Üniversite

Çırağan Caddesi

HASKÖY

Kulaksız Mezarlığı

KASIMPAŞA

Taksim Square

Modern City

Dolmabahçe Caddesi

Naval Museum (Deniz Müzesi)

Kasımpaşa-Hasköy Yolu

Caddesi

TEPEBAŞI

Dolmabahçe Palace

Tepebaşı Park

Evliya Çelebi Caddesi

BEYOĞLU

İstanbul Boğazı (Bosphorus)

Golden Horn

Tünel

Nusretiye Camii

Semsi Pasa Camii

UNKAPANI

Sultan Sâlim Camii

Atatürk Bridge (Köprüsü)

(Haliç)

Galata Bridge (Köprüsü)

ÜS

Fatih Camii

Zeyrek Camii

KÜÇÜKPAZAR

EMİNÖNÜ

Belediye Müzesi

Rüstem Paşa Camii

Yeni Camii (New Mosque)

Süleymaniye Camii

Spice Market (Mısır Çarşısı) Egyptian Market

Sirkeci Gen. (Train Station)

İstanbul University

Büyük Postanesi

Topkapı Palace

BEYAZIT

Beyazıt Kulesi

Arkeoloji Müzesi

Gülhane Park

Grand Bazaar (Kapalı Çarşı)

Nuruosmaniye Camii

Aya-İrine Kilisesi

Şehzade Camii

Lâleli Camii

Beyazıt Camii

Atik Ali Paşa Camii

Aya Sofia (Ayasofya)

Ordu Caddesi

Yeniçeriler

Sultanahmet Square

Divan

Ağa Camii

Ayasofya Hamamı

KUMKAPI

Blue Mosque (Sultanahmet Camii)

Museum of Turkish and Islamic Arts

Mosaic Museum

Küçük Ayasofya Camii

Kennedy Caddesi (Florya Sahil Yolu)

MARMARA DENİZİ (MARMARA SEA)

ISTANBUL BOSPHORUS (BOGAZI)

KARA DENİZ (BLACK SEA)

Bahçeköy

Kemerburgaz

AVRUPA (EUROPE)

ASYA

Alibeyköy

(ASIA)

BEYOGLU

FATİH

EMİNÖNÜ

HAREM

İSTANBUL

MARMARA DENİZİ (SEA OF MARMARA)

500 m
0.31 miles

5 km
2.1 miles

Maltepe

N

ISTANBUL

Any great city is a study in contrasts. Luxury exists side by side with poverty, beauty with ugliness, glamour with squalor, sanitation with filth, serenity with violence, the cultured with the philistine, the sacred with the profane, the ancient with the modern. But even by this reckoning, Istanbul stands out among the world's great cities. For, historically, it has the added contrast of having been the capital of both a great Christian empire and a great Muslim empire. And geographically it embodies the unique contrast of being both Western and Eastern, European and Asian, the only city in the world built on two continents.

Whether you arrive in Istanbul by air, by land or, best of all, by sea, you know at once that you have arrived in a very special place. Its distinctive blend of sights, sounds, and smells — a blend which has been 2,700 years in the making — is impossible to ignore or, once experienced, to forget.

BACKGROUND

According to tradition, the ancient city of Byzantium was founded in 667 BC by Byzas, a Greek from Megara near Corinth, who established a colony on the hill overlooking the Bosphorus where the Topkapı Palace now stands. Legend has it that before setting out on his expedition, Byzas consulted the oracle at Delphi and was told that he should found a new settlement "opposite the land of the blind." Later, when Byzas and his followers reached the Bosphorus, they noticed an earlier Greek colony at Chalcedon (modern Kadıköy) on the Asian side. Thinking these people must have been blind not to have seen the enormous advantages of settling on the other side of the strait — a splendid natural harbor, an easily defensible site high above the water, a commanding position with regard to shipping passing between the Sea of Marmara and the Black Sea — Byzas established his settlement there.

For the next three centuries, with the exception of a few decades under Persian control after falling to Darius in 512 BC, Byzan-

tium alternately fought with and against the Athenians, until in 334 BC Byzantium surrendered to the Macedonians under Alexander the Great. During the 200 years that followed, Byzantium was gradually absorbed into the spreading Roman empire and officially became a part of the Roman province of Asia in 133 BC. After the final triumph of Rome over the troublesome Mithridates, King of Pontus, in 63 BC Byzantium enjoyed more than 250 years of peace and prosperity under the *Pax Romana*. But the Byzantines joined in an unsuccessful rebellion against Emperor Septimius Severus in 194 AD and two years later the emperor razed the city walls and burned down the city. Then, a few years afterwards, he had second thoughts and rebuilt the city on an even grander scale.

The bitter power struggle following the abdication of the Roman emperor Diocletian in 305 finally ended with Constantine's victory in 324. Thus began a new era in the history of the city — and of the world. Constantine immediately began reorganizing the Roman Empire with Byzantium as its new capital. A vast building program was launched, quadrupling the size of the city, and in a magnificent ceremony on May 11, 330 Constantine declared his capital to be New Rome, though it soon came to be known as Constantinople. As such it was the capital of the Byzantine Empire, the most important city in the world, for the next thousand years.

Even before the sack of Constantinople by the Crusaders in 1204 the Byzantine Empire was tottering, but afterwards it was so weak and fragmented, and its leadership so ineffective, that Constantinople should have been easy pickings for the massed forces of Ottoman Turks under Sultan Mehmet II who laid siege to the city in 1453. With the building of two huge fortresses on either side of the Bosphorus north of the city, and with the Ottoman navy anchored in the Sea of Marmara, and with giant cannon emplacements outside the city walls to the west, the Turks had Constantinople completely cut off from the outside world. Nonetheless, despite being outnumbered by 10 to one, and despite the almost continual artillery bombardment, the Byzantines held out for seven weeks. Finally, on May 29, 1453, after an all-out assault, the city fell to the Turks. That afternoon Mehmet rode triumphantly through the city, where he was hailed as *Fatih* ("Conqueror") by his troops, and then rode into Aya Sofia, the greatest church in Christendom, and declared it a mosque.

Subsequently Mehmet made the city the capital of his empire and rebuilt it into the great Ottoman city of Istanbul. Among the buildings he erected were the Topkapı Palace and the great Fatih Camii, the Mosque of the Conqueror. Not surprisingly, the period of the most lavish building in Istanbul coincided with the period of the greatest empire-building, which took place during the reign of Süleyman the Magnificent (1520–1566). The most impressive of the mosques and palaces built during this period is the Süleymaniye, the largest mosque in Turkey, which was completed in 1557. Later sultans, when they weren't presiding over the crumbling of the empire, supervised the erection of many more grand palaces and mosques, until today there are no fewer than 1,300 minarets puncturing the sky above Istanbul.

Inevitably, when after 16 centuries Istanbul ceased to be an imperial capital, it lost much of the cosmopolitan glitter and ethnic diversity that are the hallmarks of the hub of a great empire; and when with the advent of the Turkish Republic in 1923 it ceased to be the national capital it lost some of the worldliness and excitement that goes with being the center of political power. But one thing it has not lost is its timeless allure, its power to enthrall and enchant the most jaded traveler — in a word, its uniqueness.

GENERAL INFORMATION

Your best source of information in Istanbul, as elsewhere in Turkey, is one of the Tourist Information offices operated by the Ministry of Tourism. There are four offices in Istanbul. One is at Atatürk Airport, (573-2920 or (573-7399. Another is at the Maritime Passenger Terminal in the Karaköy district, (149-5776. In Beyoğlu, where most of the big hotels are, there is an office in the Hilton Hotel arcade off Cumhuriyet Caddesi, near

Taksim Square, (133-0592. And the fourth is on the western side of Sultanahmet Square, between Aya Sofia and the Blue Mosque, (522-4903. The regional directorate of the Ministry itself is at Meşrutiyet Caddesi 57, in the Tepebaşı District, just up the street from the Etap Istanbul and Pera Palas hotels, (145-6875 or (143-3472.

For specific travel inquires, the following telephone numbers might prove useful:

Atatürk Airport (domestic routes): (573-1331 or (573-7388 (international routes): (573-3500 or (573-7145.

Sirkeci Railway Station (European lines) (527-0050.

Haydarpaşa Railway Station (Asian lines) (338-3050 or (336-2063.

Topkapı Bus Terminal (European side) (577-5617 or (582-1010.

Harem Bus Terminal (Asian side) (333-3763.

Karaköy Maritime Terminal (144-4233.

The main office of **Turkish Airlines** (THY) is at Abide-i Hürriyet Caddesi, Vakif Işhani Kat 2, 154-156, (147-1388 or (573-3525. The headquarters of Turkish Maritime Lines is on Rıhtım Caddesi in Karaköy, near the passenger terminal, (144-0207 or (149-9222.

Motorists with questions should contact the very helpful Touring and Automobile Club of Turkey (TTOK). Their head office is in the Şişli district at Halaskargazi Caddesi 364, (131-4631 or (146-7090, and they have another office at the Topkapı gate by the walls at the western entrance to the Old City, (521-6588.

For problem-solving there is the Tourism Police, specially created to help tourists, with offices in Sirkeci at Mimar Kemalettin Caddesi 2, Şube Yanı, (527-4503, and in Sultanahmet on Alayköşkü Caddesi at the corner of Hükümet Konaği, (528-5369. For less pressing problems you can always turn to the Association of Turkish Travel Agencies (TÜRSAB) at Cumhuriyet Caddesi 187/3, just north of Taksim Square, (146-0236.

For detailed archaeological and historical information on everything the city has to offer the serious tourist-explorer, John Freely's book on Istanbul in the Blue Guide series is easily the most comprehensive and readable guidebook to the city currently available. I strongly recommend it.

WHAT TO SEE

Before beginning the daunting task of selecting which of Istanbul's many glories to urge you to see, I think a few words about the lay-out of the city might be helpful.

European Istanbul is separated from Asian Istanbul by the Bosphorus, the 16-mile strait that connects the Black Sea with the Sea of Marmara. The Bosphorus could be said to be Istanbul's main street, with its heavy traffic of tankers, warships, cargo ships, ocean-

and ancient Istanbul. This is where all of the city's most celebrated landmarks are to be found — the great mosques, museums, and monuments, as well as the Topkapı Palace and the Grand Bazaar. Indeed, if you are reasonably fit and have a reasonably good map with you, the sights to see are almost all within walking distance of each other. By contrast, Beyoğlu is where you will find the modern luxury hotels (mostly clustered around Taksim Square), and the consulates, expensive shops, airline offices, car rental firms, and travel agencies. This is also where one finds, here and

going liners, steamers, and ferryboats. Most of the sights you will want to see are on the European side, with the Asian side consisting mostly of endless suburbs from which, every day, thousands commute to work in Europe. European Istanbul is itself divided by the Golden Horn, a freshwater estuary that separates the Old City (Stamboul) to the south from Beyoğlu to the north. There are two bridges linking the Old City and Beyoğlu across the Golden Horn: the Atatürk Bridge and the famous Galata Bridge near the mouth of the estuary.

The Old City, which occupies the triangular peninsula between the Golden Horn and the Sea of Marmara, is what we mean when we talk about Byzantium and Constantinople

there, the most depressing tracts of sleaze: seedy bars and nightclubs, clip-joints, brothels and so forth.

Whatever you do decide to see in Istanbul, it's essential to know the name of the district it is in, especially if you are looking for something with which the ordinary citizen (and that includes most taxi drivers) may not be familiar. In the same way that New Yorkers routinely refer to locations in Manhattan by their district — Upper West Side, Lower East Side, Midtown, Greenwich Village, Harlem et al — and Londoners likewise

The Galata Bridge across the Golden Horn in Istanbul. Every day fishermen bring their catch to sell to the restaurants on the bridge's lower deck.

locate things according to district — Hampstead, Chelsea, Kensington, Mayfair, Soho — so, too, the natives of Istanbul identify places and addresses by the districts they are in. Indeed, as the streets of Istanbul are very poorly marked, if at all, it is important to find the right district if you want to find the right place.

Topkapı Palace

Topkapı Palace — like Aya Sofia, Sultanahmet Camii (the Blue Mosque), the Hippodrome, and the Obelisk of Theodosius — is in the Sultanahmet district, where the eastern tip of the Old City thrusts out into the Bosphorus. The original palace was built by Mehmet the Conqueror between 1459 and 1465. Süleyman the Magnificent was the first sultan to move in permanently, and for the next three centuries, until Sultan Abdül Mecit I moved into the new Dolmabahçe Palace in 1853, it was the home of the Ottoman emperors. In fact, it was much more than simply the official residence of the emperors; it grew into a sort of Ottoman Vatican City, with its own mosques, schools, libraries, Turkish baths, residences for guards and workers, hospital, bakery, arsenal, zoo, and mint. The supreme executive council of the empire, the Divan, was also based here, and the average population of the whole Topkapı complex was seldom below 5,000 and was often much higher. Today the palace is one of the world's greatest museums, and is open every day except Tuesday.

Entering through the Imperial Gate (*Bab-ı-Hümayun*), built in 1478, you come to the first court, known as the **Court of the Janissaries,** a large tree-shaded park where the imperial mint was located and where the sultan's elite praetorian guard had its barracks. On your left as you enter is the small basilica of **Aya Irene,** or Church of the Divine Peace, which was dedicated by Justinian in the same year that Aya Sofia was completed and which now houses the Mosaic Museum. At the far side of the first court is another wall and the Gate of Salutations (*Bab-üs Selam*) leading to the second court, where the official business of the empire was conducted. No one was allowed through the gate without permission, and no one but the sultan himself could pass through it on horseback.

Today's visitors only need a ticket, which you buy at this gate. The little fountain just beyond the ticket booths was where the sultan's chief executioner washed his hands and sword after beheading a prisoner.

The second court, or **Court of the Divan,** is a beautiful enclosed park full of cypresses and plane trees. To the right as you enter are the **palace kitchens,** most of which are now given over to the display of some of the palace's huge collection of porcelain and glassware from China, Europe, and Ottoman lands. On the opposite side of the court

is the **Imperial Council Chamber** where the Divan met.

Behind the council chamber is the **Harem,** a labyrinthine complex of 300 rooms on six different levels. To see it you will have to buy a ticket and join one of the guided tours; as these leave only at certain times, it's a good idea to get your ticket and check the tour schedule before going on to other parts of the palace.

Entering through the Carriage Gate, you pass the apartments of the black eunuchs who guarded the sultan's wives and concubines before passing through another gate and coming upon the courtyard of the Valide Sultan (the sultan's mother). Here was the center of the web of murderous intrigues and political scheming for which the Ottomans were famous, or infamous, and for which the empire paid a terrible price. Beyond are the ladies' quarters and the private chambers of the sultan and the apartment of the crown prince, all now beautifully restored to their former glory.

The **third court,** yet another lovely park with plane trees, was the sultan's personal domain and was approached (by the few who were permitted to approach) through the Gate of Felicity *(Bab-ı Saadet)*. Just beyond it is the audience chamber where the sultan

received high officials, ambassadors and foreign dignitaries; to the right, opposite the entrance from the Harem, is the Treasury. This is where you will find what you are probably looking for: the most dazzling collection of jewels in the world, including the enormous, 86-carat Spoonmaker's Diamond, surrounded by 49 smaller stones, and the Emerald Dagger featured in the film *Topkapı*. Whatever else this breathtaking exhibition does for you, it will give you a whole new definition of what it means to be rich.

One last gate leads to the **fourth court.** This is occupied by four individual pavilions which the sultans used for entertaining and as parts of the imperial residence. Two of them, the Erivan Kiosk and the Baghdad

Kiosk, are among the most beautiful examples of Turkish architecture to be found anywhere. In a third, the Kiosk of Sultan Abdülmecit, is the entrance to the palace restaurant and café, with wonderful views of the Bosphorus.

Still within the palace grounds, conveniently enough, are three of Istanbul's most fascinating museums. The first, and most famous, is the **Archaeological Museum (Arkeoloji Müzesi),** which has one of the world's finest collections of sarcophagi. Across a small courtyard is the **Museum of the Ancient Orient (Eski Şark Eserleri Müzesi),** where the treasures include the Ishtar gate of Babylon from the time of Nebuchadnezzar II (sixth century BC) and clay tablets on which are inscribed the law code of Hammurabi in cuneiform. The third museum in the complex is the **Museum of Turkish Ceramics (Çinili Köşkü),** built by Mehmet the Conqueror in 1472, with exterior tiles from the Seljuk period. The museum houses Turkish ceramics dating back to Seljuk times, with an exceptionally good collection of Iznik tiles from the seventeenth and eighteenth centuries. All three museums are open every day except Mondays.

Aya Sofia

Aya Sofia — also known as Hagia Sophia or Sancta Sophia — stands just outside the Topkapı walls in Sultanahmet. From its completion in 548 until 1453 when Mehmet the Conqueror rode in and declared it a mosque, this was the greatest church in Christendom. For the next five centuries it was a great mosque. Today it is officially a museum, and still one of the architectural wonders of the world.

The architects who designed it — Anthemius of Tralles (modern Aydın) and Isidorus of Miletus — were in fact not architects at all but mathematicians, two of the greatest of the epoch. They needed to be, because nothing like Aya Sofia had ever been attempted before — and nothing like it was attempted again until St Peter's was built in Rome over a thousand years later. Unfortunately, the immensity of the dome — it

ABOVE AND OPPOSITE: Two of the 300 rooms in the Harem of the Topkapı Palace.

rises 55 m (180 ft) above the ground and is 31 m (102 ft) in diameter — has necessitated the addition of buttresses and other forms of support over the centuries, which detract somewhat from the exterior lines of the building but not from its grandeur.

Although no less than four acres of the interior were originally covered by the most stunning Byzantine mosaics, they were all plastered over after the church became a mosque. Happily, many of the mosaics have now been partially restored, and restoration of the others continues. What can never be

restored are the precious treasures looted by the Crusaders in 1204. This gives the interior a certain austerity that you don't find in other great buildings, but that in turn serves to emphasize the majesty of the building itself.

Of the surviving mosaics, the largest is on the apse above the spot where the altar originally stood; it depicts the Virgin Mary holding the infant Jesus. The best of the other mosaics are to be found in the galleries around the nave, which you reach by going up the ramps from the corner of the narthex at the atrium end. From these galleries you also get a splendid overall view of the great internal spaces of the church.

ABOVE: The Serpentine Column across from the Blue Mosque, which originally stood at the Temple of Apollo at Delphi, is one of the three surviving monuments on the site of the old Hippodrome. OPPOSITE TOP: The Sultan Ahmet Camii, otherwise — and better — known as the Blue Mosque. One of the world's most famous landmarks, it derives its popular name from the thousands of blue Iznik tiles which adorn the interior. BOTTOM: The faithful at prayer in the Blue Mosque.

The Blue Mosque

Across the delightful gardens of Sultan-ahmet Square from Aya Sofia is **Sultan Ahmet Camii,** the renowned Blue Mosque. Built by Sultan Ahmet I (1603–1617) to rival Aya Sofia, it lacks both the scale and the technical inventiveness of its great predecessor. It makes up for them, however, in its elegant symmetry and in its color: inside are 21,043 blue Iznik tiles, from which the mosque derives its colloquial name.

Outside, the mosque is distinguished by the domes and half-domes that from whatever perspective seem to bubble up above it, and by the six needle-like minarets that surround it. When the mosque was built, only the sacred shrine of the Ka'aba in Mecca had as many as six minarets, and such was the outcry from all corners of Islam that Ahmet was obliged to dispatch his architect to Mecca to build a seventh minaret there. The Blue Mosque is still the only one in Turkey with six minarets.

The Hippodrome

Begun in 203 under Septimius Severus, only seven years after he had destroyed the city, the Hippodrome was not completed until the reign of Constantine over a century later. It then went on to become the most famous stadium in the world, and by the time of Justinian had seating for up to 100,000 spectators. Not only chariot races and sporting events were held here; it was the center of the city's life, and as such had great ceremonial importance, whether the ceremonies involved celebrating famous victories or executing failed enemies.

The Hippodrome was almost totally destroyed by the orgiastic pillagers of the Fourth Crusade, who stripped it of everything of any value that could possibly be moved — the most famous example being the four bronze horses of Lysippus that were taken back to St. Mark's Basilica in Venice. The ruins of the stadium itself were quarried in the seventeenth century to help build the Blue Mosque.

All that's left of the Hippodrome today is the granite Obelisk of Theodosius and two lesser monuments that stand to the west of the Blue Mosque (to your left when facing Aya Sofia). First erected in Helio-

polis around 1500 BC to commemorate the victories of Pharaoh Thutmose III, the obelisk was brought from Egypt by the emperor Theodosius in 390 AD specifically to adorn the Hippodrome. It is remarkable today for the clarity of the hieroglyphs with which it was inscribed 3,500 years ago as well as for the engraved marble pedestal on which it stands.

The Grand Bazaar

If you go west from the northern end of the Hippodrome along Divan Yolu — the Old

City's principal thoroughfare, though it changes its name several times before it reaches the city walls in the west — you will come upon the **Çemberlitaş** (the "bound stone") after about one kilometer, on the right. Also known as the Burnt Column, it was the first monument erected by Constantine to celebrate the city's dedication as the capital of the Roman Empire in 330. Though it has been rattled by earthquakes and scorched by fires, it has

survived thanks to the bronze bands that hold it together. The street that runs beside it leads to the Grand Bazaar.

Mehmet the Conqueror built a covered market on this site in 1461, before he began building either his mosque (the *Fatih Camii*) or his Topkapı Palace. It was only a pair of small warehouses (*bedestens*) to begin with, but it grew… and grew… until today it is the largest covered market in the world. It has over 4,000 shops, as well as cafés, restaurants, mosques, banks, police stations, a post office, and a school: a city within a city.

The streets are each given over to shops selling a single product — shoes, furs, brass, carpets, *kilims*, leather goods, jewelry, etc. — and they are all named after trades. Some of the trades have died out — for example, there are no longer any fezmakers along Fezmaker's Street — and others have moved to different parts of the bazaar, but half the fun of being there is wandering around and coming upon the totally unexpected. One area you should definitely aim for, though, is the Old Bedesten at the center. Quite apart from having an impressive array of valuable antiques, it also features copperware, jewelry, tiles, and glassware.

If the noise and the crowds get too much for you, you can get away from both at the Havuzlu restaurant, near the post office, which has a small pool. Or you can retreat to the **Old Book Market** (*Sahaflar Çarşısı*) just outside the Beyazit Square entrance to the Grand Bazaar. There, in a delightful little courtyard with a fountain, you will find a lot of small bookshops selling both new and used books in all languages.

The Süleymaniye

The Süleymaniye, or Mosque of Süleyman the Magnificent, is considered the most beautiful of all the imperial mosques in Istanbul. It is also the largest and, because it rises majestically on top of a hill overlooking the Golden Horn, the most conspicuous. It is only fitting that the greatest of all Turkish mosques should have been built for the greatest of Turkish rulers by the greatest of Turkish architects, Sinan.

Started in 1550 and completed seven years later, over 5,000 workmen were employed in its construction. The awesomeness of its

ABOVE: One of the streets in the Grand Bazaar. With over 4,000 shops, its is the largest covered market in the world. OPPOSITE: The magnificent interior of the Süleymaniye, or Mosque of Süleyman the Magnificent. Completed in 1557, it is widely considered to be the most beautiful of all Istanbul's imperial mosques.

exterior, accentuated by four tall minarets rising from the four corners of the courtyard, is matched by the simple grandeur of the interior, where the vast spaces are colored by the light streaming through the glorious stained-glass windows (which were created by a sixteenth-century glazier known as Ibrahim the Drunkard). The *mihrab* (prayer-niche) is of finely-carved white marble and decorated on either side with Iznik tiles.

The eight large buildings surrounding the mosque belong to its *külliye* (complex) of institutions designed to serve the local

down to its essence: it is perpetually thronged with people and cars challenging each other's territorial rights, it resonates with the sounds and smells of a great maritime metropolis, it has more pigeons and street vendors than some entire cities, and its skyline is dominated by the domes and minarets of a great imperial mosque.

If Eminönü is the gateway to the Old City from the north, the Galata Bridge is the key that unlocks it. Built in 1912 by German engineers, it is a metal drawbridge floating on pontoons, though it is only ever opened

community. Every imperial mosque had its own külliye — which would typically include a hospital, a library, an orphanage, a hospice for travelers, and a cemetery — but the Süleymaniye is almost unique in that its külliye is still intact and still serving the needs of the neighborhood. In the walled garden behind the mosque are the tombs of Süleyman and his wife Roxelana, and of the man who designed it all, the great Sinan.

Eminönü

If Istanbul can be said to have a city center, it is the district of Eminönü, where the **Galata Bridge** links the Old City with "modern" Istanbul across the Golden Horn to the north. Here is where Istanbul has been distilled

for about an hour before dawn to allow ships in and out. At either end of the bridge are the docks from which the ferries leave to go up the Bosphorus, or over to the Asian side, or to the Prince's Islands in the Sea of Marmara. Beneath the bridge there is a lower deck packed with cafés serving fish bought straight from the fishing boats that come to the bridge. At this writing, a new stationary bridge is under construction alongside the present one, and I'm told that when the new one is completed the old bridge will be towed around to Seraglio Point, atop which is Topkapı Palace, where it will spend the rest of its days as the home of a row of restaurants.

According to tradition, the Galata Bridge — or more precisely its predecessor, built in

1845 — has an unusual and amusing claim to fame. In the 1880s, so the story goes, there were two English families living in Istanbul who used to meet regularly for a game of cards resembling dummy whist. As they lived on opposite sides of the Golden Horn, they took turns crossing the bridge to play cards. Depending on whose turn it was, one of the families would have "to bridge" in order to have a game. Thus did the game get its name.

Yeni Cami

The most familiar landmark of Eminönü is the Yeni Cami ("New Mosque") which looms straight ahead of you as you cross the Galata Bridge. It was begun in 1597 at the behest of Valide Sultan Safiye, the mother of Sultan Mehmet III, whose death in 1603 put both his mother and the laborers on the mosque out of a job. It wasn't finally completed until 60 years later, by which time three different architects had fiddled with the plan.

The plan is not dissimilar to that of most imperial mosques, though less distinguished in execution than the finest ones. There is an elegant fountain for ablutions in the large courtyard, and inside there is some quite stunning decorative work in gold and carved marble. Upstairs the royal gallery is adorned with beautifully colored Iznik tiles.

Spice Market

The Spice Market, known locally as the Mısır Carşısı or "Egyptian Market", is right beside the Yeni Cami. It was built just after the mosque was completed in 1663 and was intended to be part of the mosque's *külliye;* today the rents from its shops still go towards the upkeep of the mosque. It is open every day except Sunday.

Once you enter the big L-shaped hall there is no point in trying to follow your nose, because you will be in the midst of a tournament of aromas, with the various herbs and spices and other comestibles all competing for your nose's attention. However, just because the foodstuffs have taken over the market's airspace this doesn't mean that everything for sale in the market is organic. On the contrary, you will come across shops selling all kinds of things: clothing, footwear, toys, electrical gadgets, household goods, jewelry, cosmetics, tools, you name it.

Meanwhile, outside in the courtyard, there are endless varieties of seeds, bulbs, flowers, and plants for sale. Somewhat incongruously, there are also a number of men perched patiently in front of typewriters, whose business consists of writing letters and filling out forms for the illiterate.

Rüstem Paşa Camii

If you go west for about 150 m (490 ft) on Hasırcılar Caddesi, the street that runs alongside the main stretch of the market, you will

come to the Rüstem Paşa Camii, or rather you will come to the steps leading up to it. Climb them. At the top is a little mosque of surpassing elegance, built by Sinan in the 1550s for Rüstem Paşa, the Grand Vezir and, not coincidentally, son-in-law of Süleyman the Magnificent. What makes this mosque particularly worth a visit is the fact that its interior is covered with the most spectacularly beautiful Iznik tiles to be seen anywhere in Istanbul.

OPPOSITE: The underground Basilica Cistern, built by Justinian in 532 AD, just off Sultanahmet Square between Aya Sofia and the Blue Mosque. ABOVE: Wooden houses, or *Yali*, along the Asian side of the Bosphorus.

The Tünel

When you cross the Galata Bridge to Beyoğlu, you are almost immediately confronted with a cityscape of dereliction and ugliness. This is more than a little ironic, considering that in the twilight of the Ottoman Empire it was in Beyoğlu that one found the greatest concentration of wealth, the latest in fashion, the newest inventions (electric lights, telephones), the most glamorous neighborhoods, and the most sophisticated inhabitants. You can still find pockets of luxury and modernity here, especially around Taksim Square, but the old opulence and romance are no more than faded memories. And to visit those memories you still have to get past the grim present that greets you at the north end of the bridge. The best way is by subway.

That's right. What is probably the world's oldest (1875) and certainly the world's shortest (600 m or 1,970 ft) subway, the Tünel, runs between Tersane Caddesi, a block from the bridge, and the beginning of Istiklâl Caddesi. By taking it from the station near the bridge you will not only save yourself a fairly steep walk uphill through an insalubrious area, but you will also get a glimpse of how Beyoğlu has gone downhill. When it was built, the Tünel combined technological innovation with great charm; today, the system hasn't advanced one inch, either literally or figuratively, while all the charm has been "modernized" out of it by replacing the elegant old train carriages with characterless new ones. Oh well. It's a short journey.

Çiçek Pasajı

Istiklâl Caddesi, Beyoğlu's main street, runs from the upper Tünel station to Taksim Square, with a dogleg to the right at Galatasaray Square. Walking along the floor of this narrow gorge of peeling plaster, darkened windows, hanging dust, honking horns, and exhaust fumes, it is startling, and saddening, to think that only a century ago this was the Grand Rue de Pera, a delightful promenade where the cosmopolitan elite of the city went shopping in the street's elegant shops, had meals in its stylish restaurants, and attended functions in its gilded embassies.

Nevertheless, the street has its compensations today in the form of all the little alleyways and side streets that branch off it.

Easily the most famous, and notorious, of these is the Çiçek Pasajı or "Flower Passage". Just above Galatasaray Square on the left, it has only a few flower stalls but is lined on either side with cafés and taverns, all of which have tables outside, making the narrow passage even narrower for the stream of people flowing in and out. In this noisy, unprepossessing arcade beats the real heart of Istanbul.

It attracts Turks from all over the city (and all over the country) as well as the more adventurous tourists; they in turn attract a wonderfully motley collection of strolling musicians, would-be singers, unjustly neglected poets, dancers, acrobats, magicians, and street vendors. During the day, when the place is at its quietest, it is still quite merry; during the evening, to borrow Fats Waller's phrase, the joint is jumpin'. And as the evening wears on, such is the contagion of merriment, it gets harder and harder to tell the entertainers from the entertained. Which is what makes it such fun, if you like that sort of thing.

Dolmabahçe Palace

From Bohemian boisterousness to Ottoman extravagance is a journey of only three kilometers. If you go down to the Bosphorus from Taksim Square and turn left at İnönü Stadium you will quickly arrive at the Dolmabahçe Palace. It was built between 1843 and 1856 by the reforming Sultan Abdül Mecit as the symbolic centerpiece of his campaign to "Europeanize" the running of the Ottoman Empire. In the end, having bankrupted the empire to put up this enormous marble confection, what he got was a repository for possibly the gaudiest *mélange* of bad taste ever assembled under one roof.

Speaking of the roof, there are 36 chandeliers dripping from it — one of which, a gift from Queen Victoria, is the largest in the world, weighing in at four and a half tons. Wherever you look there is crystal; there is even a crystal staircase. And there is gold, and silver, and porphyry, and alabaster, and

TOP: A Janissary band marching in the grounds of the Dolmabahçe Palace. BOTTOM: Guards outside the doors of Istanbul's Military Museum, which features exhibits from all periods of Ottoman military history.

silk, and damask, and so on. The reception salon alone is so huge that it contains 56 columns. Atatürk kept a small apartment here, where he died at precisely 9:05 am on November 10, 1938. You will notice that all the clocks in the palace are stopped at 9:05. The palace is closed on Mondays and Thursdays, and visitors are required to take a guided tour, which lasts about an hour. It could be one of the most, well, glassy-eyed hours you will ever spend.

The Bosphorus
No visit to Istanbul would be complete without a cruise up the Bosphorus. It is one of the most beautiful, and restful, excursions imaginable. The cruise ferries leave regularly from the Eminönü end of the Galata Bridge and then zigzag slowly up the strait, stopping alternately on each shore, as if the boats are trying to stitch the two continents back together. The trip takes about two and a half hours each way, but if you are pressed for time you can get off at any stop and return by other means.

Other Sights
Of the **mosques,** the most interesting is out of the way, but worth the trouble. It is the **Kahriye Camii,** near the Edirnekapı gate in the Old City's land walls. Built in the eleventh century as the church of St. Savior in Chora, it has the most magnificent collection of Byzantine frescoes and mosaics in the entire country. More accessible but less enthralling is the giant **Fatih Camii,** built by Mehmet the Conqueror and finished in 1470, though it had to be rebuilt 300 years later after an earthquake.

Among the museums, I would particularly recommend a visit to the **Naval Museum** just north of the Dolmabahçe Palace. And when in Sultanahmet you should see the **Museum of Turkish Carpets,** near the Blue Mosque, and the **Museum of Turkish and Islamic Arts,** on the western side of the Hippodrome. The latter is especially fascinating because it has so many types of exhibits — ethnographic, calligraphic, textiles — from so many different periods.

When you get tired of sightseeing, a real sight for sore eyes (and sore feet) is **Gülhane Park,** which is in the grounds of Topkapı

Palace. It is lovely and peaceful here. Even more lovely, and with a better view as well as several charming restaurants and cafés, is **Yıldız Park** on the hillside above Çırağan, a little way up the Bosphorus from the Dolmabahçe Palace.

WHERE TO STAY

There are so many hotels in Istanbul — hundreds of them, catering for every taste and every budget — that singling out a few for mention is a decidedly invidious exercise. But it has to be done. Read on.

Luxury
If among the amenities you require are television, air conditioning, a swimming pool, a sauna, a choice of restaurants, a nightclub, and a rooftop bar, to name only a few, then you should head straight for Taksim Square, where you will find the **Sheraton** (☏ 148-9000), the **Etap Marmara** (☏ 151-4696) and, just north of the square on Cumhuriyet Caddesi, the **Hilton** (☏ 146-7050). All three are exactly what you would expect of luxury chain hotels: modern, extremely comfortable, efficient, expertly staffed, and furnished in the international hotel idiom. And the prices charged by all three are also exactly what you would expect: high. Depending on the time of year and the type of view, a single room in any of them will cost from $110 to $170 a night, doubles $170 to $250.

A few steps from the Sheraton, on Cumhuriyet Caddesi, and a step down in price is the **Divan Oteli** (☏ 146-4020). You lose nothing in comfort here, and you gain a superior restaurant; singles start at about $75, doubles at $100. In the same price range is the **Etap Istanbul** on Meşrutiyet Caddesi in Tepebası (☏ 151-4646), which has a matchless view from its rooftop swimming pool. Right across the street, at Meşrutiyet Caddesi 98, you can stay for the same money at the legendary **Pera Palas** (☏ 145-2230). Built in 1892 for passengers off the Orient Express, it is splendidly old-fashioned, with high ceilings, chandeliers, period furniture, cavernous bathrooms, and an open wrought-iron elevator to the rooms upstairs. If there was a plaque outside every room where a famous personage has slept, the corridors would be covered in plaques; as it is, there is a plaque outside room 411, where Agatha Christie used to stay. And room 101, where Atatürk stayed as a young officer, is now something of a shrine. Here, too, as in the Dolmabahçe Palace, the clock is stopped at 9:05.

On the other side of the Golden Horn, but still in the same price range, are my two favorite hotels in Istanbul: the **Yeşil Ev** and the **Ayasofya Pansiyonları**. The Yeşil Ev (℡ 528-6764 or ℡ 511-1150), at Kabasakal Sokak 5 between Aya Sofia and the Blue Mosque, is a wooden Ottoman mansion that has been

the street side are $55, on the wall side $40; doubles are $90 and $70.

Middle Range

Just south of Taksim Square, at Sıraselviler Caddesi 51, is the **Hotel Keban** (℡ 143-3310). With comfortable rooms, air conditioning, a restaurant, and barber shop, it is amazingly good value considering its "upmarket" location. It also has (or had) one of the funniest notices I have ever seen in a hotel room: "It is kindly requested from our guests to avoid dirting and doing rumors in the rooms."

faithfully restored and exquisitely furnished by Çelik Gülersoy of the Turkish Touring and Automobile Club. Outside there is a lovely walled garden with a rock pool and fountain, shaded by fig and plane trees, with marble-topped tables for dining. Not far away, along the cobblestoned, traffic-less Soğukfeşme that runs behind Aya Sofia there is the **Ayasofya Pansiyonları** (℡ 513-3660), a row of nine Ottoman houses lining the walls of Topkapı Palace. Another monument to the reconstructive genius of Mr. Gülersoy, these elegant houses, painted in different colors and named after flowers, are as comfortable and well-appointed as the Yeşil Ev and offer a truly startling close-up view of Aya Sofia from the rooms on the street side. Singles on

That alone is worth the price, which is about $20 for a single and $25 for a double. Almost next door, at N⁰ 49, is the **Dilson Hotel** (℡ 143-2032), which has much the same to offer but costs more. Singles are about $33, doubles $44. In between these two in price, and over near the Pera Palas and Etap Istanbul in location, is the **Grand Hotel de Londres (Büyük Londra Oteli)** at Meşrutiyet Caddesi 117 (℡ 145-0670). This is a smaller, less opulent version of the Pera Palas and makes much smaller demands on your wallet. A single room here is about $25, a double room

Outdoor dining in Beyoğlu, the newer part of the city north of the Golden Horn.

$35. Further down Meşrutiyet Caddesi, near the British Consulate and right behind the American Consulate, at Refik Saydam Caddesi 62 is the modern, clean **Bale Oteli** (℃ 150-4912) which is very reasonably priced at about $20 for a single and $25 for a double.

In the Old City the **Hotel Akgün** (℃ 512-0260) off Ordu Caddesi at Hazdenadar Sokak 6 in Aksaray offers old-fashioned comfort for about $20 single and $25 double. Similarly comfortable and similarly priced is the **Hotel Eyfel** (℃ 520-9788) in Beyazit at Kurultay Sokak 19, a few minutes' walk from the

Grand Bazaar. It's a very friendly place, and features an American-style cocktail lounge. Smaller and newer than either of these is the **Hotel Barın** (℃ 522-8426) at Fevziye Caddesi 25 in Şehzadebaşi. It's also cheaper, with singles from $15 and doubles from $20. A couple of streets to the west, at Gençtürk Caddesi 44, is another small, modern hotel with roughly the same prices, the **Hotel Doru** (℃ 527-6928).

Inexpensive

There are quite a few decent one-star hotels near the five-star sights in Sultanahmet, but easily the most popular is the **Hotel Klodfarer** (℃ 528-4850) at Klodfarer Caddesi 22, off Divan Yolu. It has rooms for under $10 single and under $15 double. If you continue along westward on Divan Yolu until it

ABOVE: The Sirkeci district, between the Topkapı Palace and the Galata Bridge, has many delightful little hotels such as this one.
OPPOSITE: You need never go hungry in Istanbul, because on virtually every street there is a café selling *döner kebap*, which you can either eat on the spot or take away with you.

changes its name to Ordu Caddesi, you will come to the district of Lâleli to the north and, a little further on, the district of Aksaray to the south. For the traveler on a tight budget, this is the Promised Land. The whole area is packed with economy hotels.

If you take any of the streets going into Lâleli from Ordu Caddesi — Büyük Reşit Paşa Caddesi, Harıkzadeler Sokak, Fetihbey Caddesi, Gençtürk Caddesi — you will find dozens of hotels to choose from. There is, for example, the **Hotel München** (℃ 526-5343) at Gençtürk Caddesi 55, which charges about $7 for a single and $10 for a double. The **Hotel Oran** (℃ 528-5813) at Harıkzadeler Sokak 40 charges the same, as does **Hotel Neşet** (℃ 526-7412) accross the street from the Oran. Slightly dearer is the **Metro Oteli** (℃ 520-6448) at Ahmet Suayip Sokak 17, but it is (or was) worth it for the notice next to the telephone: "Dear Guests, We are very pleased to inform you that the electronic witch has been connected to your service."

By the same token, if you go south of Ordu Caddesi into Aksaray you will find the streets chock-a-block with small hotels. Therefore, the best advice I can offer anyone looking for inexpensive but satisfactory accommodation — all prices quoted above include private bath, by the way — is go to the Lâleli/Aksaray area and have a look for yourself. You are bound to find something you like at a price you can afford. I promise.

Camping

Istanbul's only official campsites are out near Atatürk Airport, which may or may not be handy for you. **Yeşilyurt Kamping** (℃ 573-8408) is on the coast road, Sahil Yolu, by the village of **Yeşilköy**. **Ataköy Mokamp** (℃ 572-4961) is a few kilometers down the road towards the city. Both campsites have good facilities and excellent views of the Sea of Marmara for about $4 for a couple with a tent. And both are served by the commuter trains that run frequently to and from Sirkeci station, which is within easy walking distance of Topkapı Palace and Sultanahmet Square.

WHERE TO EAT

One of the joys of eating in Turkey is that you don't have to pay more to eat better. In fact,

I would argue that in certain circumstances you will do better by seeking out the less salubrious eating places. Accordingly, I will group Istanbul's restaurants by area rather than by price, so that the emphasis is on eating well wherever you happen to be rather than on buying meals according to what the prices happen to be.

As might be expected in an area teeming with small, inexpensive hotels, **Lâleli** and **Aksaray** are full of small, inexpensive restaurants. On Ordu Caddesi itself there is the **Murat Restaurant** at N⁰ 212 and the **Kardeşler Restaurant** at N⁰ 202, on the corner of Büyük Reşit Paşa Caddesi. At both places you can eat well for under $4. If you go on up Büyük Reşit Paşa Caddesi you will find several more little places, including the **Altuğ Köfte Salonu** and the **Şar Lokantası,** where you can eat well for under $2. Similarly, the **Gaziantep Emek Saray Kebapfısı** just off Ordu Caddesi at Gençtürk Caddesi 6 and the **Çavuşoğlu** at Şair Fitnat Sokak 4/11 both serve excellent food at bargain prices. But then so do many places in this area. Look and sniff around; you won't be disappointed.

The same goes, by the way, for every area: your chances of finding a memorably delicious repast are much greater if you go exploring than if you simply go by the recommendations of someone who can't be there with you.

Near the Lâleli/Aksaray area is the district of Kumkapı. At the Beyazıt Mosque, by the Grand Bazaar, Divan Yolu changes its name to Yeniçeriler Caddesi. If you go to the corner where the mosque stands and cross Yeniçeriler you will find yourself on Tiyatro Caddesi; follow this south for 600 m (1,970 ft) or so and you will arrive at Kumkapı Square, in and around which are numerous seafood restaurants (the sea itself is only about 200 m, or 656 ft away). The **Üçler Restaurant** in the square is one of the better known, as well as being one of the higher-priced. A meal there will set you back $15 to $20. Cheaper (and in some cases better) restaurants fill the little streets around the square; of these perhaps the best is **Kemal,** which has a mouth-watering array of fish dishes. An evening there should set you back no more than $12. Ditto for most of the other restaurants nearby. Again, check them all out for the one that best suits your appetite.

In the Grand Bazaar itself there is quite a nice place for lunch, the **Havuzlu Lokantası.** Located next to the post office (PTT), it provides not only a retreat from the hurly-burly of the market, but also some unpredictable and tasty refinements on the usual restaurant fare — all for about $7.

Not surprisingly for an area where there is a high concentration of tourist sights, and therefore of tourists, **Sultanahmet** is liberally sprinkled with cafés, snack bars, and tea houses. These are especially in evidence as Divan Yolu nears Sultanahmet Square. At

Divan Yolu 6, across from the Hippodrome, is the famous **Pudding Shop,** purveyor of cheap goodies to the flower children who transplanted themselves here in the sixties. Today, no longer the habitat of spaced-out ragamuffins calling each other Man, it still serves delicious puddings at low prices and now also serves regular meals for around $3. For only a little more you can get an excellent meal at the **Vitamin Restaurant,** Divan Yolu 16, a bright and breezy establishment where the chef has been known to take his place in the window alongside his creations. Continuing up the street you come upon the **Çinar Restaurant,** where you will pay a little more again for very good food and courteous service. But all along this stretch, and in the side streets branching off to the north, you will find no shortage of places with very edible, very affordable food.

For dining in more elegant surroundings you will have to go back to the other side of Sultanahmet Square. The **Yeşil Ev Hotel** (℡ 528-6764), about which I have already rhapsodized, has a splendid restaurant with a wide selection of dishes, superbly prepared. Prices are in the $15-$20 range, as they are at the **Sarnıç** (☎ 512-5732) in Soğukçeşme Sokağı, where my other favorite hotel, the Ayasofya Pansiyonları, is situated. This, too, is a fine restaurant, and has the unusual added attraction of being in a converted cistern.

Before crossing over the **Galata Bridge** to consider the restaurant situation in Beyoğlu, we should pause to consider the bridge itself. Its lower deck is packed with little fish restaurants. While the furniture and fittings tend to be Early Cafeterian, the fish could hardly be fresher or cheaper. A meal, drinks included, should cost no more than $7 here.

For equally good fish in a rather more refined atmosphere you should try the **Liman Lokantası** (☎ 144-1033) in **Karaköy.** Located upstairs in the Turkish Maritime Lines building, its spacious dining area has a splendid view over the mouth of the Golden Horn to the Old City beyond. Open for lunch only, it has a quiet, above-it-all quality that is enhanced by the excellent service. A delicious lunch here, with wine and coffee, will cost you about $15. For outdoor dining go to the **Geçit Restaurant** (☎ 144-3035) in Karaköy Square. It has a vast terrace overlooking the Galata Bridge, and its prices are slightly lower than the Liman's.

Most of the interesting restaurants in **Beyoğlu** are either along Istiklâl Caddesi or around Taksim Square. On Istiklâl Caddesi you will find a host of snack bars, kebap places, and cafeterias. You will also find two very good pudding shops — **Lalê** at № 71 and **Saray** at № 102. And for a whole cluster of little restaurants, lest we forget, there is the Çiçek Pasajı (the "Flower Passage" described under WHAT TO SEE P.52 above) just north of Galatasaray Square on the left as you go towards Taksim. Here you will be able to eat very well for under $10, with the best floor show in town thrown in for free. The **Piknik** (☎ 144-6703) at № 40 is quite nice, and moderately priced, but for something a little more special you should go to the **Hacı Baba** (☎ 144-1886) at № 49. Not only is the food better than you will find in the Çiçek Pasajı, and as reasonably priced, but the restaurant has a quiet little terrace at the back overlooking the courtyard of the Greek Orthodox Church — an oasis of calm in stark contrast to the laughter-filled hubbub of the Çiçek

Pasajı. It does, however, tend to get crowded on weekend evenings, so if you plan to go then it would be wise to book in advance.

Just south of Galatasaray Square, on the same side of the street, there is a little passageway at № 244 running between Istiklâl Caddesi and Meşrutiyet Caddesi. Down this passageway and up a set of stairs, at Olivo Gefidi 15, is the famous but slightly faded **Rejans Restaurant** (☎ 144-1610). Founded before the Second World War by White Russian emigrés, Rejans first achieved prominence as one of Atatürk's favorite restaurants. The cuisine is Russian, the food is scrumptious, especially when preceded by or washed down with Rejans' special lemon vodka, and the bill is always surprisingly low — around $10. Further south on Istiklâl Caddesi, at № 509, is the **Dört Mevsim** ("Four Seasons", ☎ 145-8941). A favorite with people from the nearby consulates, it serves both French and Turkish cuisine. A typical meal here will be quite delicious — and quite good value at around $15. Reservations are advisable.

The vicinity of **Taksim Square** is so densely populated with inexpensive places to eat that as far as restaurants are concerned it could be called Lâleli North. Among the many places one could mention are the **Yuva** at Recep Paşa Caddesi 23, the **Arzu** at Meyve Sokak 18, the **Bey** at Meşelik Sokak, and the **Antep** and **Pehlivan** restaurants, next-door neighbors at the beginning of Istiklâl Caddesi. At the other end of the scale are the restaurants in the big hotels, the best of which is in the **Divan** (☎ 146-4020). It is expensive, of course, and you may have to endure the musical stylings of a so-so pianist (as I did), and you may have to put up with service that borders on the churlish (as I did), but the food is undeniably of the highest order.

The establishment that has long had the reputation of being Istanbul's premier restaurant is not actually in Istanbul, but in the hills above the Bosphorus near the little town of **Emirgan,** about 10 km (6.2 miles) up the coast from Taksim. The restaurant is the **Abdullah** (☎ 163-6406) and its reputation is generally well-deserved. With its gorgeous setting, its imaginative menu, its long-standing insistence on using nothing but the freshest ingredients, and its sophisticated blending of Turkish and Continental cuisines, it can-

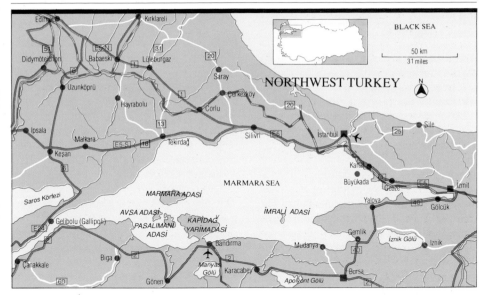

not help but provide a memorable gastronomic experience. The experience will set you back about $25; reservations are essential.

The villages of **Arnavutköy** and **Bebek,** south of Emirgan, and **Tarabya,** to the north, are all known for their excellent seafood restaurants overlooking the Bosphorus. Believe me, there are few more delightful ways to pass a summer evening than over dinner at one of these restaurants.

EDIRNE

Edirne is easily the most important Turkish city in Thrace, that corner of Europe above the Aegean, but it has one serious problem as far as would-be visitors are concerned: its location. You could say it's neither here nor there.

It is close enough to Istanbul to be overshadowed by it, yet far enough away to be overlooked. It is too close to have its own airport, yet too far for a comfortable day excursion by road. And, if you are already in Turkey, unless you are planning to leave the country Edirne is not on the way to anywhere. This is a pity, because it deserves a visit.

BACKGROUND

Somewhat ironically, it is Edirne's location that accounts for its historical importance. For the Romans, it was the gateway to By-

zantium and Asia Minor. For the Ottomans, it was the gateway to the rest of Europe. Founded as Hadrianopolis by the emperor Hadrian in 125 AD, it served as a principal outpost of defense for Byzantium/Constantinople until it was captured by the Ottomans in 1363. Having moved their capital here from Bursa, the Ottomans then used it as a springboard for expansion westward. And it was from here that Mehmet the Conqueror set out in 1453 to begin the siege of Constantinople that marked the end of the Byzantine Empire.

For the next 400 years, Edirne — as the Turks called it; Europeans called it Adrianople — maintained its strategic importance as a military post, until the shrinking of the Ottoman Empire in the nineteenth century left it increasingly exposed and vulnerable. Twice it was occupied by the Russians and once by the Bulgarians, and then in 1920 by the Greeks. They were driven out by Atatürk's armies in 1922, whereupon the city and the rest of eastern Thrace was restored to the Turks by the Treaty of Lausanne.

GENERAL INFORMATION

There is a Tourist Information office at the Bulgarian border crossing, and another by the main square at Talat Paşa Caddesi 76/A (℄ 15260 or ℄ 21490). There is also an office of the Turkish Touring and Automobile Club at the border crossing (℄ 1034).

WHAT TO SEE

From whatever direction you approach Edirne, the first sight you glimpse is the cluster of four tall, pencil-thin minarets surrounding the wide dome of the **Selimiye Camii.** It is altogether fitting that this great mosque should be the first thing you should be able to see from over the border when you are entering Turkey, as well as the last image you carry with you as you depart, for the Selimiye is widely regarded as the most exquisite of all Ottoman mosques. The architect himself, the incomparable Sinan, considered it his masterpiece.

Built for Sultan Selim II and completed in 1575, when Sinan was 86 years old, it has a dome larger in diameter than Aya Sofia's. This, together with the 999 windows through which the light is filtered from every angle, creates a glorious sense of space inside, at once majestic and peaceful. The *mimber* (pulpit) is of intricately carved marble, while the *mihrab* (prayer-niche) is set in an apse decorated with Iznik tiles. The imperial loge contains even finer examples of Iznik tilework, as well as a *mihrab* with a shuttered window opening towards Mecca. As always with Sinan, the grandeur of the building is matched by the beauty of its detail, but in the case of the Selimiye it is the harmony and symmetry of the whole that make it a work of perfection.

Outside the mosque, and also worth a visit, are the **Museum of Turkish and Islamic Art** and the new **Archaeological and Ethnographic Museum.**

Downhill from the Selimiye is the **Eski Camii** ("Old Mosque"), a nine-domed rectangle with two minarets, completed in 1414. It is noted for the huge Arabic inscriptions on its walls. On the other side of the street is the **Üç Şerefeli Camii** or "Three-balconied Mosque". The three balconies in question are actually on one of the mosque's four minarets, which are themselves distinguished by the fact that no two are alike. Across from the mosque is the **Sokullu Hamamı,** a Turkish bath designed by Sinan for the Grand Vezir of Süleyman the Magnificent, Mehmet Sokullu. Just south of Edirne's main square is another of Sinan's works — the **Ali Paşa Çarşisi,** a covered market with wares that span the centuries.

WHERE TO STAY

You don't have much choice, really. You can either stay at the **Kervan Oteli,** Talat Paşa Caddesi 134 (℃ 1355 or ℃ 1382) or the **Sultan Oteli,** Talat Paşa Caddesi 170 (℃ 1372 or ℃ 2156). Both are comfortable and well-run, both are in the center of town, both have restaurants, and both are reasonably priced. The Kervan charges about $15 for a single room and $20 for a double; the larger Sultan charges a bit more.

If you are looking for something cheaper, there are dozens of *pansiyons* and little *otels* dotted around town. For something cheaper still, there are two campsites near Edirne: **Kervansaray Ayşekadin Mokamp** (℃ 1290) and **Fifi Mokamp** (℃ 1554). The Tourist Information office in the middle of town will be able to give you directions.

WHERE TO EAT

Besides the restaurants in the two hotels I mentioned, there are lots of little *kebap* and *köfte* places in Edirne, especially in the area behind the covered market.

HOW TO GET THERE

If you are coming to Turkey by car from western or central Europe you will almost certainly be taking the main E5 highway that runs through Yugoslavia and Bulgaria, in which case you can't avoid Edirne. Likewise, from Istanbul you would take the E5 (or *Londra Asfaltı,* as it is still sometimes known) to Edirne, a distance of about 235 km (146 miles). If you are driving from anywhere along Turkey's Aegean coast, the shortest route would be via Çanakkale–Eceabat (there is a regular car ferry service across the Dardanelles) and then straight up to the E5, where you turn left at Havsa for the last 27 km (17 miles) into Edirne.

If you don't have a car, there are frequent buses to and from Istanbul's Topkapı gate bus station by the city walls. The trip takes about four hours and costs about $2. As for going by train, unless you are a masochist or an insomniac or both, don't even *think* about it.

IZNIK

BACKGROUND

For a slightly down-at-heel lakeside village, Iznik has a long and illustrious past. Founded possibly as long ago as 1000 BC, it was given the name Nicaea by one of Alexander the Great's generals, Lysimachus, in 316 BC. It was not, however, until 325 AD that it came to prominence, when Constantine convened the First Ecumenical Council here. Christians ever since have adhered to the Nicene Creed. In 787 another great Ecumenical Council met here in the cathedral of Aya Sofia and codified rituals and beliefs, particularly regarding icons, into the form still observed by the Greek Orthodox Church.

In 1078 the city passed briefly into the hands of the Seljuk Turks, who made it their capital, and then in 1331 it fell finally to the Ottoman leader Orhan and was renamed Iznik. In the early sixteenth century the armies of Sultan Selim I conquered the Persian city of Tabriz, where 500 of the area's best artisans in ceramics were rounded up together with their families and sent back to Iznik, making it almost overnight a center for the manufacture of colored tiles. By the end of the century there were 400 kilns here turning out the now-famous Iznik tiles. The industry went into decline from about 1700 onwards, but it is having a modest revival today, and some very attractive examples are available in the shops.

GENERAL INFORMATION

The Tourist Information office (℃ 1933) is at Kılıçaslan Caddesi 168, near the eastern end of Iznik's main east-west thoroughfare (the lake is at the western end).

WHAT TO SEE

In the heart of Iznik, where Kılıçaslan Caddesi intersects with Atatürk Caddesi, is what's left of Aya Sofia. Of principal interest in the ruins are the sixth-century mosaic floor and the remains of wall mosaics which were added when the church was rebuilt following the earthquake of 1065. If you go east from Aya Sofia along Kılıfçaslan Caddesi you will come to the **Yeşil Cami** ("Green Mosque") on your left, just beyond the Tourist Information office. Built in 1392, it has a particularly lovely minaret covered in blue and green tiles. Across the street from it is the Nilüfer Hatun Imareti, which now houses the **Iznik Museum**. Here you will find some very intriguing Hellenistic and Byzantine grave steles, as well as displays of Ottoman calligraphy and weaponry. Most interesting of all, not surprisingly, is the ceramics exhibit, which features tiles and other artifacts going back to 2500 BC. Back on Kılıçaslan Caddesi, a bit further along is the **Lefke Gate** (or gates, for there are three of them in a row, the middle one being a Roman triumphal arch), built in 123 AD.

WHERE TO STAY

There are two nice little motels on the lakefront, the **Burcum** (℃ 1011), just north of Kılıçaslan Caddesi, and the **Camlık** (℃ 1631), to the south. Both are very clean and, at about $12 for a double room with breakfast, very reasonably priced. In addition, each has a restaurant and a camping area.

WHERE TO EAT

There are several places where one can eat quite cheaply on Kılıçaslan Caddesi, of which the best is probably the **Köşk.** The most pleasant places, however, are along the lakefront. Two worth mentioning are the **Dallas** and the **Dostlar,** both of which serve meals featuring freshwater fish for around $7.

HOW TO GET THERE

Unless you happen to be driving between Bursa and Yalova, and make a detour of some 70 km (43 miles) around the lake to take in Iznik, you will want to go by bus from either Bursa or Yalova. Buses leave regularly from both cities, and the trip takes about an hour and a half. Note, however, that if you plan to leave Iznik the same day you should get on a bus out by 5 pm, as the buses stop running in the early evening.

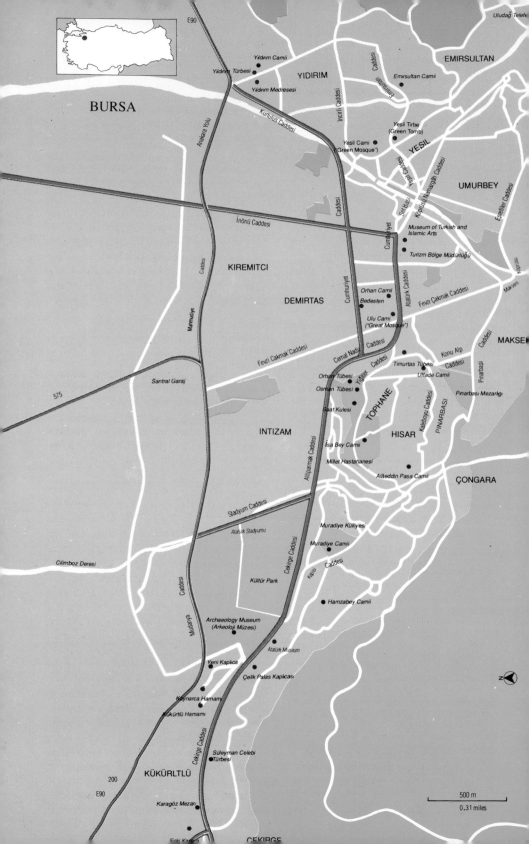

BURSA

BACKGROUND

Bursa's founding has been variously dated from the sixth to the second century BC, but in any case it was not until the fourteenth century AD that it began to enjoy a reputation as anything other than the home of some hot springs and of the Turkish silk industry. For it was in 1326 that Orhan, the son of Osman from whom the Ottomans took their name, captured Bursa and made it his capital. Although the capital was later moved to Edirne, and ultimately to Istanbul, Bursa remained in a sense the spiritual home of the Ottoman Empire.

Today Bursa is not only the proud custodian of a great deal of Ottoman history, but it is also a booming industrial city with a population of almost a million. Spread across the lower northern slopes of Uludagv, the highest mountain in northwest Anatolia (2,543 m or 8,350 ft), Bursa is known fondly among Turks as "Green Bursa". The epithet is thoroughly deserved: with its verdant backdrop, tree-lined streets, and lovingly tended parks and gardens, it is a very attractive city indeed.

GENERAL INFORMATION

There are three Tourist Information offices in Bursa. One is near the main plaza, Cumhuriyet Alanı (known locally as Heykel), at Atatürk Caddesi 82 (☏ 12359). There is another one (☏ 13368) where Cemal Nadir Caddesi curls into Altıparmak Caddesi, below the park holding the tombs of sultans Osman and Orhan. The third is off Fevzi Çakmak Caddesi at Ahmet Hamdi Tanpınar Caddesi, Saydam Iş Merkezi 31 (☏ 28005).

There is a Turkish Airlines (THY) office at Cemal Nadir Caddesi 8/A (☏ 21866), and a Sönmez Airlines office (☏ 10099) in Kızılay Pasajı off Cemal Nadir Caddesi.

WHAT TO SEE

The best known religious landmark in Bursa is the **Yeşil Cami** ("Green Mosque"), about a kilometer from Heykel — just follow the yellow signs. Built for Sultan Mehmet I and finished in 1424, it is considered by some to be the finest mosque in Turkey, surpassing even the Selimiye in Edirne. The exterior is almost entirely marble, delicately carved, while the interior is covered with green, blue, and turquoise tiles, many with floral designs. Under the dome near the entrance is a lovely fountain carved from a single block of marble. Directly across the street from the Green Mosque is the **Yeşil Türbe,** or Green Tomb. Designed by the same architect who built the Green Mosque, Hacı Ivaz Pasa, it is decorated inside and out with the same turquoise Iznik tiles. Within, there is the huge, ornately-tiled sarcophagus of Mehmet I. Down the street from the Green Mosque, its *medrese* (theological school) has been converted to house the **Museum of Turkish and Islamic Arts.** It has a large ethnographic collection, including pottery, silverware, swords, and carpets.

If you go back to Heykel and continue westward along Atatürk Caddesi you will come to the **Ulu Cami** ("Great Mosque") on the right. Monolithic and austere from the outside, and capped by no fewer than 20 small domes, its interior is noted for the carved walnut *mimber* and the wonderfully stylized calligraphy on the walls and pillars. It was originally built in 1399–1400, but has twice had to be restored.

The area to the north and east of the Great Mosque is taken up by the **market district,** at the heart of which is the **Bedesten,** or Covered Bazaar. In this labyrinth of little streets, alleys, and passages you will find all the usual market items — copper, brass, gold, silver, carpets, *kilims*, leather goods, jewelry, antiques, etc. — as well as the things for which Bursa is famous: towels, knives, and silk. The silk in particular makes the visit worthwhile. And while you're there pay a visit to the **Koza Han,** a two-storied stone building built up around a courtyard near the eastern entrance to the bazaar. This is where villagers bring their silkworm cocoons in June and September to sell to the silk traders. It makes for a fascinating spectacle, and ultimately for some splendid bargains in the shops nearby.

WHERE TO STAY

Luxury

All of the top hotels are concentrated in the the suburb of Çekirge, west of the city center, because this is where Bursa's famed hot springs bubble to the surface. The oldest and still the best of these hotels is the **Çelik Palas,** the Art Nouveau "Steel Palace" which takes its name from the steel dome over the hotel's thermal baths. A grand Old World hotel with every New World amenity, including tennis courts, the Çelik Palas (☎ 61900) is at Çekirge Caddesi 79, next to the **Atatürk Museum** and across the street from the **Archaeological Museum.** Rooms at the Çelik Palas go for approximately $75 single and $110 double. A little less luxurious, and less expensive, is the **Anatolia** (☎ 67110) on Çekirge Meydanı, where several hotels are grouped near Çekirge's Thermal Center, each one with its own thermal baths.

Middle Range
In this same group you will find the following hotels. The **Dilmen** (☎ 66114 or ☎ 21701) on Hamamlar Caddesi has rooms with wonderful views of the valley below and charges about $45 for a single and $60 for a double; the same goes for the **Gönlü Ferah** next door. The **Akdoğan** (☎ 60610) at 1 Murat Caddesi 5 is particularly good value with a Turkish bath and swimming pool, plus television and refrigerators in the rooms, for about $27 single and $35 double. The **Ada Palas** (☎ 19200) at 1 Murat Caddesi 21 is probably the best bargain for thermal bathers with single rooms for about $15 and doubles for about $20.

Inexpensive
For cheaper accommodation you are better off staying in the center of town. Among the lower-priced hotels here is the **Dikmen** (☎ 14995) at Maksem Caddesi 78, up the hill behind the main post office, which is across from the Ulu Cami. It has rooms for $16 single and $22 double. At the bottom of Maksem Caddesi, where it is now also called Fevzi Çakmak Caddesi just to confuse you, opposite the post office is the **Artıç Oteli** (☎ 19500), which charges about $13 for a single room and $16 for a double. A block west of the post office, if you turn left on Inebey Caddesi you will come to the **Otel Çamlıbel** a couple of blocks up on the right. Single rooms with private shower are about $9, doubles about $14.

Camping
The **Kervansaray Kumluk Mokamp** (☎ 13965) is six kilometers (3.7 miles) north of Bursa on the Bursa-Yalova road.

WHERE TO EAT
Bursa could have been custom-designed for the hungry tourist, for wherever you turn there is a little restaurant or *lokanta* where you can eat cheaply, deliciously and, if you like, quickly. The local speciality is *Iskender kebap* or *Bursa kebap* — slices of lamb on pieces of flat bread covered in tomato sauce and topped with brown butter — and consequently it is the star attraction at every *kebapçı* in town. Considering that it was invented in the **Kebapçı Iskenderoğlu** at Atatürk Caddesi 60, that is probably the place to try it first, but you can hardly go wrong ordering it anywhere. Another good place to stop by is the **Nazar** restaurant inside the Koza Han in the market district. The only problem with these little restaurants in the middle of town — in my experience, at least — is that many of them do not serve beer or wine, so if this is a drawback for you it would be a good idea to check before ordering.

For delicious food in a beautiful and restful setting you should go to the **Kültür Park,** where there are a number of delightful restaurants. Among them I would single out the **Özkent Lokanta,** where you can expect to pay up to $15 for a meal. Much cheaper, but still good, are the **Selçuk** and **Hacı Bey** restaurants.

HOW TO GET THERE
Sönmez Airlines has a daily flight from (and to) Istanbul, otherwise you will arrive (and depart) by road. Buses all come into the Şehir Garajı just off the main highway, a couple of kilometers from the city center, from which you can get a taxi, city bus, or *dolmuş* into town. Buses for Ankara, Yalova, Çanakkale, and Izmir leave regularly from the Şehir Garajı.

OPPOSITE TOP: The entrance to the Green Tomb of Mehmet I in Bursa. BOTTOM: The interior of the Green Tomb.

The
Northern
Aegean

TURKEY'S northern Aegean coast, the western-most part of Asia, has the combined appeal of ancient ruins and modern resorts, with a beautiful azure sea on one side and a succession of fields, orchards, olive groves, and pine forests on the other.

ÇANAKKALE

Çanakkale, at the narrowest point of the Dardanelles, is used by most tourists as the base from which to visit the battlefields of Gallipoli across the straits and the ruins of Troy and Assos down the coast. The town's name in Turkish means "saucer castle", after the castle built there by Mehmet the Conqueror in 1452, but it could with equal justification have been named after a turnstile, given its long history as a crossing point for invading armies from both directions.

BACKGROUND

Probably the most famous crossing made here was by the Persian King Xerxes in 480 BC.

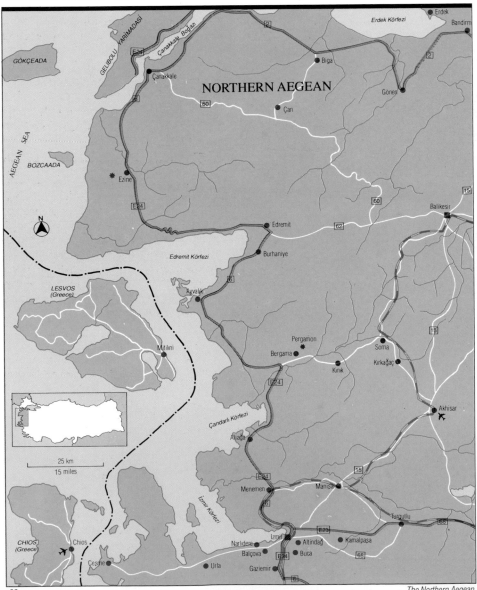

At the head of an army of 400,000 men, he crossed on a bridge of boats on his way to the climactic battles of Thermopylae and Salamis, where his dreams of conquering Europe were thwarted by the Greeks. Other celebrated crossings near here were made by the mythical Leander, who swam across every night in order to be with Hero, until one night he drowned in a storm, and by Byron, who swam across on May 3, 1810. During the nineteenth century Çanakkale was a thriving international port and boasted a large number of consulates in recognition of its strategic geographical importance. During this century its importance and its cosmopolitanism both diminished — until recently, that is, when it got a second wind as a center of agriculture and tourism.

GENERAL INFORMATION

The Tourist Information office ((1187) is at Iskele Meydanı 67, in a booth in the main square by the ferry docks.

WHAT TO SEE

The principal sights are, of course, on that long finger of land across the straits known as **Gallipoli** (in Turkish, *Gelibolu*). This is where British, Australian, and New Zealand forces landed in April, 1915 with the intention of ultimately capturing Istanbul and thereby opening up a sea lane for the Allies to Russia and eastern Europe. Unfortunately for them, the Allies landed in an area where Turkish troops were under the command of a junior officer who was about to become a legend, Lieutenant-Colonel Mustafa Kemal. After nine bloody months of fighting, the decimated Allied forces withdrew, and young Mustafa Kemal was on his way to becoming Kemal Atatürk. Today there is an enormous **Turkish War Memorial,** with a museum attached, honoring those who fell in the Gallipoli campaign. Travel agencies in Çanakkale also offer guided tours by car of the battlefields and cemeteries.

At the edge of town, on the road to Troy, is the new **Archaeological Museum,** which houses, among other exhibits, a fine collection of artifacts from Troy. There is also a **Military and Naval Museum** at the southern end of the quays near the castle. Both museums are closed on Mondays.

WHERE TO STAY

The best hotel is the **Büyük Truva** ((1024) on the waterfront, several blocks from the main square. It has very comfortable rooms, with a view over the straits, for $20 single and $26 double. It also has a very good restaurant. Similarly priced is the new **Anafartalar Oteli** ((4454) on the waterfront just north of the ferry docks. It has a nice roof restaurant. Also on the waterfront, the **Bakır** ((4088) at Yalı Caddesi 12, just south of the clock tower, is a modern, friendly hotel with rooms for about $16 single and $23 double.

A block inland, at Kızılay Sokak 20, is the new **Otel Yıldız** ((1793), which offers modern rooms for $9 single and $12 double. Even less expensive is the **Hotel Konak** ((1150) near the clock tower; rooms here go for $6 single and $9 double.

WHERE TO EAT

There are dozens of cheap and cheerful places to eat in Çanakkale, but the most interesting and the most fun are along the quayside south of the ferry docks. Here you will find the **Çanakkale,** the **Rıhtım,** the **Boğaz,** and others, all serving meals with fresh fish for $5 and under. For a little more ($8 to $12) you can have an excellent meal on the third-floor terrace of the **Yalova Liman,** overlooking the water.

HOW TO GET THERE

There are frequent buses from Istanbul, Bursa, and Izmir (and points in between), as well as two buses a day from Edirne. If you are driving from Europe, there is a car ferry from Eceabat, just across the straits, every hour.

TROY

As this is the setting for the first great work of Western literature, Homer's *Iliad,* let's start with the poetic version of Troy's past. Here in the mid-thirteenth century BC, so the story goes, King Priam presided over a kingdom at peace with the world, until his son Paris was moved to abduct the most beautiful woman in the world, Helen, the wife of the Spartan king Menelaus. With help from the other Greek states, Menelaus launched a thousand ships to bring her back. Thus began the Trojan War, in which Priam's other son Hector killed Patroclus, and Achilles killed Hector, and Paris killed Achilles. The war lasted for ten years, until Odysseus hit upon the stratagem of pretending to abandon the siege of Troy and leaving behind a giant wooden horse. The Trojans, taking the horse to be a religious offering, brought it within the city's high walls, whereupon Greek soldiers spilled out and sacked the city.

The archaeological versions of the city's distant past don't necessarily contradict the Homeric version, nor do the known historical facts. But they do introduce — in some cases literally — layers of evidence that confuse as much as they clarify. In fact, there was no archaeological version at all until 1871 when a German merchant named Heinrich Schliemann, who had made his fortune in America during the California Gold Rush, began digging here for a different kind of gold. With a team of 150 workers, paid for out of his own pocket, the Homer-loving Schliemann carried out his excavations at a mound which the Turks called Hisarlık. Here he found not one Troy but several, one superimposed on another; subsequent excavations have revealed nine cities in all, dating back to 3600 BC. Now if the historians are right in dating the Trojan War at around 1250 BC, then the city which the scholars call Troy VII would be the city of Priam. But if Homer's descriptions of the city are anything to go by, and some of them are quite precise, the earlier Troy VI is the one that fell to the soldiers of Agamemnon. This is where the complications, and the arguments, begin.

Whichever of these stones did become the foundation stones of our literature, when you visit the site you would do well to remember the epic struggle they were a part of, and the epic poetry they helped to inspire, because the stones themselves are not all that impressive. For sheer visual impact, they have nothing on the huge wooden reconstruction of the **Trojan Horse** that dominates the entrance to the site. (Visitors can enter the horse by a set of stairs underneath that lead up to windows,

and to the horse's eyes, where one can look out over the plain.) Still, the site, which is well signposted, repays close attention, and will continue to repay it long after you have left.

ASSOS

About 40 km (25 miles) south of Troy on the main highway (E24) is the village of Ayvacık; here there is a turning for Behramkale (Assos), 20 winding kilometers away to the southwest. As you approach Assos, or Behramkale, there is a perfectly-preserved Ottoman bridge at the foot of the hill that you climb to reach the village.

BACKGROUND

Assos was founded sometime around 900 BC by Aeolians from the nearby island of Lesvos. By 540 BC there was a Doric Temple of Athena at the summit of the acropolis, and two centuries later Aristotle lived here for three years, doing his seminal work on the new sciences of biology and botany. In 334 BC Aristotle's pupil, Alexander the Great, crossed the Dardanelles and captured Assos on his way to conquering half the world. It later came under the sway of the kings of Pergamon, and then was a Byzantine city until it was captured by the Ottomans in 1330 AD. Off the beaten track, it has remained in quiet obscurity ever since.

WHAT TO SEE

Now that the Temple of Athena has been reduced to rubble there is little left to see in the citadel itself except the great stone walls extending for three kilometers and reaching a height of 14 m (46 ft) in places. These are among the best preserved ancient walls anywhere in the Aegean. Outside the walls is the ancient **necropolis**, strewn with the fragments of sarcophagi. But easily the most impressive sight is the one you see *from* here: the blue seascape of the Aegean, with the large island of Lesvos rising out of the middle of it.

WHERE TO STAY

Down the cobbled road from the clifftop village is the rest of Behramkale, a huddle of houses and little restaurants along the pebbled shore. Here you will find the **Behram Oteli** (℅ 16), a delightful place under the careful supervision of its convivial owner, Mr Öcal Elmacıoğlu. It also has a first-rate restaurant. A very comfortable double room facing the ancient breakwater, with breakfast and dinner included, will cost about $28 here. If that is a bit steep for your budget, the **Motel Assos** and the **Yıldız Oteli** nearby have double rooms for about $12. There are also little areas set aside for camping near the shore.

WHERE TO EAT

The **Behram** has the best restaurant, where you can eat very well indeed for about $7. The **Assos** and the **Yıldız** also have good restaurants, and there are a number of other very inexpensive places dotted along the waterfront.

HOW TO GET THERE

By road. If you don't have a car of your own, it is not difficult to hitch a ride from Ayvacık and back again. Alternatively, you can take a *dolmuş* from Ayvacık, but you may have a wait as they run only irregularly. In the peak season there are buses to Assos from Ayvalık; if you inquire at the Tourist Information office there (see below) they will be able to tell you when the buses run.

AYVALIK

Around the curve of the Gulf of Edremit from Assos, and across a narrow strait from Lesvos, is the pretty seaside town of Ayvalık. The town itself is basically a fishing port, with pine forests and olive groves behind it, a large beach resort area just south of it, and no less than 23 emerald islets — plus one large island, Lesvos — in the bay in front of it.

BACKGROUND

Given the life span of most Turkish towns and cities, Ayvalık is still in its infancy. Founded as recently as the mid-seventeenth century, it only became a truly Turkish town in 1923 when, in an exchange of populations

following the Greek defeat in the war with Turkey, Greek-speaking Turks from Crete were brought to Ayvalık to replace the town's Ottoman Greeks who were "repatriated" to Greece. Ayvalık still retains some of its Greek flavor, and one can occasionally hear Greek being spoken here.

GENERAL INFORMATION

The Tourist Information office (℅ 2122) is located by the yacht harbor at the southern end of town.

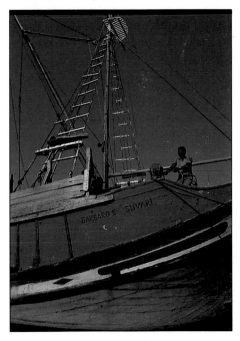

WHAT TO SEE

Because of the town's relative youth, there are no man-made sights worth seeing here, but there is more than enough natural beauty around to compensate. There are boats all the time to **Ali Bey** island across the bay, which is fringed with marvelous little seafood restaurants, as well as boat tours to the other, smaller islands scattered in the water. And for an interesting change of scene, there are daily ferries to and from **Lesvos**. Tickets, which are about $22 one-

A fishing boat pulls into Izmir with the day's catch.

way and $35 for a round trip, can be bought at almost any of the travel agencies near the main square.

WHERE TO STAY

There are quite a few very cheap, very basic hostelries in Ayvalık, but all the more comfortable hotels and motels are a few kilometers to the south. Perhaps the most splendid of these is the **Murat Reis** ((1680), on its own little bay, surrounded by pine trees, with its own private beach. Double rooms

here are from about $35. Further along you come to Sarmısaklı beach, an 11-km (7-mile) stretch of white sand lined with hotels and restaurants. Of these the best is the **Büyük Berk Oteli** ((2311). Its amenities include a swimming pool, playground, games room, disco, and restaurant. All of its rooms have balconies overlooking the sea, and are priced at about $40, breakfast and dinner included. Just down the beach is the **Ankara Oteli** ((1195), which is about half the size of the Büyük Berk and almost as nice. Its rooms range from $20 single and $27 double, with breakfast. For about the same price the **Başkent Motel** offers rooms with balconies on the seafront, very friendly service, and a very good restaurant. Among the less expensive hotels on the beach, the **Aytaş** and the **Sevo** are both recommended.

ABOVE: The acropolis at Pergamon, where the great library is now being painstakingly reconstructed. OPPOSITE: Pergamon — not only the birthplace of modern books but also of modern holistic medicine.

WHERE TO EAT

As with the hotels, all of the cheap restaurants are grouped in the town near the harbor, while the fancier places are strung out along the beach at Sarmısaklı. There is no shortage of either, and no real difference in quality among those in each group, so it's just a matter of deciding what you would like — and how much you would like to pay for it.

HOW TO GET THERE

It is very easy to get *almost* there, as there are frequent buses from Bursa, Çanakkale, and Izmir arriving along the E24. The trouble is that the E24 does not actually go through Ayvalık, so you may be dropped off five kilometers away from the center of town. And even if your bus does go all the way to the Ayvalık bus station (and be sure to confirm this with the bus company in advance), you will still be almost one and a half kilometers away from the town center. From the station, however, you can get a local bus to take you to the main square — and beyond, all the way to Sarmısaklı beach.

PERGAMON

The rise and fall of most great cities can be charted along a fairly predictable curve, but not in the case of Pergamon. It flickered dimly for centuries, then blazed into glory for a hundred years or so, smoldered on for another 300 years, then flickered again and died out, leaving behind the dead embers that thousands still visit every year.

BACKGROUND

Although we know that Pergamon (modern Bergama) dates back to 1000 BC, and perhaps earlier, there is no mention of its existence until 399 BC, after Xenophon had paused here on his long march home. The city would then probably have returned to permanent semi-oblivion but for a stroke of luck: Alexander's general Lysimachus, who was hugely successful in the internecine wars that followed Alexander's death, decided to deposit

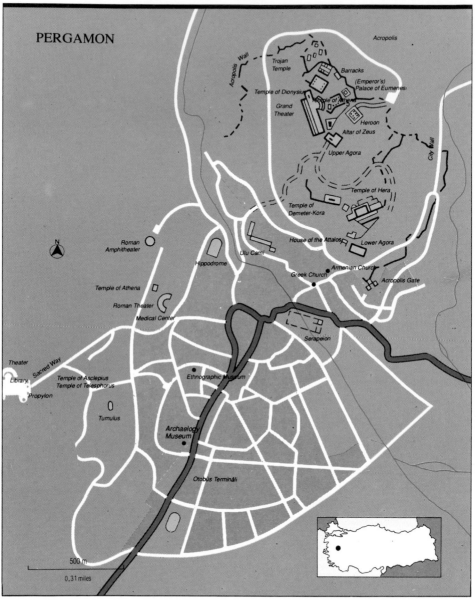

PERGAMON

his considerable war treasure in Pergamon for safekeeping. Thus, when Lysimachus died without an heir in 281 BC, Pergamon, the city on the hill, found itself sitting on a fortune. Within two decades Pergamon had a king, Eumenes I, and an ambitious building program. Under Eumenes' adopted son, Attalus I (241–197 BC), Pergamon acquired a proper kingdom.

It was Attalus' son, Eumenes II (197–159 BC), who made Pergamon not only a great power in the land but also a renowned center of art and learning. He consolidated his father's military alliance with Rome, and presided over the expansion of his kingdom all the way to Konya, 500 km (310 miles) to the southeast. He also expanded the Asclepion, Pergamon's celebrated medical center, and erected the great Altar of Zeus. But it is chiefly for his library that the world remembers Pergamon. An obsessive bibliophile, Eumenes collected 200,000 volumes for his library, making it the only rival in the world to the great library at Alexandria. Indeed, its eminence so worried the Egyptians, who feared that it would enable Pergamon to challenge and possibly supplant Alexandria as the world's foremost center of scholarship, that they banned the export of papyrus, on which all books were written. Whereupon Pergamon's scientists, at Eumenes' instigation, came up with a substitute: dried and specially treated animal skins, or parchment. As the new "paper" was too thick and stiff to be rolled up in scrolls, it was cut and stacked in leaves; thus were books as we know them invented.

On Eumenes' death in 159 BC his brother Attalus II acceded to the throne. If his 21-year reign was something of an anti-climax, the brief reign of his nephew Attalus III, who succeeded him, was a disaster. In only five years, 138-133 BC, he allowed the kingdom to crumble, and when he died he stunned the world by leaving the kingdom to Rome in his will. Four years later, in 129 BC, it officially became the Roman province of Asia.

The city was to suffer two further humiliations in fairly short order. In 88 BC it was stripped of its rights after it supported Mithridates in his "war of liberation" against the Romans, and four decades later, after fire had destroyed part of the library at Alexandria, Mark Antony stripped Pergamon's library of its books in order to give them to Cleopatra to replace the ones lost in the fire. Nevertheless, Pergamon remained a seat of learning into the Christian era. The Asclepion, in fact, enjoyed its period of greatest renown in the second century AD under Galen, the most influential physician of the ancient world. Then it, too, went into decline.

GENERAL INFORMATION

The Tourist Information office (℡ 1862) is on the main road into Bergama from the highway, just beyond the turning on the left for the Asclepion, at Zafer Mahallesi, Izmir Caddesi 54.

WHAT TO SEE

In Bergama itself there is a very good little **Archaeological Museum** on Cumhuriyet Caddesi in the middle of town. Apart from its fascinating collection of artifacts from the ancient site, it has a model of the Altar of Zeus which is of particular interest as most

of the original is now in the Pergamon Museum in East Berlin. Farther on, before you head up the hill to the acropolis, you will come across the **Red Courtyard (Kızıl Avlu)**, a large red-brick structure straddling the Selinos River. Built in the second century AD as a temple to the Egyptian god Serapis, or Osiris, it was later converted into a Christian basilica. One of its towers now contains a small mosque.

At the **acropolis,** rising almost 400 m (1,300 ft) above the surrounding plain, the most important remains are those of the **library,** which is now being reconstructed, and the enormous **Altar of Zeus,** of which only the foundation is left. Most impressive is the steep **theater** carved into the hillside, with its 80 rows of seats capable of holding up to 10,000 spectators. Looking westward across the valley from here you can see the Asclepion.

To reach the **Asclepion** you have to go back through town and turn right at the Tourist Information office; it is then another one and a half kilometers along the road. From the parking lot you approach the ancient medical center along the Sacred Way, which leads to the ceremonial area between the library and the temple to Asclepius, the god of medicine. Inside you will find the Sacred Fountain and the entrance to the underground passageway that leads to the temple of Telesphorus. On the other side of the center is the Roman theater. All of these are well signposted.

The most impressive thing about the Asclepion, for me anyway, is not the antiquity of the ruins but the modernity of the medical treatment that was offered here. The Pergamenes practiced holistic medicine to a degree that would make many contemporary clinics seem outdated. During a patient's stay at the Asclepion his dreams were analyzed for diagnostic purposes, his diet was closely supervised, he was given mud baths and massages, he was treated with herbal medicines, he spent time in the healing springs, and he had access to a library and a theater to help him relax and deal with stress. This was 2,000 years ago.

WHERE TO STAY

It's a pity the Asclepion is not still in business, because that would be the place to stay.

As it is, Bergama's accommodation illustrates the problem with the law of supply and demand: its circularity. Because for a long time there were no decent hotels in Bergama, visitors only came on day trips from Izmir or Ayvalık, and because visitors didn't come to stay, there was no point building hotels for them to stay in. Now the circle seems to have been broken. There is the **Tusan Bergama Moteli** ((1173), where the E24 meets the road into Bergama, which has pleasant rooms for $16 single and $20 double. Further along the road into Bergama is the new **Berksoy Oteli,**

How to Get There

Buses go to Bergama every half-hour during the day from Izmir's main bus terminal, and four or five times a day from Ayvalık. But here again, as with buses to Ayvalık, check in advance to make sure the bus goes all the way to the Bergama bus station, or you could find yourself standing on the E24 waiting for a lift to take you the last seven kilometers into town.

where you can stay in greater comfort for $20 single and $25 double. And in the middle of town, near the bus station, the **Park Oteli** has been extensively refurbished and now offers very nice rooms at $20 for a double. There is also a campsite just outside town.

Where to Eat

There are little *lokantas* offering cheap but tasty meals all along the main street. None of them rates a special mention, but then you didn't come here to eat.

Izmir as seen from Kadifekale, the "Velvet Fortress".

IZMIR

If ever a city should have been named Phoenix, it is Izmir, for one can hardly count the number of times it has risen from the ashes. The most recent time was in 1922, when a terrible fire of mysterious origins engulfed the city following the evacuation of the defeated Greek armies. It is this last in a long line of calamities that accounts for the fact that today Izmir is Turkey's most thoroughly modern city.

Background

Izmir, which until 1922 was known as Smyrna, probably was settled as early as the third millennium BC, but it did not take its place in the history books until around 1000 BC when the Aeolians were ousted by the Ionians. The city then had four centuries of relative peace, during the middle of which period it was the birthplace and home of Homer, before it was destroyed by the Lydians around 600 BC. It remained moribund until Alexander the Great arrived in 333 BC and breathed new life into it by encouraging nearby communities to settle on Mt. Pagus (now Kadifekale, "Velvet Fortress") in the heart of today's city. There followed a long spell of peace and prosperity, thanks mainly to Smyrna's links with Pergamon and Rome, until it was destroyed by an earthquake in 178 AD. It flourished again as a Byzantine city until it was taken by the Seljuk Turks early in the eleventh century, and then by the Crusaders, and then by Tamerlane, who demolished it in 1402.

Again, however, it rose up, this time under the Ottomans, becoming over the next few centuries a great international port. In the process it acquired a cosmopolitan air and a distinctly European accent. Then, in September 1922, Smyrna went up in flames for the last time. Out of the rubble grew contemporary Izmir, Turkey's third largest city and busiest port, a thriving metropolis of modern buildings and wide, palm-lined boulevards.

GENERAL INFORMATION

The Tourist Information office (℡ 142147) is on Gaziosmanpaşa Bulvarı next to the Büyük Efes Hotel. There you will also find the Turkish Airlines (THY) office (℡ 141226). The Turkish Maritime Lines number at the Alsancak Harbor is 210077, and the Turkish Railways (TCDD) number at Basmane Station is ℡ 148638. The number of the main bus station is ℡ 162266. The Turkish Touring and Automobile Club (TTOK) has an office at Atatürk Bulvarı 370, near the Alsancak Harbor at the northern end of the street, ℡ 217149.

WHAT TO SEE

Because of Izmir's historical cycle of catastrophe and regeneration, it has little to offer the tourist in the way of sightseeing. What it offers instead is a comfortable and con-

venient hub from which to explore all the ruins of classical civilization to the north and south of the city. The only sight definitely worth seeing in the city itself, in my opinion, is the **bazaar**, which occupies Anafartalar Caddesi (and its little tributaries) as it meanders from Basmane railway station all the way to the Ottoman clock tower on the seafront in Konak. Here you will find many excellent bargains in the one part of the city that has a genuine personality of its own.

WHERE TO STAY

Luxury
Cumhuriyet Meydanı, the bayside plaza with the equestrian statue of Atatürk, is to Izmir what Taksim Square is to Istanbul: here is where all the luxury hotels are. Foremost among them is the distinguished old **Büyük Efes** (℡ 144300). With its large enclosed gardens, its glass-sided (sic!) swimming pool, its tennis courts, its Turkish bath and sauna, its restaurants and nightclub, and its attentive service, it is certainly worth the $70-90 that it charges for a single room and $90-$110 for a double. Around the corner at Cumhuriyet Bulvarı 138 is the **Etap Izmir** (℡ 104290), which has all the amenities one takes for granted in an international chain hotel. Single rooms here are about $70, doubles $85. Still luxurious, but less expensive, is my personal favorite in Izmir, the **Otel Karaca** (℡ 144445 or 144426). It is right behind the Büyük Efes, at Necatibey Bulvarı 1379 Sokak № 55. A single room is about $45; a double is about $60, and that includes television, refrigerator, and a lounge area next to the small balcony.

Middle Range
In the same vicinity are three fine hotels offering comfortable, air-conditioned rooms at moderate prices. North of Cumhuriyet Meydanı at 1377 Sokak № 9 is the **Kısmet Oteli** (℡ 217050). A block south of the plaza at Cumhuriyet Bulvarı 124 is the **Anba Oteli** (℡ 144380). And there is the **Kilim Oteli** (℡ 145340) a block over on Atatürk Bulvarı, facing the bay. All three hotels charge from $28 single and $38 double.

Inexpensive
If you cross Anafartalar Caddesi from the Basmane railway station and keep going

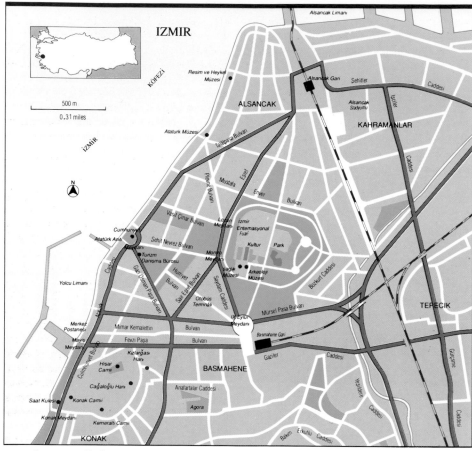

west down any little street you can, you will soon find yourself in the middle of an area teeming with inexpensive hotels. Walk along any of these numbered streets — 1294, 1295, 1296, 1297, 1298, or 1301 — and you will soon conclude that they are named after the number of hotels they have. If for some reason you can't find something suitable here, go over to Fevzipaşa Bulvarı, which is the big boulevard that runs from Basmane to the waterfront. Here, a block from the station on the north side of the street, is the unpromisingly named **Hotel Nil** ((135228). At only $10 for a single and $15 double, it's a bargain. So is the **Babadan** ((139640) at Gaziosmanpaşa Bulvarı 50, some eight blocks down Fevzipaşa Bulvarı from the Hotel Nil. It is a bit pricier, with singles for $15 and doubles for $20. The street that runs parallel to Fevzipaşa Bulvarı to the north, 1369 Sokak, also has a string of attractively priced hotels.

WHERE TO EAT

On the waterfront. Yes, it really is as simple as that. If you go north from Cumhuriyet Meydanı along Atatürk Bulvarı you will find restaurants and cafés of every description, many with outdoor tables. Of these the best are the **Kordelya** ((148686) at Atatürk Bulvarı № 148/A, the **Deniz** ((220601) at № 188/B, the **Erol'un Yeri** ((133238) at № 272, the **Imbat** ((211229) at № 278/A, the **Kaktıs** ((220548) at № 306/A, the **Yengeç** ((217368) at № 314, the **Kemal'in Yeri** ((217255) at № 344, and the **Madam** ((22327) at № 348.

On the other hand, if you want a cheap meal with a large side helping of local color, you should head for the bazaar district, especially that stretch of Anafartalar Caddesi between Gaziosmanpaşa Bulvarı and the Basmane station. Your third option (which probably ought to be your first) is to check out the restaurants on your doorstep. That's the way I found my own, idiosyncratic favorite in Izmir: the **Chinese Restaurant** (that's its name) next to the Otel Karaca on Necatibey Bulvarı.

HOW TO GET THERE

From Istanbul or Ankara the easiest way is to fly (although the *nicest* way from Istanbul is by sea). From anywhere else in the country you have a choice of coming by road or rail, or a combination of the two. If you're coming by bus, you will arrive at the Otogar Garajı, a huge complex out in the Halkapınar district next to Atatürk Stadium. From here you can take a taxi, a *dolmuş*, or the Nº 50 bus into the center of town. If you're coming by train, you will arrive at the Basmane railway station, which is already in — or very near — the center of town. It is also very near 9 Eylül Meydanı, the big square a few meters from the entrance to the station, which is where the bus companies have their ticket offices. That's worth remembering when you are planning your onward journey.

ÇEŞME

Eighty kilometers (50 miles) out along the peninsula west of Izmir is Çeşme ("fountain"), so named because of all the hot springs nearby. The hot springs are one reason why people go to this coastal village. The beautiful sandy beaches and lavish resort facilities are another. The third is the ferry to Chios.

GENERAL INFORMATION

There is a Tourist Information office (℄ 1653) by the ferry dock in Çeşme at Iskele Meydanı 8, and another one at the Altın Yunus Marina (℄ 125082).

WHAT TO SEE

The only man-made sight that warrants a visit is the fourteenth century Genoese **castle,** which was expanded and fortified by Sultan Beyazit II in 1508. After that, head for the **beaches.** The most popular is the talcum powdery beach at Ilıca, but there are also lovely beaches at Şifne, Ildırı, Boyalık, Ertan, Pırlanta, Sakızlı, Altınkum, Tursite, Çatal Azmak — all nearby. Ilıca and Şifne are also noted for their thermal spas. The remaining sight is eight kilometers (five miles) to the west of Çeşme: the Greek island of Chios. Ferries run daily to and from Chios; tickets are on sale in the square by the docks.

WHERE TO STAY

If you like luxury combined with yachting or water sports, you will have struck it rich here. There are spectacular hotels by all the main beaches, but the most spectacular of all is the **Altın Yunus Tatilköyü**, the Golden Dolphin Holiday Village (℄ 1250). Along with its luxury accommodation it provides a wide range of recreational facilities, especially for water sports, plus thermal baths and a yacht marina. A single room here is $40, a double $50. For about the same price you can stay at the delightful **Turban Çeşme** (℄ 1240) on Ilıca beach which also has a swimming pool and tennis courts in addition to its thermal baths. And there are many other smaller hotels crowded around each of the major beaches.

In Çeşme itself there is the splendid **Çeşme Kervansaray** (℄ 6490), just south of the main square by the harbor. Originally built as a caravanserai by Süleyman the Magnificent in 1528, this two-story, U-shaped building has been beautifully and tastefully converted into a hotel. Prices are again about $40 for a single and $50 for a double. On the other side of the square, near the water, is the **Ertan Oteli** (℄ 6795) with rooms for $30 single and $35 double. The nearest official campsite is the **U Kamp** at Çeşmealtı (℄ 21), but there are unofficial camping areas just north of Çeşme in the Ildırı area, which is much nearer.

The
Southern
Aegean

THIS IS my favorite corner of the world. Nowhere else can you find quite the same combination of the fashionable and the timeless, of sensuality and antiquity, of attractive people and attractive places. Here the same sun that bronzes the skin of visitors whitens the marble of history. Here camels, the ancient ships of the desert, look on inscrutably as sleek yachts trail chevrons in the blue-green water. Here the routine dazzle of sunflowers and bougainvillea gives way after dark to the scent of jasmine and honeysuckle, as the searingly bright days fade into soft, balmy nights. I like it here.

EPHESUS

Of all the great cities of the classical world, Ephesus is the best preserved. At most ancient sites you need a fair amount of imagination to fill in the gaps between the stones; at Ephesus you need only your eyes to appreciate the beauty and grandeur of the place.

BACKGROUND

Ephesus was already a busy port when the Ionians colonized it in the eleventh century BC, replacing the ancient Anatolian cult of Cybele, the fertility goddess, with their own cult of Artemis. They went on to build a temple to Artemis that was four times the size of the Parthenon and surrounded by 129 columns, of which only one is still standing. This magnificent building, the first major edifice to be built entirely of marble, was widely held to be the most wondrous of the Seven Wonders of the Ancient World.

Unlike the temple, the city was moved around several times as the nearby River Cayster silted up its harbor, finally arriving at its present site around 300 BC. Here, under Roman rule, Ephesus enjoyed its golden age. As the capital of the Roman province of Asia, it was a great center of trade and banking — indeed, it had the world's first bank — and its population of 250,000 made it the second largest city in the world, after Alexandria. It was also one of the earliest centers of Christianity, as St. Paul lived and preached here for three years around 50 AD, after which he wrote his stirring epistle to the Ephesians,

and legend has it that both St. John and the Virgin Mary spent their last days here.

Ephesus survived being pillaged by rampaging Goths in 262 AD, but it couldn't survive the gradual silting up of its harbor (the sea today is seven kilometers away). Ephesus' trade began to dry up, literally, and by the sixth century its harbor had become a malarial swamp. The city was abandoned.

GENERAL INFORMATION

The nearest Tourist Information office is four

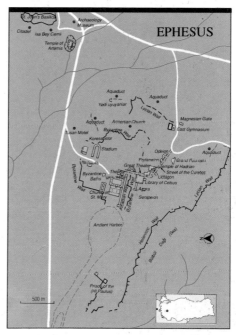

kilometers away in Selçuk, across the street from the Ephesus Museum (Efes Müzesi), (1328 or 1945.

WHAT TO SEE

As you approach Ephesus (Efes) from the main Selçuk–Kuşadası road, you will see on your left the walls of the second-century **Gymnasium of Vedius.** The gymnasium, or school, had adjoining baths which are quite well preserved. A little further on are the remains of a horseshoe-shaped **stadium.** At

The imposing Library of Celsus at Ephesus, now being restored to its former glory by Austrian archaeologists.

the entrance to the site there is a bus-clogged parking lot, toilets, cafés, souvenir stalls, and at least one mobile bank for the changing of money. Once inside the entrance gate you go down a paved road flanked by tall trees which delivers you to the eastern end of the **Arcadian Way.** This great colonnaded avenue of marble was once lined with shops and even had street lighting as it proceeded grandly to the harbor at its western end.

Gouged out of the hillside at the eastern end of the street, as if you could miss it, is the **Great Theatre.** Built in the first century AD, it holds up to 25,000 spectators — in surprising comfort, too, its stone seats having been grooved by 1,900 years of shifting buttocks. (Note: Under a starry sky, with the columns of the Arcadian Way lit in the background, this is one of the most romantic spots on earth to attend a concert.)

In front of the theater is the **Sacred Way,** more descriptively if prosaically known as the Marble Road. This leads past an open area to the right which was once occupied by the **agora,** Ephesus' booming marketplace, and up to the glorious façade of the **Library of Celsus,** built in 110 BC and restored by Austrian archaeologists. At the library the Sacred Way turns left and becomes the **Street of the Curetes.** Here, on the corner, was the **brothel.** It contains some delightful mosaics and a hand pump that still delivers cool spring water. On the other side of the street, and climbing the slope, are the **private residences** of some of the city's wealthier merchants.

Further up the street on the left is the partially-reconstructed **Temple of Hadrian,** completed in 138 AD. The four friezes in the archway are part of the reconstruction; the originals are in the Ephesus Museum. Continuing on up, you come to the ruins of the **Fountain of Trajan,** also on your left. A giant statue of the emperor once stood by the fountain, but all that remains today are his feet. From here on the Street of the Curetes is lined with plinths on which there once stood statues of various Ephesian worthies.

Back in Selçuk, you should definitely pay a visit to the splendid little **Ephesus Museum.** Very well laid-out and beautifully lit, it has a superb collection of artifacts and statuary unearthed at Ephesus. Included are two statues of Artemis with her rows of breasts (or eggs:

there is some dispute), several statues of Priapus with his amazing distended phallus, pieces of carved ivory furniture, a collection of ancient coins, various friezes and mosaics, and an entire wall given over to the (fascinating) history of the oil lamp in Ephesus from the sixth century BC to the third century AD.

Also in Selçuk, or rather overlooking it, is the huge marble-columned **Basilica of St. John,** erected in the sixth century by the emperor Justinian. As it was built over the tomb of the Apostle, it is one of the most sacred shrines in Christendom. Seven kilo-

meters (4.3 miles) south of Selçuk is an even more hallowed place of pilgrimage for Christians, the **House of the Virgin Mary,** or Meryemana. The site was discovered in 1891 by clergymen from Izmir following detailed directions and descriptions that had come to a German woman in a series of visions. On the first-century foundations of the house a small chapel has been built, where two popes, Paul VI and John Paul II, have celebrated mass. Every August 15 there is a service to mark the Assumption of Mary into heaven.

WHERE TO STAY

In Selçuk, I am personally very fond of the **Kale Han** ((1154) on the main highway

(E24) a couple of blocks north of the turning for Ephesus. Formerly a stone inn, it has been charmingly renovated — and is charmingly run — by the Ergir family. It also has a very good restaurant, and a swimming pool in the back, though it must be said that rooms on the street side can be a bit noisy. Singles are $24 here and doubles $36. The **Hotel Aksoy** (℃ 1040), on the other side of the highway at Namık Kemal Caddesi 17, near the railway station, has rooms for $8 single and $16 double. A few doors down from the museum, at Kuşadası Caddesi Atatürk

This is Cengiz Topel Caddesi, and most of the time it is just one big outdoor restaurant, as the tables from all the little restaurants spill out into the street. If you would like a tasty meal in wonderful surroundings, the best place is the **Piknik Restaurant** about seven kilometers (4.3 miles) along the road to Kuşadası, on the right-hand side, where the outdoor tables are surrounded by towering pines.

HOW TO GET THERE

As Selçuk clings to the main north-south high-

Mah. 10, is the **Ak Otel** (℃ 2161). It has a good indoor/outdoor restaurant, American bar, and bright rooms with balconies. Prices are $20 single and $36 double. If you want to be right next to Ephesus, there is the small **Tusan Efes Moteli** (℃ 1060) on the Selçuk–Kuşadası road at the turning for the ruins. You can expect to pay about $20 for a double room here. You can also camp next to the motel.

WHERE TO EAT

To eat well, your best bets are the **Kale Han** and the **Ak Otel,** where you will pay about $5 for a good meal. To eat very cheaply, but not badly, go to the street behind the clock tower on the east side of the main highway.

way along the Aegean, it is well served by buses from all directions. The bus station is right on the highway. From there you can get a minibus to Ephesus (or elsewhere nearby), or you can cross the road and walk a block to the Tourist Information office: across the street from it, up to the right past the museum and the Ak Otel, you can catch either a *dolmuş* or a taxi.

KUŞADASI

There is something odd about Kuşadası. With most attractive seaside towns — and

Displays at the Ephesus Museum.

Kuşadası is a very attractive seaside town —
you can't help feeling that the town would
be so much more agreeable if all the tourists
would go away. With Kuşadası, you can't
help feeling that if all the tourists went away
the town would cease to exist.

In fact, it just barely did exist a few years
ago before the upsurge in tourism created
the classic boom town. Then the tourists
began to arrive, lured by the proximity of
so many classical sites; then the yachtsmen
began to arrive, attracted by the large
new yacht marina; then the shopkeepers

WHERE TO STAY

Kuşadası is so crammed with hotels and
pensions, with new ones going up all the
time, that you could find a place to stay here
blindfolded. Among them:

The **Club Caravanserai,** or **Öküz Mehmet Paşa Kervansaray** ((2415), is a splen-
didly-restored seventeenth-century caravanserai in the heart of town where the waterfront street bends to the right to go out to the
dock. It has a lovely garden restaurant in its

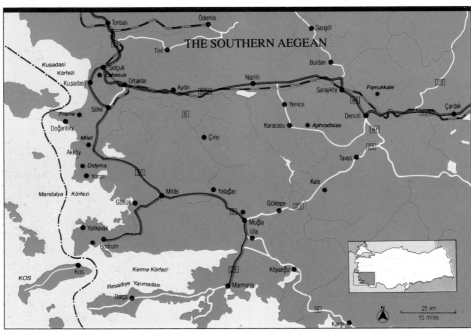

and hoteliers began to arrive, to cater to
the needs of the new arrivals; then the cruise
ships began to arrive with passengers who
wanted to be catered to; then more shopkeepers… You get the idea. Today Kuşadası's *raison d'être* is to feed you, entertain
you, and put you up while it sells things to
you.

GENERAL INFORMATION

The Tourist Information office ((1103) is
down by the quay where the cruise ships
dock. The multilingual staff are very helpful
and will be happy to provide you with information about hotels and campsites as
well as bus schedules.

tree-lined courtyard, and more than a whiff
of Ottoman luxury. Rates are about $45 for a
single room, about $65 for a double. The big
stair-stepped building facing the dock is the
Hotel Efe ((3660), Güvercin Ada Caddesi 37,
which offers spectacular views from its
flower-bedecked balconies. Rooms here are
priced about the same as at the Club Caravanserai. At the other end of the harbor,
by the yacht marina, is the **Hotel Kısmet**
((2005), which offers the same luxury, and an
excellent restaurant, for roughly the same
prices. Still in this price range, but well out of
walking range, is the **Tusan Oteli** ((1094) at
31'ler Beach north of town. The Tusan is big
and comfortable, with its own private beach
as well as a swimming pool and all sorts of

recreational facilities, but the moment the tour groups depart it becomes mortuarial in its isolation.

Less expensive places abound. The **Hotel Akman** ((C 1501) at Istiklâl Caddesi 13, near the yacht marina at the northern end of the harbor, is modern and well-appointed, with a restaurant, bar, and terrace for sunbathing. It charges $25 for a single and $35 for a double. Nearby on Istiklâl Caddesi are four nice little places — the **Özer Pansiyon,** the **Grup Pansiyon,** the **Yunus Pansiyon,** and the **Çiğdem Pansiyon** — of which the Çiğdem ((C 1895) is probably the nicest. It has rooms for $16 single and $20 double. A few meters away, on the waterfront at Atatürk Bulvarı 52, is the **Günhan Hotel** ((C 1050), which charges about the same.

If you go to Barbaros Caddesi, the main shopping street which runs into the harbor next to the Club Caravanserai, you will find dozens of little hotels packed into the side streets. On Cephane Sokak, for instance, there is the **Alkış Hotel**((C 1245) with double rooms for $17, and the larger **Minik** ((C 2359) with double rooms for $20, and the newer **Bahar Pansiyon** ((C 1191) with doubles for $25. If you continue on up Barbaros Caddesi you will come to the **Akdeniz Hotel** ((C 1120); not to be confused with the Akdeniz Hotel Club at Karaova Beach south of town. A nice double room here will cost about $25. If you follow Barbaros Caddesi up to the mosque and turn left, you will come to the bus station and the market area. All around here, and uphill to the east (away from the harbor), are more hotels. And tomorrow there will be even more.

If you would rather camp out than stay in a hotel, you are still in luck: Kuşadası has more than its fair share of campsites as well. Just north of town, on the Selçuk road, you will find **Cennet Camping** ((C 1500) and **Diana Mokamp** ((C 1457) side by side, and a bit further on **Önder Camping** ((C 2413), which has bungalows as well. Another four kilometers (2.5 miles) or so towards Selçuk is the **Kervansaray Mokamp** ((C 1106). Closer in, across from the marina, is **Yat**

A seventeenth-century caravanserai in Kuşadası has been converted into one of the most charming hotels on the Aegean coast.

Camping ((C 1333). In the unlikely event that all these are full, there are more campsites scattered along the shore south of town.

WHERE TO EAT

As a rule of thumb, you can expect restaurant prices, like hotel prices, to get lower as you get further away from the water, yet without a corresponding drop in quality. Having said that, I would myself prefer to eat at one of the quayside fish restaurants. They are all more or less equally good, as well as being more

fun and more reasonably priced than the better hotel restaurants. For simple eating, as opposed to dining, you will find Kuşadası honeycombed with cheap *kebapçıs*. My favorite establishment at this end of the scale is the **Özurfa** ((C 3244), just off Barbaros Caddesi, a block up on the left as you walk from the waterfront. It's fairly large and fairly noisy, with a good selection of hot dishes on display and a small army of friendly waiters in attendance. When I was last there three of us feasted for $21, including two bottles of wine.

HOW TO GET THERE

There are about a dozen buses a day from Izmir, plus *dolmuş* all the time from Selçuk.

To use Kuşadası as a base for visiting the archaeological sites at Priene, Miletus, and Didyma, you can either book a day tour at one of the travel agencies or you can catch a *dolmuş* to Söke, where you catch another *dolmuş* to Priene, then another, then another… Take a tour. Or rent a car from Toya-Sun Rent-A-Car at Atatürk Bulvarı 60, which is much cheaper than Avis down the street. Also, during the summer, there are boats every day to and from the island of Samos. Information and tickets are available from all the local travel agents.

PRIENE, MILETUS, AND DIDYMA

Conveniently arrayed in a line below Kuşadası are the remains of three important cities of antiquity, all three of which can be comfortably explored in a day.

PRIENE

Situated on the lower slopes of Mt. Mycale, overlooking the broad plains of the Meander River Valley, Priene occupies the most spectacular location of the three cities. Founded in the tenth century BC, it was built in more or less its present configuration in the fourth century BC, when it was laid out in a grid devised by Hippodamos of Miletus. For centuries thereafter it was an important Ionian commercial port, but, like Ephesus and other coastal cities, it fell victim to the alluvial deposits of its neighboring river, which slowly pushed the shoreline out of reach.

As you enter the site through the main gate you will approach what was once the princi-

pal thoroughfare, where on your right you will see the **Boeuleterion,** a large square council chamber where city officials met. Further up the hill is the small, horseshoe-shaped **theater** in a grove of pine trees. Occupying the city's highest point is the **Temple of Athena,** designed by Pythius of Halicarnassus (who also designed his city's famous Mausoleum). The temple is still regarded as the perfect example of Ionian monumental architecture.

Below the temple are the ruins of quite a few **private residences,** also designed by Pythius, which are considered to be among the best surviving examples of Ionian architecture.

MILETUS

Miletus was once the greatest of the Ionian cities, until it, too, succumbed to the silting up of its harbor (the sea continues to move away from Miletus at the rate of six meters, or 19.7 feet, a year). Apart from being a great center of commerce, it played a key role in the advance of Greek culture. The Ionian school of philosophers — which included Thales, Anaximenes, and Anaximander — was based here, and in the fifth century BC the Milesian alphabet was adopted as the standard Greek script.

The city's most notable ruin is its well-preserved **theater,** which dates from Hellenistic times but which was expanded by the Romans to its present capacity of 15,000. The seat of honor in the front row is flanked by two marble columns, and still visible on many of the other front-row seats are the inscribed names of their owners. From the hillside above the theater you get a splendid view of the plain where the sea once was, and where you can still see two pieces of white rock, about 150 m (492 ft) apart, which once belonged to the marble lions guarding the entrance to the harbor.

Of the other ruins perhaps the most interesting are the **Baths of Faustina,** behind the theater, erected by the wife of Emperor Marcus Aurelius. Here you can see a very fine headless reclining statue.

DIDYMA

Didyma, the southernmost of the three sites, was not a city but the home of the god Apollo. Only priests were allowed to enter here — for the sole purpose of consulting the oracle in the great **Temple of Apollo.** The temple, which was begun in 300 BC and never finished, was the third largest religious structure in the ancient Greek world, after the Temple of Artemis at Ephesus and the Temple of Hera on Samos, both of which it has outlasted. Of the temple's original 120-columns, many have been restored by French and German archaeological teams. There can also still be seen sizable bits and pieces of the temple's elaborate decoration, including a large head of Medusa which was once part of a frieze that adorned the exterior of the temple.

PAMUKKALE AND APHRODISIAS

Pamukkale (Turkish for "cotton castle") has long occupied a spot on every tourist's itinerary and every travel agent's wall, but it is no less enchanting for that. As you approach it, however, the mental image you have formed from dozens of travel brochures scarcely matches the undistinguished terrain; only the large number of campsites along the road and the columns of backpackers suggest that you are nearing a place of pilgrimage. Then, in the distance, an escarpment comes into view with what appears to be a white smudge near the top.

When you get there the white smudge assumes the shape of a series of petrified waterfalls, great white stalactites of calcium hanging from the edges of shallow aquamarine pools, all against a cliffside bleached snow-white by the mineral waters that have spilled down it for thousands of years. The road winds up through the middle of this to the plateau at the top, which is shared by several modern motels and the ruins of ancient Hierapolis.

Whether you want a cure for rheumatism, asthma, or dermatitis, for which the thermal springs of Pamukkale are noted, or simply a relaxing swim in a warm pool, all of the motels have spring-fed pools which anyone can use on payment of a nominal fee. There is also a large public bath and, of course, the natural wading pools perched beneath the top of the ridge which you passed on the way up.

Behind the motels are the ruins of Hierapolis, founded as a spa in the second century by the Pergamene king Eumenes II. The

most interesting, and certainly the most dominant, sight here is the imposing Roman **theater,** which is still being excavated and restored. In front of the theater is what's left of the third-century **Temple of Apollo.** Outside the ancient city walls is what is thought to have once been the largest necropolis in Anatolia, with over a thousand tombs and sarcophagi.

WHERE TO STAY

The **Pamukkale Motel** (℃ 1024) would be my first choice here. Not only is it friendly and

comfortable, but its swimming pool is the ancient Sacred Fountain, whose warm mineral water washes over the fallen fragments of Roman columns from Hierapolis. It is also very reasonably priced at $23 for a single room and $28 double. Nearby are the **Tusan Motel** (℃ 1010) and the **Koru Motel** (℃ 1020), both of which charge about $33 single and $37 double. The Koru is much the nicer of the two, with a wonderful swimming pool and an exceptionally fine restaurant. And for sheer luxury there is the **Beltes Motel** (℃ 1014), where you will pay about $60 for a double room, but that includes breakfast and dinner, an unsurpassed view over the ridge, and, with some rooms, your own private bit of swimming pool sectioned off outside your door.

Back down at the foot of the ridge is Pamukkale Village, a crowded, noisy jumble of

OPPOSITE: The remains of the Temple of Apollo at Didyma, dating from 300 BC, once the third largest religious structure in the classical world. ABOVE: A carved head of Medusa that was originally part of a frieze on the Temple of Apollo.

little hotels and pensions and shops and restaurants, with the tourist mobs in the streets being regularly scattered by big buses shouldering their way down into the village to disgorge more tourists. Beginning with the **Hotel Nebioğlu** (℅ 1031), on the corner at the turning into the village, which charges $12 for a double, there are more places to stay than you can count. The best known is **Ali's,** which also has a restaurant, a swimming pool, and a campground, and which charges $18 for a single and $26 for a double. But, depending on your budget, you would be advised either to reserve a room in advance at one of the motels up the hill or come to the village and see for yourself the range of accommodation available, remembering that the prices you are quoted in many cases will be highly flexible. For those traveling with a tent, there are campsites all over the place, including two on top of the ridge.

WHERE TO EAT

The place to eat here is one of the motels up the hill, preferably the **Koru.** If for some reason you want to eat in the village, there is no shortage of places, although there is — unusually for Turkey — a shortage of decent food and decent service. I suppose you can always try the **Pizzeria Restaurant** in the middle of the village. At least it has a well-stocked bar, and you can hardly be disappointed by a place with a sign inviting you to *COME IN FOR A PIZZA THE ACTION!* No, indeed.

HOW TO GET THERE

Strangely, none of the large inter-city bus companies has a service to Pamukkale, but there are frequent minibuses and *dolmuşes* from nearby Denizli, which as a provincial capital is served by buses from all over. The minibuses and *dolmuşes* for Pamukkale (and taxis too, for that matter) leave from in front of the Denizli bus station, which is itself just down the street from the train station, where there is a Tourist Information office (℅ (6128) 13393).

Pamukkale: Bathers enjoy the warm, calcium-enriched waters of the "Cotton Castle".

APHRODISIAS

A hundred kilometers west of Denizli (and 38 km, or 24 miles south of the main E24 highway) is the fascinating site of Aphrodisias. The city, which was named after Aphrodite, the Goddess of Love, in the sixth century BC, has only been excavated recently — hence only partially. But what has been unearthed so far is enough to give us a tantalizing glimpse of a most intriguing ancient city.

The **Temple of Aphrodite,** of which a

few Corinthian columns have been restored, once held a famous statue of the goddess as well as thousands of worshipful orgiasts who came to show their respects, so to speak. More impressive today are the remains of the 30,000-seat **stadium,** probably the best preserved Greco-Roman stadium in the world, and an **odeon** with a stage of blue marble. There is also a fine little museum which houses the growing number of artefacts that have been coaxed to the surface by the teams of archaeologists working there.

One of the courtyards in Bodrum's Castle of St. Peter, the best preserved Crusader castle in the world. OPPOSITE: Sleek yachts may now rule the waves around Bodrum, but the venerable "ships of the desert" still move people and things overland.

BODRUM

The people of Bodrum are now learning the lesson that the people of American towns like Key West and Provincetown and Carmel, or any number of towns in the south of France, learned some time ago: that if you have a charming town, with an interesting past, in a beautiful but somewhat remote location, it will probably attract a handful of writers and artists, whose bohemian presence, by some perverse alchemy, transforms the whole town into a fashionable resort. So it has been with Bodrum. It is now one of the most fashionable resorts in the entire Mediterranean.

Happily, though, unlike other resorts — St. Tropez comes to mind — it has lost none of its charm or personality. And, while it may have lost its innocence — it is sometimes winkingly referred to as "Bedroom" — that is not necessarily a bad thing.

BACKGROUND

There is evidence that there was a Dorian settlement here as early as 1100 BC, but the first historical record we have of Bodrum is from the seventh century BC, by which time it was known as Halicarnassus. Over the next two centuries it became more Ionian in character, in line with the coastal cities to the north. Herodotus, the "Father of History", who was born here in the early fifth century BC, wrote in Ionian. A century later the Persian satrap of the region, Mausolus, moved his capital to Halicarnassus, where he died in 353 BC. It was his death that led to his subsequent fame, and that of Halicarnassus, because his widow (who was also his sister) built a giant tomb — or "mausoleum" — in his honor which was to become one of the Seven Wonders of the Ancient World.

Not long afterwards Halicarnassus fell to Alexander the Great, then faded into relative obscurity until 1402 when the Crusader order of the Knights of St. John, having lost their castle at Smyrna to the invading Mongols under Tamerlane, were given Halicarnassus by Sultan Mehmet Celebi. Immediately they began building the mighty Castle of St. Peter on the bit of land dividing the twin bays. The castle remained in Christian hands until 1523 when it fell to the Ottoman armies of Süleyman the Magnificent. Today it houses the enthralling Museum of Underwater Archaeology.

GENERAL INFORMATION

The Tourist Information office ((1091) is in the plaza next to the entrance to the castle. For maps of the city and the peninsula, as well as books in English, go to the Haset A. S. bookshop underneath the mosque at the top of the street leading to the castle.

Güven, who for over 20 years has been Bodrum's premier sandalmaker. Each pair of his sandals is meticulously crafted from drawings he makes of the customer's feet, and some of the most famous feet in the world — including Mick Jagger's and Brigitte Bardot's — have been adorned by his sandals. The other craftsman is Kemal Utku, a jeweler and silversmith who teaches jewelry-making in Florence in the winter and makes it himself in Bodrum in the summer. Not only is his jewelry ravishingly beautiful, but the conversation you get with

WHAT TO SEE

Your first stop must be the **castle**. Here you will find displayed in the castle's halls and towers a magnificent collection of artefacts recovered from some of the world's oldest known shipwrecks: amphoras and various other forms of pottery, glassware, swords, daggers, spearheads, gold jewelry, coins — an unparalleled trove of sunken treasure.

For more modern treasure Bodrum has, in keeping with its reputation as a center for arts and crafts, two "official" **craftsmen,** designated as such by the municipal government, who you can watch at work and who will make things to order for you. One is Ali

it is delightful: he is, it should be added, almost certainly the only jeweler in the world with a Ph.D. in political science from New York University. These two master craftsmen work in a space provided by the local authorities, but as its location changes from year to year you will have to ask where to find them.

The nearest offshore attraction is **Karaada** ("Black Island"), just across the bay, where hot springs flow from a shoreline cave into a rock pool in the sea. There are lots of little boats docked along the quays that will take you there for a few hours or for the day. Further away — about an hour and a half by ferry — is the Greek island of **Kos**. Boats go over and back daily; tickets, which cost about

$25 for a round trip, can be bought from any travel agency along the waterfront.

Another pleasure for which Bodrum is well known is the **Blue Voyage (Mavi Yolculuk):** you charter a yacht and its crew (including, most importantly, a cook) and go for a leisurely cruise in the crystal-clear waters of Turkey's gorgeous Turquoise Coast, stopping wherever you like for swimming or snorkelling or fishing, dropping anchor overnight in any of the beautiful coves with which the coast is indented. There are boats of all shapes and sizes available for charter,

but I would suggest you check first with Nigel Speedy at Gulet Yachting, Hamam Sokak 7, Tepecik Mahallesi, (4489 or Annie Onursan at **Uncle Sun Yachting and Travel,** Atatürk Caddesi 61, (2659 or 5501.

The **Bodrum Peninsula** is a further source of delight, offering many lovely beaches and charming villages. The nearest beach to Bodrum, **Gümbet,** is unfortunately the least attractive, though it does have a very good windsurfing school, and the shallow, gradual slope of the seabed makes it ideal for small children who just want to splash in the water. **Bitez** beach, in the next bay to the west, is nicer and has better restaurants. The beach at **Ortakent,** further west, is probably the nicest (and sandiest) of all, while

the beach at **Turgutreis** is the widest, though the village itself is touristy and boring. Heading north up the edge of the peninsula you come to **Gümüşlük** which has a lovely little beach embracing a bay. In the middle of the bay, approachable by a barely submerged causeway, is **Rabbit Island,** the home of a large family of rabbits; under the waters of the bay, clearly visible from the island, are some of the ruins of ancient Myndos. Continuing along the coast towards the northeast you will pass above several secluded little bays (and you will also pass very near my house) as you wind your way the 10 km (6.2 miles) to **Yalıkavak,** a delightful fishing village that clings to one corner of a spectacular bay. Eastward from Yalıkavak are more villages, of which **Türkbükü** is especially attractive, and more lovely bays with little islands floating offshore. Finally, just before you join the main north-south highway that takes you back into Bodrum, there is the lavish resort complex of **Torba** with luxury accommodation, recreational facilities, a large beach, restaurants, casino, the works.

WHERE TO STAY

At the upper end of the scale is the **Torba Tatil Köyü** ((2343) at Torba Bay, which has singles for $30, doubles for $38, and suites for $61. In Bodrum itself there is the **TMT Tatil Köyü** ((1440 or 1222) at Akfebuk Mevkii, which has singles for $27, doubles for $35, and suites for $52. The trendiest place — and the noisiest, because it has a strobe-lit, seaside, open-air disco attached — is the **Halikarnas Hotel** ((1073) around the eastern bay at Cumhuriyet Caddesi 128. It has double rooms for $33 to $45. Below these three in price the choice is staggering: there are over 150 hotels and pensions in Bodrum alone, plus another 200 in clusters by the beaches around the peninsula, as well as two dozen officially licensed campsites.

At the western end of Neyzen Tevfik Caddesi, the street that runs alongside the yacht harbor, there is the **Seçkin Konaklar** ((1351), an "apartotel" which has apartments as well as rooms with up to three beds. The rooms average about $20 for a double, while the apartments are $30 and up. Next to it is the **Gala Oteli** ((1673), also modern and comfortable, with rooms for $9 single and $13 double. On the same street, across from the marina, with the same prices, you will find the **Herodot Pansiyon** (☎ 1093). Along Cumhuriyet Caddesi, which borders the eastern bay, there are many, many places. Among the best: **Mylasa Pansiyon** (☎ 1846), managed by a friendly Australian couple, has doubles for $25; **Artemis Pansiyon** (☎ 2530) charges $16 for a single and $20 for a double, as does the **Baraz Oteli** (☎ 1857); the **Dino Pansiyon** (☎ 1141) charges $18 for a single and $23 for a double.

The beaches and seaside villages around the peninsula are as well-served as Bodrum by lodgings of different kinds, offering the same comfort and amenities for the same range of prices. There are, however, two places worth singling out. One is the **Hotel Dost** (☎ 4226 or 4749) at Gümbet. What makes this place special is that its owner, Özcan Oraz, also owns Bodrum Rent-A-Car, which has the lowest car rental rates in Bodrum, so that he is able to offer a double room and a car for the same price that some of the better hotels charge for just a room. For example, you can get a double room at the hotel (which has a swimming pool), plus a car, for two weeks for under $500. If there is a better bargain on the peninsula, I don't know about it. The other place I should mention is the **Hotel Metur** (☎ 1003) in Yalıkavak. If it was in Bodrum, it would rate a mention on any one of several counts: the modern rooms, the new swimming pool, the superb restaurant and bar, the proximity to the beach, the exceptional cordiality and solicitude of the Kadiköy family who run it. But what makes it worth a special mention is that it offers all of those things — for about $17 single and $24 double — in the delightful, unspoiled setting of Yalıkavak.

WHERE TO EAT

It is probably possible to eat badly in Bodrum, but you would have to work at it. Eating well, on the other hand, generally involves nothing more complicated than sitting down at the first restaurant you come to. Emerging from the yacht marina the first restaurant you come to is the **Chinese Restaurant** (☎ 3136). The offspring of the Chinese Restaurant in Izmir, it has now outgrown its

parent: it is hugely (and deservedly) popular, with meals averaging about $10 per person. A bit further along Neyzen Tevfik Caddesi towards the castle is the **Gemibaşi** (☎ 1220), a small place with good food at very reasonable prices. Then comes the **Amphora** (☎ 2368), a wonderful restaurant (with bar) presided over by the estimable Mete Turgut and his wife Hatice. Still on Neyzen Tevfik Caddesi, next to the Avis office, is the very friendly **Liman Lokantası**, where you can eat quite well for under $5. Then, closer in to the middle of town, there is the venerable **Kör-**

fez Restaurant, where the $10 that a meal will probably cost you will be money very well spent.

Along the bay to the east of the castle my two favorite restaurants are the **Fora** (☎ 2244), which opens on to Hilmi Uran Square but has tables at the back right on the water, and has service as delightful as its food, and the **Hey Yavrum Hey** on the beach off Cumhuriyet Caddesi. Both charge about $10 for a delicious meal with wine.

OPPOSITE: Along with jewelry and leather, Bodrum specializes in the one gift item ideally suited for packing: sponges. ABOVE: Small meals on wheels: a *simit* vendor pushes his bread rings through the streets of Bodrum.

Uniquely among Turkish towns, Bodrum is also known for having a number of outstanding bars. East of the castle the pick of the crop is the **Hadigari Bar** (℄ 2959) at Dr. Alimbey Caddesi 28, although the **Mavi Bar** out at Cumhuriyet Caddesi 171 has its loyalists. Personally, I am partial to the **Jazz Café** (℄ 1533) near the little mosque on Neyzen Tevfik Caddesi, and to its owners, Cengiz and Mete, who have created one of the most convivial watering holes anywhere.

Outside Bodrum there are two restaurants worth making a special trip to visit. One is the **Karafaki** on Bitez Beach, ℄ 1082, a splendid restaurant and bar run by the mountainous, bearded Osman Tartan, who has the happy knack of always seeming pleased to see you. The other is **Çimentepe**, perched on top of a small cliff overlooking the bay two kilometers west of Yalìkavak. The restaurant is run by two brothers, Ali and Erdoğan Çetin, marvelous characters, who regularly produce delicious and reasonably priced meals in a glorious setting.

How to Get There

Unless you are traveling around by car or yacht, you will arrive in Bodrum either on the ferry from Kos or on one of the buses that come lumbering into Bodrum at frequent intervals. Regular inter-city buses and minibuses go into the busy bus station on Cevat Şakir Caddesi, while coaches meeting charter flights to Izmir or Dalaman (the nearest airports) will take you either to your tour operator or directly to your accommodation.

If you are coming from Istanbul, you should know that there is a small airline, Em Air, that during the summer flies a Cessna daily betweeen Istanbul and an airstrip outside Bodrum. The flight costs about $75 each way.

Once you are in Bodrum, you still have the problem of getting around the peninsula. Fortunately, it is not a major problem because the *dolmuş* service between the towns and villages is generally excellent, while taxis are both plentiful and comparatively cheap (though you should always agree on the price of an out-of-town trip in advance). If you want the flexibility and convenience of a rented car, there is an Avis office (℄ 2333) at Neyzen Tevfik Caddesi 80, where the staff is extremely helpful and efficient. This is the place to go if you want to be able to return the car in another city or at one of the airports. For the best rates, however, see Özcan Oraz at Bodrum Rent-A-Car, Azmakbaşı 22, ℄ 5932 or ℄ 4609.

MARMARIS

I must admit to having a soft spot for Marmaris, because it is where I first stepped ashore in Turkey. Otherwise, I am frequently

assured, I wouldn't like it as much as I do. There may be some truth to this: certainly Marmaris' newfound status as the preferred holiday haunt of Turkey's *nouveaux riches* has done nothing to enhance its charm. At the same time, it is a lively little place, in a scenic location, with an abundance of comfortable accommodation.

General Information

The Tourist Information office (℄ 1035) is at Iskele Meydanı 39, next to the yacht harbor.

One of the many fine seaside restaurants in Marmaris.

WHAT TO SEE

The best sights, as well as the nicest beaches, all have to be approached by boat. Every morning swarms of little boats, rather like Venetian *vaporetti*, leave the harbor to take tourists to various destinations around the bay: gem-like inlets scooped out of the shoreline, handsome beaches, phosphorescent caves, thermal springs. All you have to do is decide what sort of place or places you would like to visit, then stroll along the harbor and decide which boat you would like to take you there.

The most interesting place within immediate range of Marmaris is the island of **Rhodes.** In Rhodes Town itself, the medieval **Old Town** — massively fortified by the Knights of St. John and exquisitely restored by Italian archaeologists — is worth a day or two of anyone's time. (The Turks, under Süleyman the Magnificent, went to Rhodes from Marmaris in 1522 and stayed for 400 years.) There are ferries over and back daily, with tickets on sale at all travel agencies.

WHERE TO STAY

Outside Marmaris there are two lavishly equipped hotel complexes. The **Turban Marmaris Tatil Köyü** ((1843), seven kilometers away to the southwest, has 246 bungalows scattered among the pines, with its own private beach, tennis and basketball courts, water sports facilities, snack bars, beer gardens, and restaurants. Rates start at about $50 for a couple. More expensive still is the **Martı Tatil Köyü** ((4910), a few kilometers further on at Içmeler Köyü, which offers much the same amenities. Closer to town is the **Hotel Lidya** ((2940) at Siteler Mahallesi 130. It is large and comfortable, with a casino, lovely gardens, a good beach, and a range of different types of accommodation beginning at about $34 double.

In the middle of Marmaris, near the Rhodes ferry dock and the Tourist Information office, is a large cluster of inexpensive hotels (which get even cheaper the further away from the water you go). The better hotels, predictably, are mostly strung out along the waterfront on Atatürk Caddesi.

The **Yavuz Oteli** ((2937) at No. 10, which has a swimming (well, splashing) pool on its roof, charges $32 for a double room, as does the new **Otel 47** ((1700) next to it. The **Atlantik Oteli** ((1218) at Nº 11 is older and charges slightly less. The **Otel Marmaris** ((1308) at Nº 30 has singles for $15, doubles for $30. The **Karadeniz** ((2837) at Nº 46 has clean, modern rooms for under $30 double, as does the **Karaca** (1663) at Nº 48.

Most of the best campsites are by the sea on either side of the Hotel Lidya, which can be reached by one of the frequent *dolmuşes* marked "Içmeler".

WHERE TO EAT

Apart from the restaurants in the hotels, which are generally reliable but unexciting, the best eateries in Marmaris are lined up along the yacht harbor. Perhaps because the competition is so close by, they all serve delicious food at reasonable prices. The **Birtat** ((1076) is one such, with the added bonus (in a seaside town) of having very decent steak. Others are the **Tilla** ((1088), **Bomboo** ((1339), **Zuhal** ((4792), **Kumkapı**, and the **Yat Restoran.** But even in this galaxy of good restaurants, there are two that shine not only brightly but unusually. One is **The Green House** ((4896), which is that rarity in Turkey, a vegetarian restaurant. The other is **Kemal's Hangout,** which might be described as half-diner and half-bar. In the morning, Kemal, an ex-Chicagoan, fries up some distinctly un-Turkish breakfasts, and in the evening mixes some wicked drinks.

HOW TO GET THERE

As with Bodrum, you will arrive either by ferry from a nearby Greek island, in this case Rhodes, or by road. There is frequent bus service from Bodrum, Izmir, and other points north and east as well as from Fethiye to the south. The nearest airport is Dalaman, about 100 km (62 miles) away.

The Mediterranean Coast

VISITORS familiar with other coasts around the Mediterranean are invariably unprepared for the Mediterranean coast of Turkey. Used to putting up with uninteresting buildings and undistinguished countryside (not to mention unfriendly faces and unreasonable prices) for the privilege of lying on crowded beaches next to polluted water, they find themselves almost disbelieving when they contemplate any part of the Turkish coast, from Fethiye in the west over to Alanya and beyond.

Breathtakingly beautiful coves, inlets, rock hollows, and beaches follow each other along the water's edge, where the sea is of such stunning clarity that it doesn't seem to have any depth, and where the majestic, pine-forested mountain ranges in the background form a giant wall that keeps out all unwanted weather from the north. Add some pleasant towns and villages, inhabited by pleasant people, throw in some fascinating ruins, and you have a pretty good idea of what Mediterranean Turkey is like.

FETHIYE

Fethiye, 140 km (87 miles) from Marmaris, is a modern little town built on top of an ancient little town, Telmessos, overlooking a bay dotted with 12 little islands. It has nice beaches, interesting sights, a good yacht marina, and a certain quiet charm, but its real popularity comes from the fact that it is only 15 km (9 miles) away from one of the most gorgeous beaches in the entire Mediterranean.

GENERAL INFORMATION

The Tourist Information office ((1527) is at Iskele Meydanı 1, across from the yacht marina, next to the Dedeoğlu Hotel.

WHAT TO SEE

You can hardly *avoid* seeing the large **Lycian sarcophagi** lying in the streets. These date from the fifth century BC, and the most interesting of them is the one next to the post office. Cut into the cliff behind the town, near the bus station, are several Lycian rock tombs, the grandest of which is the Tomb of Amyntas from the fourth century BC. You can also take a boat tour of the **12 islands** in the bay. The nearest beach to the town is **Çalış Beach** to the northeast.

The main attraction, though, is unquestionably the beach at **Ölü Deniz** ("Dead Sea"), where high wooded slopes descend to a warm lagoon of sparkling turquoise water surrounded by a great sweep of white sand. It really is astonishingly beautiful. In the woodlands around the lagoon and along the huge beach that stretches south of it there are many campgrounds, motels, bungalows, restaurants, and picnic areas.

WHERE TO STAY

In Fethiye, the **Likya Hotel** ((1169) beside the yacht marina is the choicest place to stay. With a swimming pool, lovely gardens, and balconies overlooking the bay, it charges $30 for a double. Back towards the center of town, across from the marina, is the **Prenses Hotel** ((1305), which has a disco but no swimming pool and is slightly less expensive than the Likya. Next to the Prenses is the **Dedeoğlu** ((4010), with the same balconied sea views as its neighbors but for only $15 single and $23 double.

There are a number of lower-priced hotels in the middle of town. Of these I would recommend the **Kordon Hotel** ((1834) at Atatürk Caddesi 8 and the **Sema Hotel** ((1015) on Çarşı Caddesi across from the statue of Atatürk. Both charge about $13 for a double room.

In Ölü Deniz, the **Meri Motel** ((4388 or (1025) has a private beach and a seaside restaurant and a lot of nerve, because it charges almost $40 single and $60 double. And still it's usually full. In any case, this is a spot that was made for camping — and there are plenty of campsites here to accommodate you, most of them with excellent facilities. There are also several free discos, quite a few good restaurants, and shops where you can buy food for picnics.

Lycian rock tombs from the fourth and fifth centuries BC carved into the cliff behind Fethiye. OVERLEAF: The turquoise waters in the lagoon at Ölü Deniz lap up against one of the most beautiful beaches in the Mediterranean.

WHERE TO EAT

In Fethiye, as in so many other seaside towns, the best meals and the best atmosphere are to be found in the seafood restaurants along the waterfront. Here, too, as elsewhere, the prices — though not the quality — of the meals decline very noticeably as you move away from the water. Probably the best of the non-waterfront restaurants is the **Rafet** (℃ 2676) by the Turkish baths behind the Kordon Hotel. You can eat very well here for $7 or less.

HOW TO GET THERE

There are regular buses from both directions along the coast road. To get to Ölü Deniz, take a *dolmuş* from Atatürk Caddesi in Fethiye (they run hourly until midnight) or a taxi (having agreed the fare beforehand).

KAŞ

A little over 100 km (62 miles) down the coast from Fethiye is Kaş, a pretty fishing village that knows just how pretty it is. With all its buildings brilliantly whitewashed, and its ancient hillside rock tombs illuminated at night, it's not embarrassed to call attention to itself either. The only question is whether it will survive all the attention it is beginning to get.

GENERAL INFORMATION

The Tourist Information office (℃ 1238) is on Cumhuriyet Meydanı, the main square. In keeping with the village's encouragement of tourists, the tourist office's director, Namık Aydın, has become almost legendary for his helpfulness.

WHAT TO SEE

The entire focus of Kaş is on its picturesque little harbor, from which boats leave regularly

Kaş — the fishing village that looked in the mirror and decided it was the fairest of them all. It could be right.

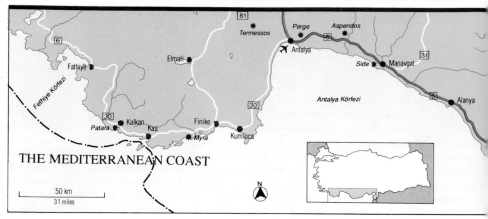

THE MEDITERRANEAN COAST

50 km
31 miles

to take visitors on sightseeing excursions. The most popular of these is to **Kekova,** an ancient Lycian city now partially submerged, and its neighboring villages on the coast east of Kaş. Another tour explores the **Blue Caves.** These large sea caves, with their strange fluorescent water, are home to the only colony of seals in the Mediterranean. There is also an excursion to tiny **Kastellorizon,** the easternmost Greek island, anchored forlornly two kilometers offshore. And there is one to **Patara,** once a Lycian port city and now the home of some haunting Roman ruins scattered among the sand dunes of a beach 18 km (11 miles) long. Other boats are simply for nosing in and out along the coast, looking for little coves where one can swim and sunbathe in splendid isolation.

These secluded coves aren't approachable only by sea. If you walk west out of town along Hastane Caddesi, past the hospital (*hastane*), you will come first to a well-preserved Hellenistic **theater.** Climb up a few rows and look out: you will see, just as you would have seen over 2,000 years ago, an impressive performance by the Mediterranean with an appearance by Kastellorizon in a small supporting role. A bit further on you will come to **Kaş Camping;** continue along this little peninsula as it curls around to form a **lagoon.** Here you will find many beautiful, secluded spots ideal for swimming or just lazing about.

By road from Kaş you are half an hour away from **Kalkan** to the west, along some of the most dramatic coastline in the world. This stretch always reminds me of Big Sur

in California — which means, if you are driving, that you will have a struggle to keep your eyes on the road. Kalkan itself is a smaller version of Kaş: white buildings huddled around a little harbor. It, too, has decided to use its charms to attract tourists. Foremost among these charms, for me anyway, is the surprisingly large number of very good restaurants.

About 40 km (25 miles) from Kaş in the opposite direction, again with spectacular scenery unwinding before you, is **Demre.** In the middle of Demre is the **Church of St. Nicholas.** As a fourth-century Byzantine basilica it would be well worth a visit in its own right, but it is the fame of the man whose tomb is here that attracts the visitors. Born in Patara around 300 AD, St. Nicholas went on to become the much-loved bishop of ancient Myra. The ruins of Myra lie nearby, but the bones of the saint now lie in the Italian city of Bari, where they were taken by relic-hunters who looted the tomb in 1087. If it was the miracles he performed that earned him his sainthood, it was his legendary acts of generosity — which included the giving of anonymous gifts to children, especially to poor girls whose families couldn't afford dowries — that earned him his place in Christian folklore. Known to the Turks as Noel Baba, St. Nicholas is better known to us as Santa Claus or Father Christmas.

WHERE TO STAY

In the last few years there has been an explosion of hotel-building in Kaş,

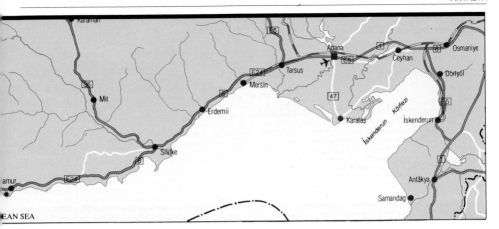

and a corresponding explosion in prices, as its popularity has grown. The **Ekici Oteli** (℡ 1417) on Hükümet Konağı Yani has a swimming pool and wonderful views for $70 double in season. The **Hotel Mimosa** (℡ 1272) up at the top of Elmalı Caddesi also has a pool (and a disco and sauna and rooftop restaurant) and charges just a little less, though prices drop by up to half out of season. Across the street from the Mimosa is the **Derya Hotel** (℡ 1304), which is not as fancy but is very friendly, where rooms go for about $25 double. A little further down the hill, the **Oriental Hotel** (℡ 1445) at Elmalı Caddesi 10 offers rooms at the same price.

If you turn right at the bottom of Elmalı Caddesi on to Hastane Caddesi, you will come upon the **Ali Baba Motel** (℡ 1126), which has double rooms for $15. Across the street, the **Kaş Hotel** charges the same but is right on the sea. Further out Hastane Caddesi, as I've already mentioned, there is **Kaş Camping** (℡ 1050), which occupies a beautiful site and has little cabins (at $8) for the tentless. Even nicer, if you can get there, is **Can Mocamp** (℡ 1541) just outside Kaş on the road to Kalkan. Run by the amiable Ahmet Kahvecioğlu, it has a motel and outdoor restaurant surrounded by bungalows (also $8) and a camping area on a terraced hillside sprinkled with olive trees.

If none of the above suits your fancy, Kaş is positively saturated with pensions offering rooms of every description and price.

WHERE TO EAT

If you go to the main square — and you can scarcely avoid going there, as it is the hub of village life — you will find most of the good restaurants not found in hotels. The **Eriş,** next to the Tourist Information office, has perhaps the nicest ambience, with quite good food for about $5 a head. Across the square, by the water, the **Mercan** is similarly attractive and reasonable. On the shady little street that runs from Cumhuriyet Caddesi up to the market, there is the **Derya Restaurant** and several others where you can watch the dishes being prepared. They are all good, and all under $5.

HOW TO GET THERE

Like Fethiye, Kaş is well served by buses going back and forth along the coast. If you are heading eastward from Kaş, however, don't be fooled by the map into thinking that Antalya is just a short hop away. What you gain in dramatic scenery you lose in time: it takes almost as long — up to five hours — to get to Antalya by bus as it does to get to Marmaris.

ANTALYA

Antalya would probably be a bustling, prosperous city under any circumstances. With its strategic location at the heart of a fertile agricultural region, its natural harbor, its unpolluted air, and its wonderful climate, it is already exceptionally well-favored. When you consider the added attractions of nearby beaches and archaeological sites you understand why tourists flock here in their thousands.

BACKGROUND

Founded early in the second century BC by Attalus II of Pergamon, and consequently named Attaleia, the city passed into Roman hands soon afterwards. The only high points of its subsequent life as a Roman city came in 6 BC when the emperor Augustus settled a colony here and in 130 AD when the emperor Hadrian paid a visit here. Then it became a Byzantine city, which it remained until 1207 when it was taken by the Seljuks, who altered its name to Antalya. It fell to the Ottomans in 1391, since when it has been content to lie back and stretch out in the sun.

GENERAL INFORMATION

The Tourist Information office (☎ 11747) is at Cumhuriyet Caddesi 73, next door to the Turkish Airlines office (☎ 23432). There is also a very helpful municipal tourist office (☎ 19925) further east on Cumhuriyet Caddesi below the remarkable equestrian statue of Atatürk.

WHAT TO SEE

The city's most famous sight is the landmark **Yivli Minare**, or Grooved Minaret, erected shortly after the Seljuk takeover in the early thirteenth century. From here, if you cross the plaza above the minaret you will come to Atatürk Caddesi, which curves down to the Old Town past **Hadrian's Gate,** built in honor of the emperor's visit in 130 AD. At the end of the street, overlooking the sea, is the beautiful **Karaali Park,** with its fountains and stately palms and colorful beds of flowers. Leaving the park, a walk down to the **harbor** through the Old Town will take you past rows of attractive Ottoman houses towards a most unusual sight: a modern yacht marina surrounded by new tourist facilities of every kind which nonetheless blend in admirably with the architecture of the **Old Town.**

The **Antalya Museum,** on Orgeneral Kenan Evren Bulvarı (the main coast road) at the western end of the city, houses one of the finest collections to be found anywhere in Turkey. Not only that, it is user-friendly: the exhibits are handsomely arranged and each is clearly labeled in English. Beginning with Stone Age and Bronze Age artefacts, the exhibits represent all periods in the country's history — including the Greek, Roman, Byzantine, Seljuk, and Ottoman eras. There is much monumental sculpture and statuary, and there is an enormous variety of smaller objects, both decorative and functional. And there is a marvelous ethnographic collection covering all aspects of urban and rural life in Anatolia, with a special section devoted to nomads. It is really not to be missed. The museum is closed on Mondays.

Near Antalya are three important archaeological sites. **Termessos**, 34 km (21 miles) inland on the road to Korkuteli, has some of the most spectacular ruins to be found along this coast. This remote mountain fastness was occupied for centuries by an Anatolian tribe whose fierceness and determination (and location) defeated every attempt — even Alexander's — to subdue them. Of the ruins here the **necropolis** is particularly intriguing, with its tombs and sarcophagi scattered around and even down the mountain slopes. **Perge** is 15 km (9 miles) east of Antalya and has extensive ruins, most of them early Byzantine. Particularly impressive is the **stadium,** which is remarkably well preserved. A further 32 km (20 miles) to the east lie the ruins of **Aspendos,** where you will find the best preserved **Roman theater** in the world. Built in the second century AD, it is still used for dramatic productions during the Antalya Festival in September. Most travel agencies in Antalya run tours to each of these sites.

WHERE TO STAY

Luxury

The **Talya Hotel** (℃ 15600), on a cliff overlooking the sea at Fevzi Çakmak Caddesi 30, is easily the best hotel in Antalya, if not on the whole Mediterranean coast. Quite apart from all the amenities you expect to find at a luxury hotel, the Talya has some unexpected ones as well — like long-distance direct dialing, and an elevator that goes from the swimming pool down the side of the cliff to a seaside bar and bathing area. Prices are about $135 single and $175 double in season, significantly less out of season.

Offering luxury of a different kind is the **Turban Adalya Oteli,** (℃ (311) 18066) in the middle of the harbor development next to the Old Town. The building's original (1869) façade has been restored, as has its wonderful lobby, while the most modern conveniences have been tastefully insinuated into all parts of the building. At $75 single/$100 double, it is actually very good value. If you care more about local sand than local color, the **Sera Oteli** (℃ 28377) out on Lara Beach, 11 km (7 miles) east of town, is luxurious, modern, and on the best beach in the area. Rooms

here are less expensive than those at the Talya.

Middle Range

The **Star Oteli** (℃ 11280), on Ali Çetinkaya Caddesi at the corner of Altay Caddesi, is very comfortable, centrally located, and has a restaurant with a very cosmopolitan menu. Rooms here are about $40 single and $55 double. A block away, at Ali Çetinkaya Caddesi 12, is the **Yayla Palas** (℃ 11913), where single rooms are $25 and doubles $35. The **Büyük Hotel** (℃ 11499) near the Yivli Minare at Cumhuriyet Caddesi 57 is very decent and unpretentious, with double rooms for $30. For the same price you can stay at the small **Antalya Motel** (℃ 14609) at Lara Yolu 84, halfway between the town center and Lara Beach.

Inexpensive

There are dozens of cheap pensions near the bus station and in the Old Town; the latter

---

OPPOSITE: A restaurant overlooking the harbor is one of the best places from which to appreciate the beauty of Antalya. ABOVE: The Byzantine ruins at Perge, east of Antalya.

are much to be preferred. Of the inexpensive hotels, the best is probably the **Asya** (☎ 12632) at Atatürk Caddesi, 1251 Sokak 7, which charges $6 for a single and $10 for a double. There are also quite a few campgrounds along Konyaaltı Beach just west of the city, but none is especially enticing.

WHERE TO EAT

Apart from the main hotels, all of which (in my experience) have good restaurants, there are three places to look for an interesting meal in Antalya. The first is Eski Sebzeciler İçi Sokak, the famous little street just south-west of the junction of Cumhuriyet Caddesi and Atatürk Caddesi. Here you will find one cheap *kebapçi* after another in chaotic, cheery array. The second place to look is along the main waterfront boulevard, which has many good seafood restaurants. The third — and best — place to look is the yacht harbor, where you will find the **Kral Sofrası** (☎ 12198), the **Hisar Tesisi** (☎ 15281), the **Yat** (☎ 24855), the **Liman** (☎ 10900), the **Orkinoz** (☎ 26736), and many others, all delightful, all costing $10 per person and up.

HOW TO GET THERE

Not surprisingly, buses pour into Antalya from all over the country, arriving at the centrally located bus terminal on Kazım Özalp Caddesi. There are also Turkish Maritime Lines cruise ships which call at Antalya during the summer. And in addition to the daily flights from Istanbul and Ankara, there are many charter flights weekly arriving from London and other European cities.

SIDE

For many people, Side is the ideal resort: a picturesque little package of leisure and culture, hotels and history, bustle and beaches. What makes Side different from other resorts-with-ruins, perhaps unique, is that here the ancient and the modern are tightly interwoven. The busy, noisy, contemporary village of Side is built in, on, and among the silent ruins of the ancient city of Side. This means, on the one hand, that everything you

might want to see or do is conveniently incorporated within the same experience of the place. On the other hand, it means that one's appreciation of Side's past is inevitably contaminated by the fungoid growth of its present. (The Turkish authorities, it must be said, are keenly aware of this problem, and as of this writing are trying to roll back some of the more vulgar development so that proper restoration work can be undertaken.)

BACKGROUND

Founded by the Ionian Greeks in the seventh century BC, Side grew up to live almost exclusively on immoral earnings — partly from the trade in stolen goods brought here for resale by the pirates that operated along this coast, and partly from the trade in people captured by the pirates and sold here in the city's busy slave market. When the Romans took over, the city went straight, and *still* prospered — for a while, until its inhabitants wearied of defending it against Arab attackers and packed up and moved to Antalya. For the next 1,000 years the city was nothing but a collection of ruins. Then in the 1890s Turkish refugees from Crete settled here and built a village among the ruins.

GENERAL INFORMATION

There is a Tourist Information office (☎ 0303) outside town on the road into Side, and another one in nearby Manavgat at Antalya Caddesi 273, ☎ 1645.

WHAT TO SEE

Your first stop should be Side's superb little **museum,** on your right as you enter the village. Its collection, all of which was unearthed here, includes some fine Roman statues and a number of beautifully, poignantly carved sarcophagi. Across the road is the **agora,** where the ancient slave market was held, next to the large **theater,** which is all the more impressive for being free-standing and not carved out of a hillside. If you continue down the main street — which you will have to imagine as it was, lined with majestic columns, rather than as it is, lined with tacky little shops and restaurants — you will come to the tip of this little beach-lined finger of land, where there are the **ruins** of the Temple of Apollo and the Temple of Athena, as well as of a Byzantine basilica which would appear to have been built over the temples.

WHERE TO STAY

The beachfront along the western side of the village is the place to look for upscale accommodation. Here you will find the **Cennet**

Oteli (℃ 1167), with attractive gardens and many water sports facilities, where rooms cost $70 double, and the **Side Motel** (℃ 1022), also very nice, where a double costs $40. Another good choice is the **Subaşi Motel** (℃ 1047), which charges $30 for a double. Further out on the beach, and further up in price, are the **Defne Hotel** (℃ 1880) and the **Turtel Tatil Köyü** (℃ 2225), two enormous holiday complexes with all the trimmings: swimming pools, tennis courts, saunas,

ABOVE LEFT: One of the most welcome sights in a Mediterranean summer: an ice cream stall. RIGHT: The conversational and mercantile arts flourish side by side in Side. OVERLEAF: The huge thirteenth-century Seljuk fortress that presides over Alanya and its bay.

discos, restaurants, etc. Prices start at $75 at the Defne and $50 at the Turtel.

In the village itself there is the **Buket Motel** (℃ 1384), a cluster of little wooden bungalows between the parking lot/bus terminal and the sea. If the vehicles arriving next door don't keep you awake, the motel's chatty manager, Canser Kılıç, will. At $30 for a double, this may not seem a bargain, and it isn't, but it's an oddly nice place to stay. Better bargains are to be found by plunging down any of the streets (especially to the left as you go towards the sea) leading from the main

street. They are full of little pensions, of which two — the **Özden Side** (℃ 1137) and the **Winter Palas** (℃ 1197) — are especially good value with comfortable doubles for only $12.

WHERE TO EAT

If you start at the end of the main street, by the sea, and work your way back inland, you will start with the **Afrodit Restaurant** and work your way generally back downwards in quality, and in price. The **Ilgi Restaurant** and the **Punta Marino,** both on the main street, are two places where I have had quite tasty meals for under $8. Anyway, the street is packed with restaurants; if you walk down it you will certainly pass a restaurant to your liking.

How to Get There

There are several buses a day to Side from both Antalya to the west and Alanya to the east, but any bus along the coast road will drop you at the turn-off for Side, from which it is only a three- kilometer (1.9-mile) *dolmuş* ride to the village.

ALANYA

Known — and not only in its own brochures — as "the pearl of the Turkish Mediterranean," Alanya has unashamedly dedicated itself to tourism. It lies at the foot of a rocky promontory dominated by a massive thirteenth-century Seljuk fortress, with sandy beaches and bright white new hotels stretching for miles in either direction, and in this glorious setting it waits to welcome visitors.

General Information

The friendly and helpful Tourist Information office (℃ 1240) is at Çarşı Mahallesi, Kalearkası Caddesi, at the northwest corner of the promontory across the street from the museum.

What to See

Down by the harbor is Alanya's landmark, the **Red Tower (Kızıl Kule)**. This five-story, octagonal structure was built in 1226 by the Seljuk sultan Alaeddin Keykubat as a defensive bastion to protect Alanya's shipyards. The crenellations at the top were for the cannons; the lancet windows further down were for the pouring of hot oil on those who hadn't got the message of the cannons. Crowning the promontory is the mighty, double-walled **fortress,** from which the view is predictably magnificent. At the harbor you can rent a boat to take you around the promontory, which you will find pitted with enchanting **sea caves.** Among them: **Damlataş Cave,** with its many stalagmites and its reputation for curing respiratory ail-

Antalya's famous Red Tower, built in 1226 to discourage raids on the port's shipyards.

ments, **Phosphorescent Cave,** with its glowing rocks, **Pirates' Cave,** where the villains kept their female captives who were not for sale, and **Lovers' Cave.** South of Damlataş Cave is **Cleopatra's Beach,** where the lady is said to have gone swimming after Antony gave her this region as a love gift.

Alanya's little **museum,** from which it is only a short walk down to Damlataş Cave, is extremely pleasant and informative. Its modest collection includes ceramics and coins, carpets and *kilims,* and some quite lovely inlaid metal work.

Where to Stay

Only a few years ago there was much grumbling about both the quantity and the quality of Alanya's accommodation. Today Alanya is said to have more hotels than any other spot on Turkey's Mediterranean coast, and it clearly has some of the most luxurious. At the upper end there are three stand-outs. One is the vast **Club Alantur** (℃ 1224), six kilometers to the east at Dim Çayı Mevkii, with an infinite range of amenities, plus wooded gardens leading to a luscious beach. Rooms here start at $100. Further out on the other side of town are **Jasmin Oteli** (℃ (3237-1180) and the **Top Otel** (℃ 3237-1235) at Incekum Mevkii. They are only slightly less luxurious than the Alantur, and charge about the same prices.

For those wanting the comfort and conveniences provided by the modern new beach hotels, but in the middle of town, there is the **Kaptan Oteli** (℃ 4900) at Iskele Caddesi 62, with a fine restaurant, swimming pool, and rooms with balconies overlooking the harbor for $40 single and $60 double. There is also the **Park Otel** (℃ 1675) on Hürriyet Meydanı, with a decent restaurant but without a swimming pool, where rooms are about half the price of the Kaptan's. Similarly priced — and placed, a short walk away — is the **Özen Oteli** (℃ 7200) at Müftüler Caddesi 35, which doesn't have a restaurant but does have a babysitting service. There are also numerous inexpensive little hotels and pensions in the middle of town, near the harbor, of which my favorite is the **Hotel Kent** (℃ 2754) at Iskele Caddesi 12, which has very nice double rooms for $15.

WHERE TO EAT

The best hotels have, by and large, very good restaurants — which is just as well if you are staying in one, since most of them include the price of at least one meal a day in addition to breakfast. Otherwise your best bet is to walk along the waterfront on Gazi Paşa Caddesi, where there are many good seafood restaurants from which to choose. You can expect to pay $8 to $10 for a meal here, and about half that if you walk a block or two inland.

ANAMUR

Anamur, at the southernmost point of Turkey's Mediterranean coast, has the best single example of the castles for which this coast is noted: the great Byzantine pile of **Marmure Kalesi.** Originally built by the Romans in the third century, the seaside castle as it now stands was erected in the mid-thirteenth century. It has 36 towers joining its ramparts and was actually in use as a fortress as late as World War I.

HOW TO GET THERE

There is bus service from all parts of the country, but most frequently from Antalya.

ANAMUR TO ANTAKYA

East of Alanya there is some spectacular coastal scenery — especially from Gazipaşa around to Silifke — and there are some large cities, but there is really very little to attract either those looking for sites of great historical interest or those looking for great places to have fun.

SILIFKE

Silifke and Taşucu, the little port that acts as Silifke's front porch, are best known as places to go *from* rather than as places to go *to*. From Silifke there are buses leaving every few minutes for Mersin and Adana to the east, and the coastal resort towns to the west; from Taşucu there are boats and hydrofoils going to the Turkish Republic of Northern Cyprus. The Tourist Information office in Silifke is at Atatürk Caddesi 1/2, (1151, and in Taşucu on the waterfront at Atatürk Caddesi, Gümrük Meydanı 18/A, (1234.

Twenty kilometers east of Silifke there stands, in all its offshore splendor, the **Kız**

Kalesi, or **Maiden's Castle.** Built by the Byzantines and re-fortified by the Armenians in the Middle Ages, the castle was originally connected to another castle on the shore by a causeway, but the other castle and the causeway have both disappeared, so you will have to swim or take a boat to reach the castle. There is an excellent beach nearby, with motels, restaurants, and campsites.

MERSIN

The modern industrial city of Mersin, Turkey's

largest port on the Mediterranean, offers little hint of its distinguished ancestry: remains have been found here of a settlement going back 6,000 years. Although the city attracts very few tourists, it nonetheless has a Tourist Information office (℅ 11265) on İnönü Bulvarı down by the harbor, across from the Turkish Maritime Lines office. At the latter you can buy tickets for the car ferry to Northern Cyprus.

ADANA

Situated in the middle of a large and fertile plain, Adana has grown fat on the agricultural richness surrounding it: it is now Turkey's fourth largest city. Unfortunately, while

this means that there is a lot of it, it doesn't mean there is a lot to see. There is something special to *eat*, though — the spicy *Adana kebap*. In fact, all of the charcoal-grilled meat dishes here have a distinctive spiciness, thanks to Adana's location on the doorstep of the Arab lands of the Middle East. The Tourist Information office (℅ 11323) is at Atatürk Caddesi 13. There are daily flights between Adana and Istanbul and Ankara; there is also frequent rail and bus service linking the city to the rest of the country.

ANTAKYA

Founded by Alexander's general Seleucus Nicator in 300 BC, ancient Antioch quickly prospered as a key link in the great trade routes between the Mediterranean world and the Far East. By the time of Christ it had a population of over half a million and was one of the great cultural centers of the Roman Empire. Here St. Peter founded a community of people dedicated to following the teachings of Jesus Christ; the Romans, already having problems with the Jews here, decided to call this new bunch "Christians". The small grotto just north of the city where St. Peter preached, now known as **St. Peter's Church,** is said to be the oldest church in Christendom still in use.

In the end, however, it was Antioch's position that was its undoing. Everybody bent on conquest — Byzantines, Persians, Arabs, Crusaders — found the city in their path; by the thirteenth century it had been reduced to rubble. The modern city of Antakya is very much a twentieth-century creation, but one which does honor to its past in the form of the **Antakya Museum,** which houses probably the finest collection of Roman mosaics in the world.

Antakya's Tourist Information office (℅ 12636) is at Atatürk Caddesi 41.

OPPOSITE: Built in the third century AD and rebuilt in the thirteenth century, the Marmure Kalesi at Anamur is the most interesting castle on Turkey's Mediterranean coast. ABOVE: It's not easy being an entrepreneur: a young apple seller in Antalya.

Central Anatolia

THE CENTRAL Anatolian plain is the heartland of Turkey, a khaki-colored plateau that stretches and wrinkles over an enormous area. Although there is abundant evidence of human cultivation in the many great rectangles carved into the land, one is still surprised to see, in the middle of all this vastness, little clumps of houses nestling into the creases of the hills, scattered like crumbs over an unmade bed. Riding the hillsides, too, are the white tents of migrant farmworkers, men and women living almost exactly as their ancestors did a thousand years ago. Meanwhile, in the first city of the region, the capital of Turkey, the twentieth century strengthens its grip.

One thing, though, that doesn't change from the countryside to the city is the enduring friendliness of the people. Recently, for example, driving towards Ankara, I passed dozens of fields of melons. Finally, unable to resist any longer, I stopped and bought some at one of the stalls lining the road. The young man who served me, having already made the sale, then insisted on giving me a free sample of what I had just bought.

ANKARA

BACKGROUND

Ankara's great antiquity, though no longer very much in evidence, is illustrated by the number of different names by which it has been known. To the Hittites it was Ankuwash, to the Phrygians Ancyra, and to the people of Europe it was long known as Angora (hence the name of the wool that still comes from the goats in this region). The city's origins, in fact, go back as far as the Paleolithic and Neolithic ages, and excavators have found evidence of settlement by both the Bronze Age Hatti and the Hittites who came after them in the second millenium BC. It would appear that as soon as one group of people had recognized the value of the town's position — above the plains and close to a major trade route — everyone else saw the desirability of living there. After the Phrygians had established Ancyra in the tenth century BC they were quickly followed by the Lydians, the Persians, and the Galatians,

who made the town their capital in the third century BC.

The Galatians (a Celtic people who seemingly spoke a language not too far removed from Welsh) made the most of the topography of the place by building the citadel that can still be seen. But no amount of natural or man-made defense could prevent the Romans adding the town to their empire, or the subsequent Arab and Byzantine conquests which ensured that Ankara's history kept pace with that of the rest of the country. The long period of Byzantine control ended in

1073 with the capture of the city by the Seljuk Turks, who were in turn ousted by the Ottomans under Yıldırım Beyazıt in 1402. After that Ankara remained a small and rather unimportant town right up until the time of the Turkish struggle for independence, when it became the focal point of the nationalist resistance led by Kemal Atatürk. If it is no exaggeration to say that Atatürk was the father of Turkey, it is even more accurate to say that he was the father of Ankara. For he it was who on October 13, 1923 declared that this small but strategically important city should be the capital and symbol of the modern nation that he was in the process of creating. He achieved his aim: Ankara today may not be the most attractive city in Turkey (with none of the atmosphere or uniqueness of Istanbul, for example), but it is the capital, the center of government, and a thriving metropolis, just as Atatürk envisaged.

Thanks to Atatürk's decision to make this the capital of the new Turkish republic, Ankara went from being an obscure town to an important city almost overnight.

Having said which, there are still some ways in which Ankara is surprisingly provincial. A small but illuminating example is the difficulty one can experience when trying to find English-language newspapers; easily available in Istanbul or the resort towns of the Aegean, they can be fiendishly difficult to track down here (see GENERAL INFORMATION for the address of the Tarhan Bookstore). You may, indeed, find yourself having difficulty tracking anything down in Ankara: although the city is intelligently laid out, navigation is complicated by the almost total absence of street signs. In addition to this, the numbers on the houses and buildings are often very tiny, and frequently followed by letters, with the consequence that Nº 29 and Nº 30 can be a whole block apart. The trick is to make sure you always know where you are in relation to Atatürk Bulvarı. This is the spine of the city, running north-south throughout its entire length. If you are on this street, or know where it is, you can't be too hopelessly lost.

GENERAL INFORMATION

There is a Tourist Information office ((230-1911 or (321-7380) at Gazi Mustafa Kemal Bulvarı 33, near the junction with Necatibey Caddesi. In the Ulus district, north of the center, there is another at Istanbul Caddesi 4,(311-2247. The offices of the Turkish Touring and Automobile Club (TTOK) are at Adakale Sokak 4/11, Yenişehir, (131-7648. The Tarhan Bookstore should also be mentioned here because it is the best place in Ankara for English-language publications: it is in the Kızılay district, just off Atatürk Bulvarı, at Sakarya Caddesi 2/A, (133-6730.

WHAT TO SEE

In the Maltepe district to the west of the city, at the end of Anıt Kabir, stands one of the finest examples of modern architecture to be seen anywhere. The vast and austere **Atatürk Mausoleum (Anıt Kabir)** houses the tomb of Kemal Atatürk. Only completed in 1953, it is built of yellow limestone in the form of a colonnaded temple, and stands on a hill which helps to make it one of the most prominent sights of Ankara. To your left as you enter

the grounds of the mausoleum is a museum containing many of Atatürk's most interesting possessions, including his fleet of cars.

Up a long set of steps is the monument itself, its walls inscribed with excerpts from Atatürk's writings and speeches. Inside, the building has the powerful simplicity of the great mosques, with nothing but simple mosaics to distract your attention from the huge marble sarcophagus in which the body of Atatürk lies. It is an extraordinarily impressive place, and a moving one as well: as you leave the mausoleum you pass by the sarcophagus of Atatürk's most loyal friend, Ismet Inönü, who outlived him by 34 years and, as his successor as president, did so much to safeguard his legacy. The mausoleum stays open until five o'clock every day except Monday.

At the north end of the city is the **Hisar** (citadel), in and around which the sights of the old city congregate. The outer walls of the fortress are of Byzantine origin, built by the emperor Michael II in the ninth century; the inner walls are some 200 years older, and even they do not date from the first fortifications, which were built by the Galatians almost two millenia ago. When you have entered the citadel through the **Parmak Kapısı** (gate), two places you should aim for are the **Şark Kulesi (Eastern Tower),** which provides an excellent vantage point for viewing the city, and the **Selçuk Alaeddin Camii,** a beautifully restored twelfth-century mosque.

Just outside the walls of the citadel you will find the **bedesten** (covered bazaar), on Çıkrıçılar Caddesi. Situated within this building is the **Museum of Anatolian Civilizations,** which has a superb collection of exhibits stretching as far back as the Paleolithic age: some finds from Çatal Höyük, the earliest human settlement yet discovered, can be seen here, including a reconstruction of a house. The museum is closed on Mondays.

Almost next door are the **Aslanhane Camii** and the **Ahi Elvan Camii,** from the thirteenth and fourteenth centuries respectively, while down the hill on the other side of the citadel are several Roman remains. The **Column of Julian** dates from the fourth century AD, the **Roman Baths** from the third, and the **Temple of Augustus** from the second century BC, though it did not adopt its present name until the emperor to be venerated had died in 8 AD — before that it was a temple to Cybele, a fertility goddess roughly equivalent to the Greek Demeter or the Roman Ceres. You will notice that the walls of the temple have large tracts of writing over them; what you may not know is that these lines of Greek and Latin constitute a document of great historical importance. The *Res Gestae* is a work written by the emperor Augustus towards the end of his life in which he enumerates the achievements of his reign. If you are wondering why this temple was singled out for the honor of bearing such a text, the answer is that it wasn't: when Augustus was buried in Rome, the *Res Gestae* was etched in bronze and attached to his mausoleum, and copies of it were made on all the temples in the empire that rushed to devote themselves to the worship of this great man. It just so happened that this was the only temple where the work survived.

The Byzantines, inevitably, turned the temple into a Christian church, and later on the Muslims built a mosque in its grounds. The fifteenth-century **Hacı Bayram Camii**, erected to the founder of the Bayramiye order of dervishes, is the most important mosque in the city.

Back past Julian's Column, on Ulus Meydanı ("Nation Square"), is the **National Assembly Museum,** an important site for anyone interested in the birth of the Turkish state. This is where the regions of Turkey that had not been invaded by the Greeks (or the British or the French, for that matter) sent their delegates in April 1920 for the first meeting of the Grand National Assembly. Logic suggested that it would also be the last, but from these unimposing headquarters Atatürk was able to unite the country and drive out its attackers. If you think about it for long enough, that is enough to give the place an air of great power and excitement.

Before you leave Ulus and the old city, take a stroll through the **bazaar,** which starts as soon as you leave the citadel. Then, as you return towards the center of town, stop in at the **Ethnographical Museum** off Atatürk Bulvarı (the entrance is from Talatpaşa Bulvarı). To find it, simply look for the statue of Atatürk astride a horse. Once inside, you will find exhibits of a more recent vintage than those in the Museum of Anatolian Civilizations; the best-represented periods here are those of the Seljuks and the Ottomans, which means that you can expect to see some fabulous artwork and jewelry, as well as highly-crafted weapons, tools, and even musical instruments. Here, too, is the room that Atatürk used as his office after the completion of the building in 1925. This museum is also closed on Mondays.

At the southern end of the city, in the grounds of the Presidential Palace, is the

Çankaya Köşkü, the chalet which Atatürk kept as a summer house. If you hand in your passport at the entrance to the Presidential Palace, you will be taken around this immaculately-kept slice of history.

WHERE TO STAY

Luxury

Ankara has three five-star hotels: the **Büyük Ankara Oteli** ((134-4920) at Atatürk Bulvarı 183, the **Etap Altınel Oteli** ((230-3235) at Gazi Mustafa Kemal Bulvarı 151 and the **Hilton International Ankara** at Tahran Caddesi 12 ((168-2900). Of these, the Büyük is, by Turkish standards, extremely expensive ($120 single, $150 double), whereas the others, at $80/$100, are merely very expensive.

At the other end of this category comes the **Dedeman** ((117-6200). It is reached by turning east off Atatürk Bulvarı and going

Among the fine exhibits at the Museum of Anatolian Civilizations (above) are finds from Çatal Höyük, the earliest human settlement yet discovered.

down Akay Sokak; the hotel's address is Büklüm Sokak 1. For a well air-conditioned room you will pay $50 single or $70 double. Further up Atatürk Bulvarı, just past Kızılay at № 80, the **Hotel Etap Mola** (℡ 133-9065) is also quite luxurious, and slightly cheaper than the Dedeman at $45 single, $55 double.

Middle Range
Still on Atatürk Bulvarı, at № 141, is the **Bulvar Palas Hotel** (℡ 134-2180). This is a likable place with some excellent rooms: if you pick carefully you can have a double room away from the street noise, complete with bath, fridge, and television, for $45 double. The **Ersan Oteli** (℡ 118-9875) at Meşrutiyet Caddesi 13, a block east of Atatürk Bulvarı, has doubles for $30.

The **Otel Gül Palas** (℡ 133-3120) is at № 15 on Bayındır Sokak, a pedestrian street in the Kızılay district with a great many restaurants. The lack of traffic makes the hotel pleasantly quiet. A double room here costs $23 double. At № 8 on the same street is the **Apaydın Oteli** (℡ 133-3135), which is a little more expensive.

Inexpensive
The back streets of Ulus are full of cheap and friendly hotels, of which the ones below are a selection. Since many of them have some rooms with bath and some without, I have given in each case the price with bath included. Be sure to check that this is what you are getting before you sign in.

Denizciler Caddesi runs north from Talatpaşa Bulvarı; here you will find the cosy and well-run **Safir Oteli** (℡ 324-1194) at № 34, and the **Paris Oteli** (℡ 324-1283) at № 14. Neither of them should set you back more than $18 for a double room. Nearby, just off Opera Meydanı, the site of the Opera House (Atatürk was a great fan of opera), are the **Otel Devran** (℡ 311-0485) at Tavus Sokak 8, and the **Otel Akman** (℡ 324-4140) at Tavus Sokak 6. The Devran is the real bargain, with lots of Old World patina for only $10 double, while the Akman, at $15 double, is still very good value.

The **Taç Hotel** (℡ 324-3095) is at Çankırı Caddesi 35, on the same side of the road as the Roman baths, and opposite the Column of Julian. A double room here costs about $19.

WHERE TO EAT
As mentioned above, Bayındır Sokak, the traffic-free avenue east of Atatürk Bulvarı and north of Ziya Gökalp Caddesi, is full of good restaurants. The pick of them is the **Körfez**, which, despite being constantly crowded, gives excellent service. Neither the waiters nor the menu here speaks English — which may strike you as a disadvantage, but it is in fact the opposite, as you will be invited in to the kitchen to inspect their dishes and choose the one you like best. One of the few drawbacks of the place is that, like many restaurants in Turkey, the waiters are a bit casual about when they bring the wine, so you may have to remind them a couple of times. Don't be put off by this, however: it really is a very charming place, with some surprisingly English fare on offer, such as beef stew and spinach. Two people can eat and drink here for $11. If the Körfez is full, scout around the other restaurants along this street, many of which manage to include "PIKNIK" in their names.

Still in Kızılay, the **Yeni Karpiç**, just off the main square, offers a patio where you can eat delicious food and watch the city go by. The **Maksim** (℡ 229-7566) at Gazi Mustafa Kemal Bulvarı 14/D is very good value at $9 for two. The **Liman** (℡ 230-2705) at İzmir Caddesi 11 is moderately expensive, but it has a good menu which features fresh fish, something of a rarity in Ankara.

When you are in Ulus I recommend you try the **Yavuz Lokantası**, which is up by the Anatolian Civilizations Museum, at Konya Sokak 13/F. The staff and the prices are both very friendly. Nearby, at № 51 on Denizciler Caddesi, is the **Uludağ Lokantası**, which will provide a full meal, based on *kebap*, for about $8. If you have been up past Ulus Meydanı to look at the Temple of Augustus or the Column of Julian, a handy point for re-grouping would be the **Çiçek Lokantası** at 12/A Çankırı Caddesi, where you can sit by a lovely fountain and eat good, cheap food.

Three places specializing in foreign cooking are: the **Italyan Restoran** at 200 Hoşdere Caddesi; **China Town**, 19 Köroğlu Caddesi; and the **Mikado**, which is in the Etap Altınel Oteli on Gazi Mustafa Kemal Bulvarı. The cuisine of the first two is in each case announced in the name, and it doesn't take too long to work out that the Mikado serves Japanese food. Of the three, the Italyan is the cheapest: you can eat and drink well for $10. China Town and the Mikado, on the other hand, are both quite fashionable and expensive: you may wish to check the prices before sitting down.

How to Get There

This should be very simple. Ankara, as you would expect, is served by every available form of transport, and in most cases it is served very well. The airport has flights to and from every other airport in Turkey, as well as most international destinations. It is also very well served by bus, and even the train, usually so unreliable, offers some good options, most notably from Istanbul: if you catch an express train you should arrive in Ankara in under eight hours.

As with most big cities, the airport is quite a long way out from the center, so be prepared to pay for a taxi or to take one of the THY buses to their terminal near the junction of Talatpaşa Bulvarı and Hipodrom Caddesi—from which you may still need to take a taxi. The railway station is behind the THY terminal, and the bus station is still further along Hipodrom Caddesi.

KONYA

Background

In a country the size of Turkey a journey of 260 km (161 miles) is not a particularly long one; yet in traveling that distance between Ankara and Konya you take the greatest imaginable leap. From the city that, above all, symbolizes modern Turkey, you now arrive in the city with the strongest attachment to Turkey's past. Konya is not the oldest city in this region: that distinction goes to the settlement of Çatal Höyük, 45 km (28 miles) to the south, which dates from the eighth millenium BC and is thought to be one of the earliest human settlements in the world. But in its attitudes Konya generally deserves its reputation as the most conservative — not to say reactionary — city in Turkey.

Evidence of prehistoric and Hittite inhabitation has been found here, but it seems to have been the Phrygians, calling the place Kuwania, who first invested it with any significance. According to their legends this was the first city to emerge after the great flood. It may have been this that established Konya as a mystical place; certainly the town seems to have exercised a strong magnetic force on holy men ever since. In the first century AD, as Iconium, capital of the Roman province of Lycaonia, it heard the sermons of both St. Paul and St. Barnabas. The battle of Manzíkert in 1076 ushered in an age of unsurpassed glory for Konya. It brought to an end hundreds of years of Byzantine and Arab tussling, in which the town had repeatedly changed hands, and gave control to the victorious Seljuk Turks. Despite the unwelcome attentions of one or two passing Crusades, the Seljuks held Konya pretty securely for the next 200 years; and it was towards the end of this period, and particularly in the reign of Sultan Alaeddin Keykubat, that the town reached its peak. It was also in the thirteenth century that Konya saw the birth of a religious order whose name was to resound throughout the world: the Whirling Dervishes.

The source of the order, and of the ritual for which it is famous, was a single man, Celaleddin Rumi. The son of a holy man, he was born in what is now Afghanistan and came with his family to Konya when he was 21. Here, after several years of meditation, he founded an order of dervishes, who called him Mevlana — "Our master" — while they came to be known as Mevlevi. Mevlana's greatest achievement was his epic poem, the *Mesnevi*; his most enduring legacy has been the *sema*.

The *sema* is a dance where everything you can see has a powerful symbolic meaning. This includes the costumes worn by the dancers — the tall, cylindrical hats they wear represent their tombstones; their white dresses, shrouds. The point of this imagery is that the dervishes are dying in order to gain new life. The movement of the dance itself, whence the name of "whirling dervishes" originates, is apparently connected with the constant rotation of the heavens: by spinning round in one direction, as the stars do, the Mevlevi are supposed to achieve the union with God that they desire. Nor is the manner of their whirling unimportant. The right hand must be stretched up to the heavens, the left down towards the earth, so that the dancer becomes a kind of conductor for all the blessings that flow from above. This dance is repeated three times, always to the accompaniment of the *ney*, a flute fashioned from a simple reed cut down and with holes burnt into it. The holes are said to represent humans who were once in paradise, and the wailing noise produced by the

forgotten, largely ignored as the order became more and more self-serving and conservative. By the time Turkey had won the War of Independence in 1922 the Mevlevi represented a powerful obstacle to the reforms Atatürk was bent on bringing about; three years later he dissolved the order. In this he was, for once, only partially successful. The order continued to exist, and even to perform every December the *sema* ceremony to commemorate Mevlana's death in 1273. Today the dervishes are officially accepted again, and are even encouraged as a

ney is the sound of their lamentations for the heaven they have lost.

If all of this sounds remarkably alien, one need only remind oneself of the Shakers, and the fundamentalist Christians known as "holy rollers". Ecstatic devotional dancing has been a feature of almost every religion at some point.

The Mevlevi order of dervishes soon became an enormously influential one, and their power was not diminished by the arrival of the Ottomans. Indeed, while Konya itself went into a gradual decline, the *çelebis* ("inheritors" of Mevlana's legacy) exercised enormous influence on successive sultans. Probably as a result of this, the liberal and humane teachings of Mevlana were, if not

part of the nation's heritage; while the Mevlevi order, in spite of everything the twentieth century has thrown at it, has retained much of the mystical force and genuine devotion that made Atatürk so uncomfortable.

For all that it lags behind the times in some respects, Konya is not doing badly on the economic front, thanks largely to the terrain in which it is situated. The land around here may seem dry and arid, but it is in fact ideal for growing the grain that goes into the making of Turkey's delicious bread.

GENERAL INFORMATION

The Tourist Information office ((11074) is at Mevlana Caddesi 21.

WHAT TO SEE

The most important building in Konya is without doubt the **Mevlana Müzesi** on Kışla Caddesi. The Mevlevi order can trace its roots back to this very plot of land, which is believed to have been donated by the sultan to Mevlana's father. After his death in 1232, this is where he was buried, and his tomb was later joined by that of Mevlana himself, and Mevlana's son, Sultan Veled. The museum began life as a Mevlevi *tekke* (convent), which explains why the building itself is as beautiful as anything inside it. The deep turquoise of the conical dome is quite stunning.

After passing through a lovely courtyard enhanced by crowds of red roses, you will be required to take your shoes off before entering the building; when you see the carpets on the floor you will know why. Once inside you can inspect the sarcophagi of Mevlana, his father, and his son, with a white turban sitting proudly at the head of each. Also on display are the earliest surviving manuscripts of Mevlana's *Mesnevi*, and some superb illuminated Korans. In addition to the carpets under your feet, you can see Mevlana's prayer carpet, and a 500-year-old Persian silk carpet which is said to have taken five years to weave, and which is reckoned by many to be the finest carpet ever made. As you examine these exhibits you will hear haunting music being played in the background: this is the sound of the *ney*, or perhaps the *rebab*, a single-stringed violin which is also used in the dancing ceremony. The room where the dance takes place, the adjacent **semahane,** is not of Seljuk origin but was a gift from the Ottoman sultans. The interior is made beautiful by its chandeliers and rich carpets.

As you head into the center of town along Kışla Caddesi to see the other major sights, you pass the **Selimiye Camii.** Completed in 1574, it is an Ottoman-style mosque built by Sultan Selim I. There is nothing inside to warrant a visit, but as you pass you might admire the refreshing simplicity of its design.

The hill in the center of town, created not by nature but by an accumulation of human settlements, is called Alaeddin Tepesi, and the mosque on it is the **Alaeddin Camii.** Dating from 1221, the mosque contains, in its *mimber* (pulpit) and *mihrab* (prayer-niche) two of the finest pieces of woodcarving to be found anywhere. It is also the resting place of eight sultans, whose sarcophagi are here. There is another tomb next door to this, which is empty. Next to the mosque are the scanty ruins of a Seljuk palace, which you pass on the way to your next stop.

Once a theological school, the **Karatay Medrese** (1251) now houses a **Museum of**

Ceramics, with rare and beautiful Seljuk artefacts depicting all sorts of weird and wonderful things — angels and fabulous animals and such like. The most exciting thing about the medrese, however, is the dome, which is covered in exquisitely-crafted tiles. Each one is shaped like a star with 24 points, and they are set in rows against a deep blue background.

When you come out of the Karatay Medrese, turn right and walk down the circular road in a counter-clockwise direction until you reach the **Ince Minareli Medrese,** built by the architect Keluk in 1258. At the entrance there is an unbelievably ornate portal, with intricate designs and bands of Arabic inscriptions twisting around each other. The museum, appropriately, exhibits stone and wood carvings, many of them reliefs or

OPPOSITE: The beautiful dome of the Mevlana Müzesi in Konya, home of the whirling dervishes. ABOVE: The Aziziye Mosque in Konya, an oasis of tranquillity next to the bustle of the city's bazaar.

statues from the Seljuk palace on Alaeddin Tepesi. The minaret here used to look much more impressive, before it had its top knocked off by a bolt of lightning in 1901.

Bear in mind that none of these museums is open on Monday.

The **bazaar** is on Çıkrıkçılar Caddesi, near the post office. There is a wide range of goods you can buy here, but the *kilims* are particularly fine, many of which have been made by "amateurs" — girls of marrying age out to prove their virtuosity (not their virtue, of course: that is assumed). A Turkish girl is much more marriageable if she can prove how adept she is.

WHERE TO STAY

For the visitor who has just arrived at the bus station feeling hot and sticky, the adjacent **Özkaymak Park Oteli** ((33770) is bound to look extremely attractive. In this case it is quite safe to follow your instincts, as the Özkaymak is as good as anything you will find in the center of town. A double room here costs $40.

If you are looking for something more central I would recommend the **Hotel Selçuk** ((11259), which is just off Alaeddin Caddesi, on Babalık Sokak. It is $36 for a double room here, but you should have no complaints. The **Başak Palas** ((11338), on the other hand, does not quite live up to its name. Situated further from the hill than the Selçuk at Hükümet Alanı 3, Başak Palas is anything but palatial: the rooms are quite tiny, and the lights cannot always be relied on to work. One advantage it has over some other places is that you can park right outside with little difficulty; parking elsewhere in Konya can be a nightmare. Here you will pay slightly less than at the Selçuk: $30 single, $35 double. Just behind the Tourist Information office, off Mevlana Caddesi, is the **Konya Otel** ((19212 or (16677). This has one of the best reputations around, and shouldn't cost more than about $30-$35 for a quiet and very comfortable double room.

Much cheaper than all the above is the **Saray Oteli** ((19990) at Mevlana Caddesi 15. This hotel is excellent value for the $15 it charges for a double room. The nearby

Hotel Tur ((19825), just around the corner from the Tourist Information office at 13 Esarizade Sokak, has perfectly good rooms that go for about the same price. Near the station, just south of Istasyon Caddesi, there is a good campsite, **Atatürk Camping**.

WHERE TO EAT

The fairgrounds to the west of Alaeddin Tepesi provide a very pleasant spot for sitting at a terrace table and surveying the domes and minarets of Konya. As to which table you do this from, there is no shortage of choice: you can have something very basic and refreshing at one of the cafés, or go somewhere more upmarket, such as the **Fuar Lokantası**, which will cost about $12 a meal.

If you are on the other side of the hill, the bazaar has plenty of cheap places where you can try the local speciality, *fırın kebap*, mutton cooked not over a fire but in an oven. The best place for sampling this dish is perhaps the **Çatal Lokantası** near the Mevlana Museum and the Tourist Information office. Two people can eat here for $4.50, including two beers. The **Şifa Restaurant** at Mevlana Caddesi 30 is also good, and only slightly more expensive than the Çatal, while the **Kösem** on Alaeddin Caddesi charges a little more again for nice food and pleasantly breezy surroundings.

HOW TO GET THERE

Konya has no airport, though there is a Turkish Airlines office here, at Alaeddin Caddesi 22, Kat. 1/106, (12000 or 12032. The town is served by trains running along the Istanbul-Adana route (it takes slightly over 12 hours to get here), but not by any direct service from Ankara; the station is on the outskirts of town, to the southwest at the end of Istasyon Caddesi, but there are plenty of buses that you can catch into the center.

To reach Konya from Ankara, your best bet is the bus, which runs direct from Ankara (taking about four hours) and which connects with every other city, though in some cases you may have to change on to another bus.

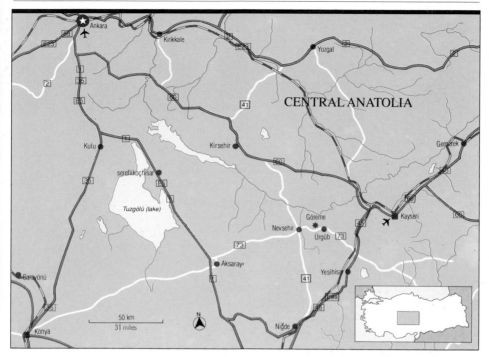

CAPPADOCIA

The region of Cappadocia has no official existence, but the Turks know where it is as surely as Americans do New England and the British do the Lake District. It is hardly surprising that a name as ancient and famous as Cappadocia has not died out, yet the region itself is actually very small: if you were to draw a triangle with Kayseri, Aksaray, and Niğde as its points, you would more or less have it.

BACKGROUND

The most historically interesting inhabitants of Cappadocia were not the Seljuks or the Ottomans but the Christians. They were converted by St. Paul, and the region remained a significant part of the Christian world for a thousand years. There were, of course, other people here first, such as the Hittites (for whom this was the base of their empire) and the Romans — and, between them, a small independent state lasting several hundred years. But the most interesting remains were left by the Christians, both the indigenous ones and those who fled here to escape persecution at the hands of the Arabs. Their churches, and the frescoes inside them, are a major contributing factor to the beauty of this region.

What really made Cappadocia the stunning experience it is today, however, is without doubt Erciyes Dağ, the volcano that looms over Kayseri (Roman Caesarea). It was the lava spewed out of this, and its companions Hasan Dağ and Melendiz Dağ many thousands of years ago that gave the area its distinctive topography: the lava, as it cooled down, became tufa, a soft and porous stone that over time was molded by the wind and the rain into the strange conical towers we see today. These shapes, with their harder layer of tufa protecting them at the top, are known as "fairy chimneys". When man arrived in the region, and had finished wondering at the weird landscape, he realized that these shapes would make very serviceable homes, particularly since other building materials were hard to come by here. So the holes that one sees ventilating these cones are in fact doors and windows, some of them still in use. Although the most common

OVERLEAF: Dwellings ancient and modern: nature's architecture and man's rise next to each other in Göreme.

practical use to which the fairy chimneys are now put is for cool storage of the lemons and apricots grown nearby, there are still some troglodytes who see no reason to modernize their mode of habitation.

GENERAL INFORMATION

The address of the Tourist Information office in Nevşehir is Meteriş Mah., Osmanlı Caddesi 37, ℂ 1137; there is also an information desk at the bus station. The office in Kayseri is at Kağnı Pazarı 41, ℂ 19295. In Ürgüp go

down the hill from the main square to Kayseri Caddesi 37 (ℂ 1059). If you want to do some advance research, there is a Cappadocia Culture and Tourism Center in Ankara, ℂ (4) 133-3223 or 133-8897.

WHAT TO SEE

The two biggest towns here are Kayseri and Nevşehir, but these are not the best places to be for sigtseeing. Kayseri's boulevards of tower blocks provide an unattractive example of modern troglodyte living, and Nev,sehir is similarly undistinguished. Neither of them is completely devoid of interest, of course, so if you find yourself in either city you can look out for the follow-

ing: in Kayseri, the most impressive object is the snow-capped volcano ErciyesDağı (3,916 m or 12,848 ft), now extinct, while the best man-made sights are the Mahperi Hatun Mausoleum, near the Byzantine fortress, the Döner Kümbet (1276), and the Sahabiye Medrese, which has a magnificent portal. Have a look, also, at the Çifte Medrese, which was the first school of anatomy built in the Middle Ages. In Nevşehir you can inspect the legacy of the Grand Vizier Ibrahim Paşa, a great fan of European culture who was responsible for the construction in 1726 of the Kurşunlu Camii.

However, the ideal spot to aim for is, without any doubt, Ürgüp. Not only is this the best-placed town from which to make the most interesting excursions, and the one with by far the best accommodation, it is also extremely charming in its own right. Nestling in among cave dwellings punched out of the mountainside, it has hardly a right-angle to its name. Best of all, it is only eight kilometers southeast of Göreme, along a road lined with superb examples of the surreal cones known as fairy chimneys. Göreme itself is a museum unlike any other you have ever seen: an open-air museum, in fact, encompassing most of a valley which will leave you breathless with its beauty. As you walk around exploring the paths and photographing the scenery, you will come across the "exhibits" — the caves and troglodyte dwellings of an ancient city.

Given that Göreme was an important center of early Christianity, it is hardly surprising that one finds a great many churches here. What is not so predictable is the way they are constructed — or rather, not constructed, but simply carved out of the hillside. Nor are they merely impressive from the outside: their interiors, though somewhat damaged by the inevitable vandalism, contain frescoes which in some cases date back to the fifth century AD, and are nonetheless remarkably vivid, thanks in part to some excellent restoration. In the Karanlık Kilise (the "Dark Church") there are some fine paintings, and also a refectory where the tables and benches have been hewn out of the rock. The most interesting of the other churches are the Elmalı Kilise (the "Church with the Apple"), the Barbara Kilise (the

"Church of St. Barbara"), and the **Yılanlı Kilise** (the "Church with the Snake"), which derives its name from its frescoes depicting serpents wrapping their coils around the damned. The **Tokalı Kilise,** on the road to the lower of Göreme's valleys, has some excellent New Testament scenes on restored thirteenth-century frescoes. If you are driving to Göreme and you take the wrong turning, don't hurry to get back on course: you will almost certainly stumble on something well worth seeing, whether it is one of the rock fortresses at Ortahisar or Uçhisar, the

who inhabited them were not particularly large; one hardly has room to turn around in the corridors. So who went to all the trouble to form these warrens, and why?

The answer is that it was the Christians who lived here, and not for spiritual reasons: in the centuries following the introduction of Christianity to the region, the Arabs to the east got into the habit of rampaging over the land periodically, slaughtering anyone who got in their way. Thus it was prudent for the Christian inhabitants, when they saw the Arabs coming, to duck into their holes and

churches carved from the tufa at Kızılçukur, or the crowds of fairy chimneys at Zelve.

If Göreme presents you with an unfamiliar mode of living, the thought of people existing in the **underground cities** at Derinkuyu and Kaymaklı is almost inconceivable. Derinkuyu, whose name means "Deep Well," is 29 km (18 miles) south of Nevşehir. The city here goes down to a depth of 120 m (394 ft), and may have as many as 15 levels (many of them overlap and crisscross, which makes it hard to calculate). A tunnel several kilometers in length connects it with Kaymaklı. Both cities were fully-equipped for long-term inhabitation, with kitchens, cisterns, store rooms and even chapels. But they can never have been comfortable places to live, even if the people

roll across the entrances the huge stones that you can still see lying about the place. These boulders could not be moved from the outside without a long struggle, during which the aggressors could be decimated by means of small slits in the rock face through which the Christians would chop them up. When you also consider all the secret entrances from which the defenders could dart out, hack down the enemy's rearguard, and disappear again as if into thin air, one can imagine how effective these defenses were. They had to be, for otherwise it is impossible

OPPOSITE: A fresco inside a church at Göreme, Cappadocia. ABOVE: The valley of Zelve, north of Göreme, where some of the most stunning rock formations are to be found.

to conceive of people wanting to live here. It must have been particularly trying when the invaders were right on top of them, for then they could not afford to light any fires for fear of the smoke giving away their position.

I say that the Christians lived here, which is true. What is not completely clear, however, is whether it was they who first created these subterranean dwellings. The assumption that they did has been thrown into doubt by the discovery of a Roman tomb, and even more by that of a grain mill that seems to have been built in the style of the Hittites. So the

in Cappadocia. My favorite stop-over here is the **Park Hotel** ((1883), PTT Karşısı, Avanos Caddesi 20, where two can stay for a little over $15. The hotel is beautifully appointed, down a little cobblestone street, and rooms come with constant hot water, towels, soap, and a lovely view.

Two rather more expensive hotels are a little way out of town. If you go up the hill along the road leading west towards Göreme and Nevşehir, you will find the **Turban Ürgüp Motel** ((1490). The rooms here are actually little bungalows, which give their occupants

origin of the cities is likely to remain obscure. What we do know is that the Christians took the cities to unprecedented levels of inhabitation: in the seventh century, not long before the Byzantines finally drove off the Arab marauders, the population of the Derinkuyu-Kaymaklı complex seems to have peaked at around 60,000.

Both of these sites are well signposted and easy to find from the main highway connecting Nevşehir and Niğde. They are open every day until 6:30 pm.

WHERE TO STAY

As I have indicated, Ürgüp is the most attractive and most convenient place to stay

the pleasant, if deluded, impression that they are living like real Turks. For this you will pay $40 single, $55 double. Further along this road, just before it turns off for Göreme, is the **Paris Motel & Camping** ((1435), with doubles from $15. On the other side of town, along the road to Kayseri, is the **Tepe Hotel** ((1154) on Teslimiye Tepesi, which has double rooms with superb views from $40.

Back in the center of Ürgüp, the old-fashioned **Büyük Otel** ((1060), near the main square on Kayseri Caddesi, provides old-fashioned (*i.e.* good) service and an excellent breakfast menu for $30 double. At Nº 24 on the same street is one of the best bargains in town, the **Pinar Otel** ((1054), which has simple and unfussy rooms for under $10.

Many of the pensions in Ürgüp have gardens where you can camp: the **Güzelgöz Pansiyon** ((1094), for instance, charges very little for you to pitch your tent there, and has shower and cooking facilities. There are also several campsites on either side of the road towards Nevşehir, so you will have no trouble finding a spare bit of grass.

If for any reason you are in Kayseri or Nevşehir and need a room for the night, I suggest you try one of the following: in Kayseri, the **Terminal Oteli** ((15864) at Istanbul Caddesi 76; in Nevşehir, the **Fatih Mehmet Oteli** ((1810) at Sebze Pazarı 40. Neither of these is anything special, but they are inexpensive and well run.

WHERE TO EAT

Ürgüp does as well for restaurants as it does for hotels. It has its own specialty, *güveç*, which is a delicious combination of lamb, eggplant, and peppers, and a wide range of fine restaurants ready to give you a taste of it: the **Sofa** in Cumhuriyet Meydanı will feed two people most satisfactorily for $7, including drinks. The same sort of prices apply at the **Cappadocia,** which is by the bus station, and the **Çırağan**, also in the center. The restaurant in the **Büyük Otel** is only a little more expensive, and good value for its reliable food.

The restaurant of the **Göreme Oteli** in Nevşehir, at Bankalar Caddesi 16, is much nicer inside than the hotel is from the outside, and the service is swift and courteous. Expect to pay at least $12 for two.

In Kayseri, try the **Kristal Lokanta,** which is right in the center, near Atatürk Parkı: this is perhaps the best place for sampling local dishes such as *pastırma*, dried beef with garlic. You can do so for about $5. Alternatively, you could eat at the **Kardeşler Lokantası** at 27 Mayıs Caddesi, where the food is good and not too expensive.

HOW TO GET THERE

Main highways connect Ankara with both Nevşehir and Kayseri, so you will have no trouble at all finding a bus to take you to either of those towns, or — perhaps after changing coaches — to Ürgüp. Kayseri's

Erkilet airport (the only one in the area) receives flights from both Istanbul and Ankara; to fly on from Kayseri, consult the THY office at Yıldırım Caddesi 1, (11001. Trains run here from Ankara and Adana, and leave here for the east; the phone number for enquiries in Kayseri is 11313. Once you are in Cappadocia, the buses, and even more the minibuses, are the best way to flit from one site to the next. You could even take a taxi to many of them, as the distances involved are often not great, and the fares very low.

It may be that you just want to make a quick excursion from Ankara. If so, you might think about getting on to an organized tour. These will usually take three days and include all the major sights of Cappadocia in the itinerary. The fares, which include full board and guide's fees etc., are quite low: **Konvoy Tur**, Atatürk Bulvarı 233/8, Kavaklıdere, Ankara, (126-1631, uses the Turban Ürgüp Motel and charges $160 for a three day tour. **Angel Tours**, Köroğlu Caddesi, Kahraman Kadın Sokak 17, Gaziosmanpaşa, Ankara, (136-1216, has lower prices ($125 for the same three day tour) but doesn't specify which hotels it uses.

OPPOSITE: Central Anatolian peasant women washing their carpets. ABOVE: A wedding day in Cappadocia.

The
Black Sea
Coast

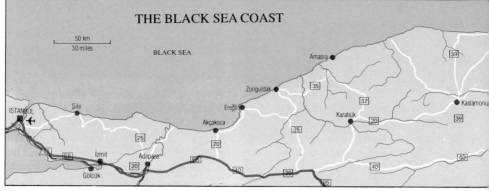

THE REGION of the Black Sea coast is unlike any other part of Turkey. It occupies a completely different climatic zone, with mild temperatures and high humidity year-round. It is this temperate climate, along with the large annual rainfall, that accounts for the extraordinary greenness of virtually the entire coast. At whatever point you venture into Turkey's upper margin, you enter a different world — a greener, denser, damper world, deeply forested, and tilted towards the sea.

Separated geographically from the rest of the country by the Black Sea mountain range, the area can also claim to have had a rather separate history. Originally colonized by the people of Miletus in the seventh century BC, the towns along the coast led an obscure existence until about 300 BC, when Mithridates, a general fleeing the carnage that followed the death of Alexander the Great, came to Amasya (then Amaseia) and started calling himself the King of Pontus. He succeeded in getting everyone else in the region to call him that as well, and his descendants ruled an increasingly large and wealthy kingdom. This was to end in the first century BC, when Mithridates IV Eupator, having conquered Cappadocia and other parts of Anatolia, grew too confident and attacked an ally of Rome. The Romans first slapped him down, and then, when he tried again, sent Lucullus to deal with him. A year later Mithridates was dead, having committed suicide, and Pontus was part of the Roman Empire.

At the beginning of the thirteenth century another exile set himself up by the sea. Alexius Comnenus came here to escape the sack of Constantinople by the Crusaders in 1204, and, like Mithridates, established a small but durable state: the diminutive Comnene Empire lasted for 250 war-torn years, managing to keep its capital Trebizond (Trabzon) out of the hands of the Seljuks at a time when every other opposing power was being swept aside. Not until 1461 and the advent of the Ottomans did it fall into line with the rest of the country.

Nowadays the region is of great importance to the Turkish economy: all of the country's tea, as well as most of its coal, steel, hazelnuts, and tobacco, comes from here. Tourism has yet to make much of an impact, despite the abundance of beautiful (and mostly deserted) beaches, but it is surely only a matter of time before this coast joins Turkey's other coasts in being discovered.

If you are coming here from Istanbul, the most pleasant form of transport is the Turkish Maritime Lines car ferry which takes two days to chug across to Trabzon, with stops at Sinop, Samsun and Giresun. If you're in a hurry, there are Turkish Airlines (THY) flights from Istanbul and Ankara to both Samsun and Trabzon. If you are coming overland, the buses to (and in) this part of the country are as fast and frequent as they are everywhere else. You should have no trouble finding a bus to take you to any of the towns mentioned below.

SILE TO SAMSUN

SILE

Driving east from Istanbul, the first resort you come to is Sile, 70 hilly and pine-covered kilometers away. Its proximity to Istanbul

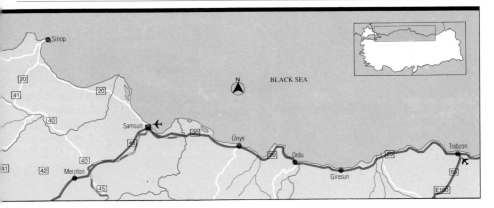

explains why its permanent population of 5,000 rises to 65,000 during the summer. Most of the visitors are here for a dose of sand and sea, but there is also something for the ruin-seeker, in the shape of the Genoese castle whose remains stand on the hill overlooking the town.

The hotel most favored by those fleeing Istanbul is the **Değirmen** ((148) at Plaj Yolu 24. It is large and modern, on the beach, with rooms for $17 single and $25 double.

AKÇAKOCA

This small fishing village was once very important to the Ottomans: it is where they first established themselves on the coast, and Akçakoca was the name of the general who did it. The town, like Şile, has a Genoese castle nearby. Otherwise it is distinguished by the wooded hills that surround it, and by a lovely, sandy beach suitable for camping. For more sophisticated accommodation, there are about a dozen hotels, in all of which the rooms have baths. The best of these is probably the modern **Deniz.**

EREĞLI AND ZONGULDAK

On the map these cities look much more significant than little towns like Şile and Akçakoca, and so they are — to the Turkish economy. These are the country's largest producers of steel and coal, which makes them important to the natives but of little interest to the visitor. Since you have Akçakoca to the west and Amasra to the east, there is no compelling reason to stop in between.

AMASRA

Eighty kilometers east of Zonguldak lies the pretty village of Amasra, once a Genoese port built around a promontory with a harbor on either side. There are the remains of a **Genoese castle** here, and the **Fatih Cami,** once a Byzantine church. The town is somewhat off the beaten track, but that needn't deter you as there are numerous hotels and pensions around, such as the Deniz, above the **Canlıbalık** restaurant on the edge of the sea. The restaurant, not surprisingly, specializes in fresh fish.

SINOP

Founded — according to legend — by an Amazon queen, Sinop has certainly been around a long time: archaeologists think it was a Hittite settlement in the third millenium BC. It was Sinop that gave the world Diogenes, the famous third-century philosopher and aphorist. After that the only part of any note that it has played in world affairs was in 1853 when, in spite of the protection afforded by Sinop's natural harbor, the Turkish fleet was destroyed in a sudden attack by a Russian squadron. The attack, which left 3,000 Turkish sailors dead, led to the start of the Crimean War four months later. Having managed to keep itself out of trouble since then, the town is now best known for its traditional nautical wood carvings and high-quality crystal.

Sinop's **museum** is worth seeing for the foundations of an old temple of Serapis that lie in the grounds, as well as for the

seventh century BC. Very little evidence of their presence, or that of subsequent generations, remains since the town was put to the torch by the Genoese in the fifteenth century. As a consequence the city makes as much as it can of the fact that Atatürk, after fleeing from Istanbul, landed here to organize nationalist resistance around the country.

Nowadays Samsun is the largest city on the coast, with a population approaching 300,000.

superb gold exhibits inside. Nearby are the **Alaeddin Camii,** a Seljuk mosque of the thirteenth century, and the **Alaiye Medrese** from the same period. The Tourist Information office (℡ 5837) is at İskele Meydanı 2/A.

You can stay in comfort at the **Melia Kasım Hotel** (℡ 1625) at Gazi Caddesi 41 for about $20 double; if you want something cheaper, the **Hotel Gülpalas** (℡ 1737) near the bus station on Cumhuriyet Caddesi has double rooms for as little as $7. For even less you can camp at sites along the shore on either side of the city.

Since the natural harbor is still used by fishing boats, you are guaranteed a delicious fish dinner at any of the quayside restaurants. *Palamut* (baby tuna) and *hamsi* (a kind of anchovy) are two of the local delicacies.

SAMSUN

The road from Sinop threads its way through maize and tobacco plantations all the way to Samsun, the city known as Amisos by the Greek colonists who settled here in the

Nor does its economy show any signs of slowing down, as demand for the cigarettes produced at its Tekel factory remains voracious. Like the similarly industrialized Ereğli and Zonguldak, the town is a bit shopsoiled, and you wouldn't want to swim in its water. On the other hand, it has retained some degree of historical interest: to the west of town, just south of Atatürk Bulvarı, are mosques from the fourteenth and nineteenth centuries (the **Pazar Cami** and the **Büyük Cami),** and on either side of Atatürk Bulvarı itself are the **Atatürk Monument** and the **Atatürk Museum,** where some of the great man's weapons, clothing, and photographs are on display. Apart from this the most interesting buildings are the more recent municipal ones, such as the **Old City Hall,** which is almost baroque in its architecture.

Rugged looks and attractive headwear form part of Turkey's ethnic mosaic.

The Tourist Information office (℡ 11228) is on the corner of 19 Mayıs Bulvarı and Irmak Caddesi, near the Atatürk Monument. Turkish Airlines (℡ 13455) have their office at Kazım Paşa Caddesi 11/A, and the office of Turkish Railways (TCDD) is on Atatürk Bulvarı (℡ 32296).

Samsun's biggest hotel is the **Turban Samsun Oteli** (℡ 10750) on Sahil Caddesi, the road that runs around the edge of the harbor. It is well equipped and modern, with a swimming pool, and charges about $40 for a single room, and $60 for a double. The **Tuğra Hotel** (℡ 31107) on Irmak Caddesi charges $22 for a double, but is one of those hotels that, annoyingly, doesn't accept the Visa card that it welcomes in its window. In any case, the **Hotel Burç** (℡ 15479) on Kazım Paşa Caddesi is better value at $20

double, while the **Otel Yafeya** (℡ 16565) on Cumhuriyet Meydanı, near the Tourist Information office and the Atatürk Monument, has excellent rooms for about the same price. For a good place to eat, try the **Cumhuriyet Restaurant** on Şeyhhamza Caddesi (℡ 12165).

Heading east from Samsun there is no view of the sea for some time: you rejoin the sea further down the coast past Terme. The coastline here becomes increasingly lush and verdant, while the mountains to your right in the middle distance are somehow made more majestic by the mist that surrounds them. By filtering out the colors and erasing the details, the mist isolates and dramatizes the outline of the mountain range against the sky.

ÜNYE TO GIRESUN

ÜNYE

Ünye's ancient name was Oenae, and, hard though it is to believe now, this relaxed and colorful port (with its purple rock and its green hazelnut plantations) once required strong fortifications, traces of which can still be seen here. The only other impressive sight for which man may claim the credit is the eighteenth-century **town hall.** You may decide to visit these places in the morning, after a night at the **Otel Kumsal** (℡ 4490), which is a few kilometers to the west of town. At $13 single and $18 double you ought to feel that you are getting value for money; if not, you can always pitch a tent at **Europa Camping** (℡ 4447) next door. As for eating, the restaurant in the **Belediye Çamlık Motel** is friendly and cheap.

ORDU

Ordu is another lovely coastal harbor that started life as a Greek colony. As Cotoyra it was the scene of a famous event: it was here that Xenophon and the bedraggled remnants of his 10,000 embarked on the ships that took them to safety. Where exactly they saw the sea first (as recorded in a moving passage of the *Anabasis*) historians have been unable to agree, but it was probably further along the coast from here, at the Zigana Pass. Nowa-

days the clearest evidence of Ordu's long history is the **Caleoğlu Castle** of King Mithridates, five kilometers to the south. The town itself boasts an eighteenth-century church, and a beach (at Güzelyalı, a short walk away) with beautiful, fine sand.

The Tourist Information office (℃ 14178) is in the town hall on Sahil Caddesi, the road where you will also find the **Turist Oteli** (℃ 1466), which has double rooms for $10.

GIRESUN

Cherry orchards abound near Giresun, and it was from here — so tradition has it — that the great Roman general and gourmet Lucullus brought back the first cherry trees to Europe. It is even possible that the town's old name of Cerasus lies behind modern words like the French *cerise* and Turkish *kiraz*, as well as the English word *cherry*.

The **Seyit Vakas Türbe,** the tomb of the Ottoman general who took Giresun in 1461, and the town's eighteenth-century **Greek**

Church are the most worthwhile outings in the town itself. Then there is the stunning view available from the top of the nearby **Byzantine fortress.** Offshore is **Giresun Island,** a place associated, in the lore of the region, with the Amazons.

The Tourist Information office (℃ 3560) is at Fatih Caddesi, Özel Idare Işhanı Kat. 2. The **Giresun Hotel** (℃ 3017), Atatürk Bulvarı 7, has double rooms from $14.

TRABZON

Trabzon is both a hillside town and a seaside town, and has the charm that accrues to each. But that's about it. Indeed, it is difficult to reconcile the cheerful ordinariness of the place with the powerful mystique it held for Westerners for so many centuries.

BACKGROUND

Trabzon has been through at least two other incarnations, both with names which echoed throughout the known world. As Trapezus (the Greek word for table, a well-deserved epithet for this high-standing city) it was an important trading center, and was held in a kind of awe as the furthest outpost of the Greek world. As Trebizond it was the capital of the Comnene Empire, and a useful place to have as a capital, with its remarkable natural defenses. One of the few Byzantine cities to resist attack by both Seljuk Turks and Mongols, the city was not even taken by the Ottomans until eight years after the fall of Constantinople. Even then its defenses were not breached: the emperor David surrendered the city without bloodshed when he saw the size of the navy brought into the harbor by Mehmet II.

As the European powers of Genoa and Venice began to muscle in on trade to the east, Trabzon inevitably began to fade out of the picture, and it seemed to be finished for good when the Russians captured and devastated it in 1916. But since then its fortunes have revived, and it is today once again a successful trading post. Nor is its importance based solely on the sea: at least half of the cargo that arrires here does so by road, on its way to and from Iran.

GENERAL INFORMATION

The Tourist Information office (☏ 12722) is at Taksim Caddesi 31. Everyone I know has a good word to say about the friendliness and efficiency of its staff. I, on the other hand, found them uncomprehending in each of the foreign languages (English, French, German) they are supposed to be able to speak, and the map of the city they gave me was indecipherable. You, however, may be luckier. The ever-helpful Turkish Touring and Automobile Club (TTOK) has offices at Devlet Caddesi 2/2 Tünel Çıkışı (☏ 17156).

WHAT TO SEE

The finest building in Trabzon is the **Church of Aya Sofia,** built in 1250 on a hill that tumbles down into the sea. It was converted into a mosque when the Ottoman sultan Mehmet II brought about the fall of the Comnene Empire in 1461, and it is now a museum. The frescoes which you will see here have only been visible again since 1957, when the paint and plaster that had been slapped over them was painstakingly removed. It was worth the trouble, as these frescoes compare well with the greatest of Byzantine art.

If you are making your sightseeing excursion from the main square (Taksim Square), you should aim to go west, along Maraş Caddesi. This takes you in the direction of the old city, affording a glimpse along the way of the **bazaar;** if you turn right before the post office you will work your way right into the heart of it. While you are there, take a look at the **Çarşı Cami,** a nineteenth-century mosque hemmed in by the traders' stalls and the **bedesten** (dating from the sixteenth century). Climbing now to the south, you will find the **fortifications** of the old city wrapped around İç Kale Caddesi, and, on either side of the fortifications, the **Yeni Cuma Camii** (once a Christian, now a Muslim place of worship) and the **Gülbahar Hatun Cami,** which is of Ottoman construction.

Two buses a day leave Trabzon for the **Sûmela Monastery.** You may prefer to take a taxi, which will wait to take you back, or to drive out there yourself; whichever method you settle on, this is a trip you must make.

The road from Trabzon winds through a steep, alpine landscape where little clouds, like balls of cotton wool, tear themselves on the treetops. Sûmela itself is 17 km (11 miles) from the main highway, up a road that becomes a single-lane dirt track for a while before reverting to asphalt. Alongside, an energetic little stream swirls and froths its way past the rocks in the opposite direction.

At the end of this road you can either carry on by car up a path to the left, or you can pull over to the right and continue by

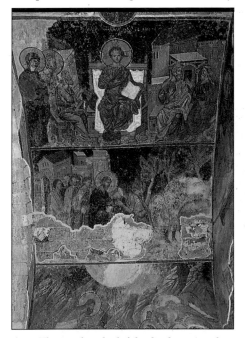

foot. The road to the left looks daunting, but in fact isn't really all that bad, whereas the climbers' route is twice as strenuous as it first appears. Whichever way you choose, you may want to park first and have something to eat in the picnic area across the stream to your right. Although there is a tea house there, just over the wooden bridge, you would do better to take your own picnic lunch to eat at one of the tables provided.

The monastery, which is carved out of a sheer rock face hundreds of meters above the floor of the mountain valley, is a

OPPOSITE: A traveling salesman displays his goods outside Samsun. ABOVE: The marvelous thirteenth-century Byzantine frescoes in the Church of Aya Sofia in Trabzon.

breathtaking place to reach in every sense of the word. Founded in the fifth century BC, most of what can now be seen was built by the Comnenes; when Alexius II Comnene decided to hold his coronation here Sûmela was the most important monastery in Asia. It housed three chapels, immense dormitories, corridors, and courtyards, and a library which was world-famous for its thousands of books in the fifteenth century. Sadly, the frescoes inside (dating from 1740) have faded, and the walls have suffered from both dereliction and vandalism. (Among the graffiti defacing these walls one cannot help noticing, writ large, the name of one Clyde Harris. Way to go, Clyde.) There is nonetheless a powerful sense of the inviolability of the place, an air of holiness, reinforced by the intermittent *plinks* in the small pool that collects the 'sacred water' (*ayazma*) dripping from the overhang of a rock cliff above, and the constant, urgent whisper of the stream below, which becomes strangely amplified after the mist has closed in.

WHERE TO STAY

There are quite a few decent hotels on or near the main square (Taksim Meydanı), where the inevitable statue of Atatürk stands in the tea gardens amidst beautiful red flowers. The **Otel Kalfa** (℄ 12690 or 16748), on the north side of the square at Atatürk Alanı 10, is one of these. It has a very friendly, English-speaking staff, but unfriendly plumbing that often refuses to give hot water after 8 pm. A double room here costs $18.

The **Hotel Özgür** (℄ 11319), also on Taksim Meydanı (Atatürk Alanı 29), will charge you slightly more than the Kalfa, and for that you will have the added pleasure of a nice restaurant on the roof with a view of the gardens. Still in the same price range, the **Usta Hotel** (℄ 12843) on Iskele Caddesi (Telegrafhane Sokak 3) has an excellent reputation. If your budget has been getting a little stretched, the **Anıl Hotel** (also near the square) is very cheap and good.

WHERE TO EAT

Only a few meters from the Kalba, at Atatürk Alanı № 6, is the **Yeşilyurt Restaurant** (℄ 23913), an American-style café or bar which gives excellent value at between $5 and $8 for a meal with drinks. It is not, however, the only nice restaurant around the square: all the places on Atatürk Alanı are good, with the **Güloğlu Restaurant** and the **Meydan Kebap ve Yemek** worthy of special mention. If you fancy perching above street level, the rooftop restaurants of the **Özgür** and **Usta** hotels both have sophisticated and appealing menus.

HOW TO GET THERE

Apart from the typically good bus service from everywhere, and the (very reasonably priced) ferry from Istanbul, there are frequent direct flights from both Ankara and Istanbul.

The Zigana Pass

If you are planning to arrive in Trabzon by car from the south or east, or to leave by that route, there is something you should know about the road between Trabzon and Aşkale to the south, that bit of road which once formed the final link in the ancient Silk Route between Persia and Trebizond. The something you should know is that it goes over the Zigana Pass, that lofty gash in the mountains where Xenophon's exhausted soldiers are said to have shouted ecstatically, memorably, "Thalassa! Thalassa!" "The sea! The sea!" Modern travelers here tend to let out rather less celebratory shouts as the road ascends in dizzying hairpin turns, inches away from precipitous drops into deep gorges, through sudden explosions of rain or sleet and equally sudden avalanches of wool as herds of sheep or goats overflow into the road just as you round a bend, through eye-straining, headlight-reflecting banks of fog and cloud upward into the dazzle of sunlight above the clouds. And down again. Be prepared.

Aya Sofia in Trabzon — originally a church, then a mosque, now a museum.

The East

A QUICK list of Turkey's neighbors in the East should suffice to demonstrate how far you have now come from Europe: Soviet Armenia, Iran, Iraq, and Syria all have their borders with eastern Turkey. This alone should help prepare you for the foreignness of the place. Whereas in the rest of Anatolia you are aware that you are in a different country, here you will sometimes feel you are in a different world.

ERZURUM

BACKGROUND

From an altitude of 1,980 m (6,500 ft), the capital of eastern Anatolia is in a position to look down on much of its region. Formerly named Theodosiopolis, after the Byzantine emperor who founded the city (c. 400 AD) on the ruins of an earlier settlement, it formed the eastern boundary of the Byzantine Empire for many centuries. As such it was the subject of a long-running game of tug-of-war between the Byzantines and, among others, the Arabs which went on until the Battle of Manzíkert in 1071 left it in the hands of the Seljuks. They had got into the habit of calling it Arz-er-rum ("Land of the Roman"), and the name somehow survived the many changes of management that took place over the next several hundred years.

Erzurum today is quiet, clean, and gray — rugged gray, not dull gray. In parts it seems safe to assume that nothing has changed for centuries: many more women wear the veil here than in most of Turkey, and some of the local industries are conducted by methods untouched by the modern age.

GENERAL INFORMATION

The main street, just for a change, is called Cumhuriyet Caddesi. Where it becomes Cemal Gürsel Caddesi, past the Havuzbaşı roundabout to the west of town, you will find the Tourist Information office at Nº 9/A (℃ 15697 or ℃ 14890).

WHAT TO SEE

Cumhuriyet Caddesi may be the main street of Erzurum, but it is far from being the whole

story. Almost as soon as you penetrate past its modern façade, you come upon the real thing: narrow, cobblestoned streets and gray stone houses. Most of the sights worth seeing here are to be found on or just off Cumhuriyet Caddesi.

The oldest mosque is the **Ulu Cami** (at the eastern end of the street), built in 1179 by the Saltuk emir Abdül Muhammad. It has an austere elegance, with its thirteen aisles, seven running north-south and six east-west. Nearby is the still more impressive **Çifte Minareli Medrese,** built as a school by Alaet-

tin Keykubat II in the thirteenth century. If you visit it look out for the superbly-carved limestone portal that leads into the courtyard, as well as for the Hatuniye Türbe, the mausoleum of Alaettin's daughter Huant.

On the north side of Cumhuriyet is the **Kale,** the citadel of Erzurum. It's not really as exciting as it sounds, as apart from its well-preserved walls and the curious clocktower (previously a Saltuk minaret) near its entrance, everything of interest in it disappeared some time ago.

OPPOSITE: The Euphrates near its headwaters between Erzincan and Erzurum. ABOVE: Erzurum, the former Theodosiopolis, with the massive Palandöken Dağı looming in the background.

Back on Cumhuriyet Caddesi, if you head west (away from the Ulu Cami) towards the City Hall you will find the **Caferiye Camii,** a mosque erected by Ebubekiroğlu Hacı Cafer in 1645. Across the intersection with Ali Ravi Caddesi is another Ottoman mosque, this one from the Golden Age of the empire. The **Lala Mustafa Paşa Camii** dates from 1563, which makes it at least possible that it was designed by the great Sinan — if not, then by one of his better pupils.

From here you are in a good position to make a detour to the **bazaar,** passing on your way the **Rüstem Paşa Çarşisi,** where they make the black prayer-beads one sees around the place. When you have finished savoring the atmosphere of one of Turkey's most unspoilt and old-fashioned markets,

come back down to the main street and continue west, pausing at the **Yakutiye Medrese,** a Mongol theological school of the fourteenth century; then turn left at Havuzbaşı and go south up Paşalar Caddesi. As the hill is quite steep, and the walk to the **Archaeological Museum** a good ten minutes, your legs may like the look of the buses that run up and down this hill. The museum has weapons, pottery, and jewelry from almost every age, as well as a splendid collection of carpets and *kilims*. It is closed on Mondays.

WHERE TO STAY

The **Otel Oral** (℡ 19740) at Terminal Caddesi 3 is probably the best in Erzurum, though quite a long way from the center

Kurdish nomad women with their children outside their tents near Erzurum.

of town and the main hotel district. Both the service and the restaurant are very pleasant, which largely makes up for the fact that you have to take a taxi to get there. Expect to pay about $14 single, $20 double.

Back in town, the majority of the hotels are situated in the quiet region near the railway station. **Buhara Oteli** (℃ 15096) charges $12 for a comfortable double, while the **Hitit Otel** (℃ 11204) at № 26 is cheaper again — $5 single, $7 double — and still perfectly acceptable.

WHERE TO EAT

If you believe, as I do, in the wisdom of going where the locals go, the **Mesud Restaurant** on Tahtacılar Caddesi should be one of your stops (a meal will cost about

$5), as should the **Tufan Restaurant** (℃ 13107) just off Cumhuriyet Caddesi. The latter is unlike many other restaurants in this part of the country in that it sells alcohol; if you avail yourself of this facility your meal will come to about $7. In the cheap and cheerful category the **Salon Çağn** (℃ 19320) on Cumhuriyet Caddesi, near the traffic roundabout by the Yakutiye Medrese, stands out. Here, for little more than a dollar, you can enjoy very tasty food in clean surroundings.

HOW TO GET THERE

Erzurum is one of the few cities in the East to have an airport, which makes it a useful starting-point for any

tour. THY has a daily flight from Istanbul, via Ankara. The flight from Ankara takes an hour and costs $60. For those wanting to fly *from* Erzurum, the Turkish Airlines office is situated, rather handily, in the hotel district, at 100 Yıl Caddesi, SSK Rant Tesisleri 24 (℡ 18530 or 11904).

A few trains from Ankara roll into the railway station, which has the advantage of being within easy reach of the hotel district. There are buses arriving from everywhere, but unfortunately the bus station is several kilometers from town, so you will have to take a taxi or a Nº 2 bus into Erzurum. (For moving around in the East the bus also provides the traveler with plenty of options: Diyarbakır, Doğubayazıt, Kars, Sivas, Malatya, Van, and Trabzon can all be reached cheaply from here.)

DOĞUBAYAZIT

BACKGROUND

Doğubayazıt itself is not very interesting, but it has an interesting location. It is near Mt. Ararat (Ağrı Dağı). So this is the place to go if you want to look at Turkey's highest (5,137 m, or just under 17,000 ft) and most famous mountain — the mountain where, according to the Book of Genesis, Noah's Ark came to rest when the waters subsided. Interestingly, it has the same role in other epics, including the *Epic of Gilgamesh,* in which Noah goes under his other name of Utnapishtim, and scientists do now believe that there was a significant flood sometime in the fourth millenium BC, but the odds against finding a boat perched on one of its ledges are thought to be very long indeed.

Doğubayazıt itself is a fairly grubby little town, with plenty of rustic charm (read: sheep and dung) about the place. As it is so near to Iran, there are usually a fair number of Iranian tourists in town.

GENERAL INFORMATION

There is no Tourist Information office in Doğubayazıt, but the Trek and Travel Agency (℡ 1981) at 53 Emniyet Caddesi can help you

if you want to climb Ararat and haven't arranged anything beforehand (see below).

WHAT TO SEE

Well, **Mt. Ararat,** of course. From Doğubayazıt you can actually see two peaks, one rising to the full height of over 5,000 m (16,400 ft), the other about 1,000 m (3,280 ft) shorter. You won't, however, see either of these peaks unless you are up early, preferably at sunrise, before the clouds obscure the view.

You can climb the mountain, but before

you even think about it you ought to know that it is for the serious climber only: it involves spiders, snakes, bears, vicious dogs, snowstorms, and bureaucrats. The last come in at the first stage, because that is when you have to write to the authorities in Ankara for permission to climb. Even with permission, you are still obliged to go with a guide. The reason they make it so difficult for you is not just out of concern for your health; the army are none too keen, either, on anyone wandering so near to the Soviet border. If none of this deters you, write to the İç İşleri Bakanlığı (Ministry of Internal Affairs) with a copy of your passport and the dates you want to climb, and then wait (two months at least) for the reply. If you haven't got two months to spare, the following agencies in Istanbul provide organized group tours with official arrangements taken care of: Trek Travel, Taksim Meydanı 10/6, and Metro Tourism, Cumhuriyet Caddesi 43/5, Platin Ap, Taksim. For those who have permission but no guide, the Trek and Travel agency in Doğubayazìt offers group tours for about $50 a day (the trip takes four days).

The other reason for going to Doğubayazıt is the Işak Paşa Sarayı. It is six kilometers out of town, and up a hill, so you can walk it, if you like, or take a *dolmuş* (before noon) for next to nothing. It is closed on Mondays. The palace, though not all intact, is still a stunning piece of work: castle and mosque, dome and minaret, courtyard and fountain, Georgian, Persian and Osmanlı architecture — and all of it, surprisingly, built in the eighteenth century. Not far away, and accessible by road, are some slightly older **Urartian fortress** ruins — 2,500 years older, to be precise — and a mosque dating probably from the reign of Selim II (1512–1520).

WHERE TO STAY

You can sleep comfortably and eat well at the **Hotel Isfahan,** Emniyet Caddesi 26, ℓ1159. It also has a Turkish bath. Rooms go for about $12 single and $17 double. The same sort of prices apply at the **Ararat Hotel** (ℓ1139), just down the road at № 48, for the same sort of facilities, including Turkish baths.

To the east of Doğubayazıt, on the E23 highway to Iran, is the **Sim-Er Moteli** (ℓ1601 or 2254). Rooms here cost $9 for a single and $15 for a double.

WHERE TO EAT

Both the **Isfahan** and the **Ararat,** above, serve good food for about $6 a meal. If you're staying at the Ararat and feel like a change of scenery, you don't have far to go: just across the street is the **Karadeniz,** a popular restaurant with the locals. Venture onto the main street and you will find the **Gaziantep**

Kebap Salonu, which is quite nice, and the **Istanbul Lokanta,** also good.

HOW TO GET THERE

This can be tricky, and more than a little time-consuming. From Van, the bus not only follows a sickle-shaped route to take in the towns of Erciş, Patnos and Ağrı but it will sometimes disgorge you when you're not expecting it to. When this happens, the point is for you to change on to another bus (usually larger), so make sure you don't lose your

ticket, and be prepared to wait a while.

VAN

Lake Van, from which the town of Van takes its name, is really two lakes, a southern (deep) one and a northern (shallow) one joined by a narrow passage in the middle. It is set in the most stunning surroundings, with huge volcanic mountains towering above it; one of these, the Süphan Dağ, is the third highest peak in Turkey — 4,430 m (14,534 ft). As if to underline the supremacy of the elements in these parts, the region is frequently shaken by earthquakes. A particularly violent one killed 4,000 people in 1976.

The water of the lake, though fine for swimming, is not recommended for drinking. That's because the lake is virtually stagnant; indeed, only one kind of fish, the small, carp-related *darekh,* can be found in these waters. Curiously enough, however, the lake is reckoned to be excellent for washing clothes in.

OPPOSITE: Inside the courtyard of the Işak Paşa Sarayi near Mt. Ararat. ABOVE: The sheep market at Doğubayazit.

BACKGROUND

Van itself is seven kilometers inland and not on the the lake at all. The first people to leave an impression on the region were the Hurrians, who arrived sometime in the third millenium BC: the Mitanni state that they established represents the beginning of recorded history in this region. When the Urartians moved in, in the ninth century BC, King Sarduri built the fortress of Tuşpa near the lake, on what is now called the Rock of Van. Very little of that city survives, partly because the Urartians were defeated by the Scythians in the sixth century BC, and partly because a fresh layer of ruins lies across the site. These are the remains of the old Van, the city which had, by the beginning of this century, sprawled all the way to the lake, only to be destroyed in fighting with Armenian rebels and Russian armies.

The rebuilding of the town took place about one and a half kilometers from the site of the previous settlement, at a healthier spot higher up the mountainside. Today, at its new altitude of 1,725 m (5,660 ft), Van has a population of 100,000. Like Erzurum, it has a modern-style main street called Cumhuriyet Caddesi; unlike Erzurum, there is not much to see when you leave it. The town, though older than some, still gives the impression of a job that someone has yet to get around to finishing. This does not mean that it is a waste of time. For one thing, Cumhuriyet Caddesi offers an excellent selection of *kilims*, many of them made by the Kurds who live in the region.

GENERAL INFORMATION

The Tourist Information office (**(** 12018 or 12530) is at Cumhuriyet Caddesi 127, at the southern end of the main street.

WHAT TO SEE

What remains of the fortifications at **Tuşpa** should definitely be seen: the steps up to the citadel, and the cuneiform inscriptions in praise of Xerxes (in Babylonian, Persian and Medic) give out the smell of history in heady doses. And the 30-km (19-mile) excursion to

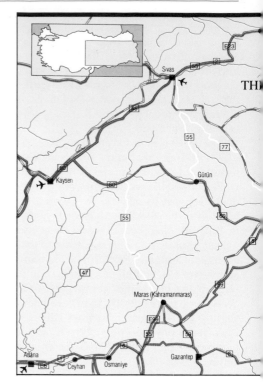

Gevaş is worthwhile (you should have no trouble finding a *dolmuş*), in part because of the quietly beautiful tomb of a fourteenth century Turkish princess that you will find there. But the best motive for arriving in Gevaş is in order to leave it, on one's way to the **Akdamar Kilisesi**. Built in 921 by the king of Vaspurakan, Gagik Artzruni, the **Church of the Holy Cross** is all that remains intact of the three buildings — palace, monastery, and church — that were originally here. It is a deep brown color on the outside, with superb Armenian relief carvings on the walls.

Back in Van, the **Museum,** just off Cumhuriyet Caddesi, has an unmatched collection of Urartian artefacts: bronze and gold belts, plates, brooches, bells, all engraved with animals or depictions of religiqus ceremonies. Upstairs are beautiful *kilims* made by the mountain-dwelling Kurdish and Turkoman tribes.

WHERE TO STAY

There are quite a few decent hotels in Van, and the **Hotel Akdamar** (**(** 3036) at Kâzım

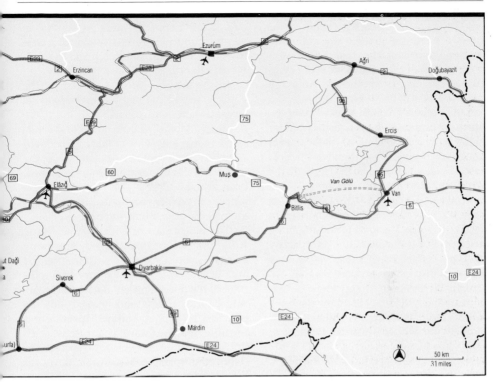

Karabekir Caddesi 16 is about the best of them. To find it, turn west off Cumhuriyet Caddesi near the tourist office. When you get there, you will discover that it is not only the best place to sleep, but it also has a terrace restaurant that is probably the nicest place to have a meal. A single room here costs $17, a double $22. If you feel like paying more for about the same, the **Büyük Urartu Hotel** (€ 20660) at Hastane Sokak 60 will relieve you of about $24 or $32 for a single or a double respectively. For those with slightly less money to spend, the **Beşkardeş Oteli** (€ 1116) at Cumhuriyet Caddesi 34 is very good value at $9 single, $12 double.

WHERE TO EAT

Apart from the ever-reliable *kebapçıs*, most of which can be found on Cumhuriyet Caddesi, the **Hotel Akdamar** is well worth the $6 a head you will pay. The **Şafak,** on Maraş Caddesi (just off Cumhuriyet, near the tourist office), has outdoor tables and a wide menu for around $4 a meal. The **Saray Lokantası** at İş Bank, off Cumhuriyet Caddesi, is popular and cheap.

HOW TO GET THERE

Van is blessed with an airport, which receives five flights from Ankara every day and one from Diyarbakır each week. Apart from the obvious advantage of saving time, flying into Van is highly recommended for the breathtaking view of the lake that it affords. The THY office here is at Cumhuriyet Caddesi 196 (€ 11241 or 11768).

There is a daily train from Istanbul which involves boarding a ferry at Tatvan and crossing over the lake to Van (TCDD € 12124); there are also bus connections to and from Erzurum, Diyarbakır, Malatya, and Doğubayazıt.

DIYARBAKIR

BACKGROUND

Diyarbakır, on the banks of the Tigris, is a confusing city with a confusing past. Its name is Arabic and means "City of the Bakır tribes", but it has in fact been occupied by no less than 20 different states and nations, suffering, like so many of these cities, from the curse of having a strategically important position. Urartians, Hurrians, Seljuks, Ottomans — all of them had control of Diyarbakır at one time or another. As Amida, it was an outpost of the Roman Empire, and it was the emperor Constantius who, in the fourth century, provided it with the walls for which it is now famous. In their present incarnation the black, basalt walls are largely Seljuk-built, and said to be the largest in the world after the Great Wall of China.

Recently the city has sprawled outside these walls as its population has risen to 250,000. The land around is nothing but a dusty plain, but the irrigation afforded by the Tigris (which by this stage has not yet grown to impressive proportions) has apparently always been enough to sustain agriculture and, ultimately, life. Nowadays the farming industry is supplemented by a little oil and light industry, but the product of which the people are most proud is the watermelon: they even have a Watermelon Festival each September.

GENERAL INFORMATION

The Tourist Information office (℅ 12173 or 17840) is located at Lise Caddesi 24/A. There is also a Diyarbakır Tourism Association office on Izzet Paşa Caddesi, in the Old Town, which is where you will also find the post office and several banks on Gazi Caddesi.

WHAT TO SEE

You may think you have already seen the **walls** just by arriving here, but if you fail to take time to wander around them, you will be missing a treat. Five and a half kilometers long, with 16 keeps and five gates, they are one of the best examples you could hope to find of medieval military architecture. But that is not all: if you examine them closely, you will see that there are all sorts of inscriptions and reliefs carved in to the walls, from many different ages. It may in some cases be no more than ancient graffiti, but there is still

a fascination in seeing history so near to the end of one's nose. Towards the southwest can be found the impressive pair of round towers, the **Evli Beden Burcu** and the **Yedi Kardeş Burcu.**

In the maze of streets enclosed by the walls you will see many examples of the stripe design that arose naturally out of the ready availability of both basalt and sandstone in this area. One of these is the **Nebi Camii** ("The Prophet's Mosque"), on the corner of Gazi Caddesi and Inönü Caddesi, built around 1530. It also provides an example of a further peculiarity of the region's architecture, the square minaret.

The oldest part of Diyarbakır is the **Iç Kale**, the **Inner Citadel,** which has many points of interest. Among them is the pointed arch at the entrance, which may be a remnant of the now-vanished Palace of the Artukid Turks. Inside the kale one finds the provincial courts, an **Atatürk Museum,** and the **Süleymaniye Camii.** This mosque, with its tall minaret, is famous for the deep underground spring whose water flows up into its courtyard.

In the center of the Old City, near the bazaar, is the **Ulu Camii,** thought to be the oldest mosque in Turkey; it was actually reconstructed out of the shell of a Byzantine church called the

The great stone faces of Nemrut Daği have stared impassively at the world for 2,000 years.

Martoma. Most of the construction work was done by the Seljuks in the eleventh century, with later worshippers chipping in. The courtyard here has a charm all its own, due to the fact that it is so obviously constructed from the stones of several different buildings.

WHERE TO STAY

There are plenty of hotels in the middle of town, and none of them is hideously expensive; a walk down Inönü Caddesi, and its continuation, Izzet Paşa Caddesi, should present you with something pleasant and affordable. Among them I recommend the **Demir Hotel** ((12315) at Izzet Paşa Caddesi 8 for its rooftop restaurant (doubles from $25), and the rather cheaper **Hotel Derya** ((14966 or (19735) at Inönü Caddesi 13. At $10 single and $15 double, it represents very good value. So, too, does the **Aslan Hotel** ((13971) at Kıbrıs Caddesi 23, which charges about the same as the Derya.

WHERE TO EAT

Most of the food you eat here will be of the simple but satisfying variety. Three places to try are the **Özgür Lokantası**, towards the southern end of Gazi Caddesi (near the *dolmuş* station), the **Kent,** and the **Baba- man,** both on Kıbrıs Cad- desi. The latter

has an open area on the upper level, overlooking the walls and tea gardens.

HOW TO GET THERE

There is an airport to the southwest of the city, with daily flights arriving from Ankara, and one a week from Van. The THY office ((10101) is on Izzet Paşa Caddesi. There is a train from Istanbul, via Ankara, four days a week, but it's unreliable. There is full bus service from Ankara, Van, Şanlıurfa, and Kâhta. The bus station is a couple of kilometers north of town, on the road to Elaziğ, but you can buy your ticket on Kıbrıs Caddesi and catch a minibus to the station.

NEMRUT DAĞI

BACKGROUND

If I were to keep to the scheme of this book, this section would be titled "Malatya" or "Kâhta" — and Nemrut Dağı would come under the heading of "What to See." But that really would be to put things in the wrong order, because there is no doubt as to why you have come to this part of Turkey.

The mountain of Nemrut Dağı (not exceptionally high at 2,150 m/7,055 ft) is one of the great sights of Turkey, not to say the world. It is the *folie de grandeur* of the first century BC Commagene king Antiochus I (69–34 BC), who built it, as he himself admits, "in commemoration of my own glory and that of the gods" (note the order). This was more than a little egotistical, as Commagene, for all its fertility and relative wealth, was a tiny kingdom entirely dependent on Rome for its survival. None of which prevented Antiochus from erecting massive statues of himself and his close personal friends Zeus, Hercules, Apollo, and Tyche (the name means "Fortune"), surrounded by eagles and lions. And there is no denying that he got the effect that he was after: one can hardly fail to be impressed by a statue which, seated and headless, is still eight meters tall. Time and the elements have, unfortunately, conspired to decapitate all the statues (Tyche was the last to lose her head, in 1926), so their heads sit in front of their bodies, where, if you are standing, you can look them in the eye.

General Information

In Malatya, the Tourist Information office (℡ 15333 or 17773) is at Izzetiye Mah. Atmalı Sokak Esnaf Sarayı 4-5. There is also a smaller version in the bus station. Kâhta is tiny and has no such office.

Kâhta and Malatya

Kâhta and Malatya, for different reasons, are the two most logical places to stay when visiting Nemrut Dağı. From Kâhta, the closer of the two, you need not worry about finding a tour to take you up the mountain; your only problem will be choosing between them. Then, once you have negotiated an acceptable deal, you go to bed early and wait for your two am alarm call. This is the time when you will have to get up to catch the minibus, which is aiming to get you to the summit in time for sunrise. Actually, it won't get you all the way to the summit, but it's only about a 20-minute walk from the bus, and as long as you brought warm clothing you will enjoy the air. After you have seen the sun come up and wandered around both sets of statues (the East Terrace gods are replicated,

and better preserved, on the West Terrace), it will be time to go down again.

From Malatya the drive is a longer one, which the tour operators try to make worth your while by giving you, in effect, two separate trips. You leave late in the morning and drive through marvelous scenery to get to the mountain in time for sunset. After that you go back a short way down the mountain and have a basic dinner and even more basic snooze on the floor, before getting up at four to watch the sun come up. After this it is back in the minibus for the drive back to Malatya.

Where to Stay

In Kâhta the **Hotel Nemrut Tur** (℡ 1459 or ℡ 1863), on the road west of town, has a swimming pool and is good value at $7 single, $10 double. There is also an area for campers to pitch their tents cheaply. The nearby **Nemrut Camping,** however, has the best facilities of all the campsites.

Near the tourist office in Malatya is the **Hotel Sinan** (Atatürk Caddesi 14, ℡ 12907 or ℡ 13007). It is big (eight floors) but not impersonal, and charges roughly $8 single, $12 double. The **Kent,** over the road and up the hill at № 151, is an equally good alternative.

Where to Eat

The choice in either town is pretty limited, though there are the standard *kebapçıs*, so you could do worse than eat in your hotel's restaurant. The Nemrut Tur in Kâhta will not let you down, nor will the Sinan in Malatya. If you feel like leaving the latter, the **Melita** is next door, friendly and cheap at about $6 for a complete dinner.

How to Get There

Malatya has the advantage of being near an airport, so that you can fly in from Ankara or Istanbul. Trains pass through the railway station going both east-west and north-south, and they too come from both Ankara and Istanbul, as well as from Kayseri, Sivas, and Adana. There are also plenty of buses running between here and all the towns above. Kâhta does not have the same transport facilities (no airport, no rail links), but it is served by buses from Malatya, Diyarbakır, and Adıyaman.

ŞANLIURFA

South of Kâhta, and along the E24 highway that skirts the border of Syria, lies the town of Urfa, as it is commonly known. The prefix Şanlı means "Glorious", and is probably the newest thing about this incredibly ancient and history-laden town. The city of Antep

known as the Cave of Job. Of these stories, the one about Abraham does at least have the backing of both Christian and Muslim tradition.

Şanlıurfa's history goes back at least as far as the second millenium BC, when it was the capital of a Hurrite state. It seems, indeed, that the name Urfa is a corrupt form of Hurri. As the focal point of endless wars in the following millenia, Urfa went through several changes of rulers and names. As Edessa it was ruled by the Seleucids who followed Alexander the Great, and as Orhai it was

to the east had been renamed Gaziantep ("Heroic Antep") for its part in Turkey's struggle for independence, so Urfa became Şanlıurfa about fifteen years ago.

BACKGROUND

Actually, the epithet "Glorious" is hardly exaggerated when one considers the history of a town so holy that it was the intended target of the Second Crusade. If you listen to the locals you will be inclined to think that "glorious" doesn't go far enough: it is widely believed here that Şanlıurfa lies on the site of the Garden of Eden, that Abraham was born (or at least stayed) in nearby Harran, and that one of the local caves is rightly

more or less independent. Not until the Ottomans took it from the Seljuks in 1643 did it become Urfa. Throughout all of this it managed to remain a great center of learning (we may well owe to Urfa the survival of many classic Greek works) as well as of religious significance. After a few centuries of sun-worship, Urfa was just about the first place in this part of the world to adopt Christianity (c. 200). By the time the Seljuks took it in 1144 it was important enough for the Pope to launch the Second Crusade, which never got anywhere near its target.

The Citadel at Şanlıurfa, one of the mightiest fortresses in Turkey.

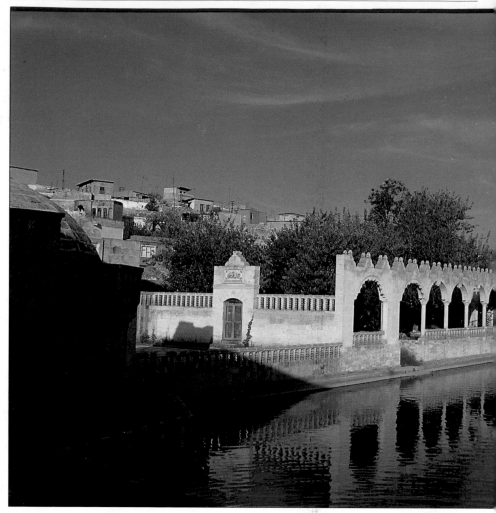

A look at Şanlıurfa today would force one to conclude that the climate must have been kinder in the time of Adam and Eve, for the dusty plains of High Mesopotamia would be no one's idea of the Garden of Eden. The city today (population 210,000) does, however, retain something of the mystique that made it so attractive to ancient pilgrims.

GENERAL INFORMATION

The Tourist Information office (℡ 1165) is at Vilayet Arkası Topçu Meydanı. There is also an office at Asfalt Caddesi 3/B (℡ 2467), which is open every day in the summer.

WHAT TO SEE

The **Museum** is at the northern end of town, quite a walk away from the best sights, which are congregated in the Old City to the south. Situated just off Atatürk Caddesi, it has an interesting collection of mosaics, relief carvings and stone cats.

The place to aim for in the Old City is the park, **Gölbaşı**, where you will find the **Pool of Abraham** and the smaller body of water fed by it, the **Ayn-i Zeliha**. This is surrounded by cafés where you can sit and feed the sacred carp who inhabit the pools and who presumably can't believe their luck: not only

The Halil Rahman Camii in Şanlıurfa, a splendid seventeenth-century mosque in an incomparable setting.

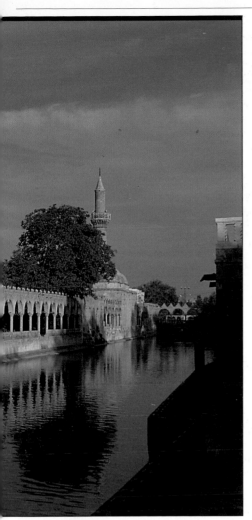

The ancient Biblical town of **Harran** does not conform to the usual idea of a tourist attraction: there is nothing huge, or conventionally beautiful, about it. True, the ancient city walls (744–750) and the ruins of the fortress are standard tourist fare, but it is not for these that you should visit Harran. The reason you should go is simply to look at the clay bee-hive houses, and at the surrounding desert, and then to marvel at what a curious place the world is. If this doesn't set you thinking about your own place in the scheme of things, nothing will.

WHERE TO STAY

The **Hotel Harran** (℃ 4918 or 2860), on Atatürk Bulvarı, near the city hall, has exactly the things you want here (like air-conditioning and a refrigerator in your room), as well as a good open-air restaurant and Turkish baths. Single $22, double $32. The **Turban Urfa Oteli** (℃ 3520 or ℃ 3521), a short walk away at Köprübaşı Caddesi 74, provides a cheaper alternative at $18 single, $26 double. Over by the tourist office is the **Hotel Kapaklı** (℃ 1430 or ℃ 2016) on Sarayönü Caddesi. Have a look at more than one room, as some are less comfortable and quiet than others — some, also, have no bathroom. For a double with a private bath, expect to pay about $12.

WHERE TO EAT

Apart from the restaurant in the **Harran,** most of the eating houses in Şanlıurfa are uncomplicated but satisfactory. Such a place is the **Lâle Lokantası**, around the corner from the city hall, where a nice meal will come to about $5. The **Eyvan Restaurant,** on Kışla Caddesi, is similarly reliable. For atmosphere you will find nothing better than that provided by the park at **Gölbaşı**, where you can wander around the cafés and restaurants and decide for yourself which of them is serving the most appetizing food.

are they constantly offered food, they are also protected by law from being disturbed. Next to the Pool of Abraham is the **Halil Rahman Camii,** a seventeenth-century mosque whose great beauty is enhanced still further by its gorgeous setting. While you're here, the **Citadel** is worth climbing the steps for. Hellenic, Byzantine, Christian, and Turkish builders have all contributed to the construction of this huge and impressive fortress.

Walking east from here you cannot fail to bump into beautiful and awe-inspiring sights, such as the **Hz. Ibrahim Mağarası** ("Birthplace of Abraham"), which must be viewed quietly as it is a place of prayer. The nearby **Hasan Paşa Camii** and **Mevlidi Halil Camii** are both superb.

HOW TO GET THERE

The only way to get to Şanlıurfa is by road, either in a car or a bus along the E24 international highway. Bus service is frequent.

GAZIANTEP

BACKGROUND

According to the archaeologists, there has been human habitation here since the Neolithic Age (roughly eight millenia BC). Naturally enough, though, none of the city's history is recoverable until one reaches about 2000 BC and the Hittites start to make their presence felt. Once things get going, there is the usual succession of more or less

Gaziantep's finest hour came in this century, when its determined, 10-month resistance to the invading French force in 1920 made an important contribution to the cause of independence. It was in recognition of this feat that the town had conferred on it the name it bears today. For many centuries previously it had been plain Antep; now it is Gaziantep, "Heroic Antep."

GENERAL INFORMATION

There is a Tourist Information office ((21858

brutal conquerors, starting with the Assyrians, whose king, Sargon II, gained control of the region in 717 BC. After lasting only a century, the Assyrians were supplanted by the Cimmerians, who in turn made way for the Persians, who ruled for the 300 years that preceded Alexander the Great. After the disintegration of Alexander's empire the Romans and the Byzantines both held sway for a while until the inevitable Seljuk conquest and the even more inevitable Ottoman one (carried out by Selim II in 1516).

or 21859) at Atatürk Bulvarı 121. An office of the Turkish Touring and Automobile Club (TTOK) can be found at Ali Fuat Cebesoy Bulvarı 5/D ((25224).

WHAT TO SEE

If you head west from the center towards the railway station, on Istasıyon Caddesi, you will pass a stadium on your right just before a turning to your left. This leads to the kale, the **citadel.** What you will see here is mostly Seljuk, though the fortress was originally built by the emperor Justinian in the sixth century. Surrounded by a dry moat, which is traversed via a wooden bridge around to the right as you approach, the kale is both

A woman dries peppers on her roof in Birecik, the ancient Roman town between Şanliurfa and Gaziantep.

impressive in itself and set in an attractive area of mosques and old houses.

As you come to Istasıyon Caddesi on your way back from the citadel, the **Archaeological Museum** (℃ 11171) is almost directly opposite you. The collection here is the largest in southeast Turkey, with Hittite reliefs joined by Roman grave steles and Ottoman *kilims*. If you have been to Nemrut Dağ you will recognize the style of Antiochus I (first century BC) in the relief carving of him greeting Apollo. The museum is closed on Monday.

WHERE TO STAY

Most of the hotels in Gaziantep are like the city, modern and businesslike. East from the crossroads in the center (where Atatürk Bulvarı becomes Suburcu Caddesi), at the junction of Hürriyet Caddesi and Güzelce Sokak, is the place to try first, the **Kaleli** (℃ 27010), which for $12 single and $13 double will provide you with comfortable and spacious rooms, an excellent restaurant on the roof, and quietly professional service. If the Kaleli is full, the **Murat** (℃ 15276), further east on Inönü Caddesi at № 39, is quite good, at $10 and $15 single/double. Back in the center of town the **Hotel Veliç**

(Atatürk Bulvarı 23, ℃ 22341 or ℃ 11726) is cheaper still at $10 for a double.

WHERE TO EAT

One thing Gaziantep is renowned for, apart from copper and pistachio nuts, is the quality of its restaurants. The reputation is deserved, and you will have no trouble finding an excellent kebap. For something a little more elaborate, the **Keyvanbey** (℃ 12651) on Hürriyet Caddesi has an open-air dining room on an upper floor, where your meal ought to cost no more than $8. Similarly elevated above the bustle of the street is the **Burç Restaurant** (℃ 13012) on the northwestern corner of the main crossroads. You will pay slightly more here for your meal, but it will be worth it.

HOW TO GET THERE

There is a rail link with both Ankara and Istanbul (known as the *Mavi Tren*, "Blue Train"), as well as the buses which arrive regularly at the terminal southwest of the city. From both the railway station and the bus station you will need to take a taxi or a minibus into town.

ABOVE: Waiting for their marching orders: a school band in Birecik.

Travelers' Tips

BÜYÜKADA
ISTANBUL

GETTING THERE

BY AIR

All major international airlines have regular flights to Istanbul's Atatürk Airport, and Turkish Airlines (THY) also flies regularly from most European capitals to Ankara and Izmir. From April to October there are regular charter flights from all over Europe to Dalaman, about an hour's drive from both Marmaris and Fethiye, and to Antalya, on the south coast, as well as to Istanbul and Izmir. Budget-conscious travelers are strongly advised to check out these charter flights before planning a trip, as they are often less than half the price charged by the scheduled carriers. For information about charter flights contact a Turkish Tourism office or one of the many travel agents and tour operators specializing in travel to Turkey (see below).

For the traveler from England with more time than money to spend, an alternative is to go on a group charter to one of the Greek islands off the Turkish coast (Lesvos, Chios, Samos, Kos, Rhodes) and then take a ferry over. Not only is this way relatively quick and painless, but it also gives you a chance to explore and enjoy a bit of Greece before continuing on to Turkey — and the whole journey can be accomplished for less than $180. Later, when you are ready to leave, any travel agent or Tourist Information office can advise you on the cheapest and easiest way to get wherever you want to go.

A word of warning, however, to the visitor to Turkey who thinks he may have just spotted the ultimate in bargain holidays. If you take a charter flight to Greece, and then go to Turkey for more than just a day trip, Greek authorities will not allow you to use the return portion of your ticket. They are not, understandably, in the business of subsidizing Turkish tourism. So the Greek-island-and-ferry route to Turkey, which I personally favor, must be regarded as a one-way option only.

BY TRAIN

Not recommended. Train journeys from Istanbul to Europe tend to be long (the Istanbul Express from Munich takes 40 hours)

and tedious (visas are required en route) and unpredictable (long delays are common) and uncomfortable (crowded, smoky) and under-provisioned (take your own food and drink) and, yes, expensive as well — the cheapest second-class fare from London for one of these ordeals on wheels is approximately $290 one way. For the same amount of money you can get a round-trip charter flight from London to Istanbul, or to any number of coastal resorts, with two weeks' lodgings included in the price!

BY BUS

This is cheaper and, surprisingly, often quicker than going by train. To go all the way from London by bus you should consult a travel agent, or any branch of Thomas Cook, as new routes and fares are being added or subtracted all the time. The trip should take four to five days and cost about $120. On the continent, Bosfor Turizm operates a weekly bus service to Istanbul from Paris, Lyon, Geneva, Milan, and Venice, and a biweekly express service from Munich and Vienna. For up-to-date timetables and fare information contact Bosfor Turizm at Mete Caddesi, Taksim, Istanbul ((143-2525), or at the international bus terminals in any of the Continental cities they serve.

BY CAR

This isn't really a good idea unless you plan to take a lot of time and visit a lot of places on the way, as well as a lot of places out of the way once you get there. Even then, you should have traveling companions to defray the high cost of gasoline, insurance, auto repairs (if necessary), and accommodation (unless you are camping). You will also require a transit visa for Bulgaria and, if you are American, Canadian, or Australian, for Yugoslavia as well. If you plan to spare yourself the unrelieved gruesomeness of Bulgaria by swinging down through northern Greece you can count on adding an extra 450 km (280 miles) to your journey, and you should plan on arriving at Ipsala, the Turkish frontier post, before midnight or you will find the border closed until eight o'clock the next morning.

A steamer sets off from Istanbul to take sightseers on a cruise up the Bosphorus.

At the border you will have to buy Turkish auto insurance if your Green Card is not valid for all of Turkey (check before you go), and details of the car will be entered in your passport. From now on you and the car are wedded to each other: you cannot leave Turkey without it and it cannot leave without you. The only exception is if you have the car bonded in Customs before you leave, which takes an interminable amount of paperwork involving half a dozen different officials, and for which you will have to pay a daily storage fee — and, of course, the fact that you have left your car with Customs is also duly recorded in your passport.

By Sea

For me, the most delightful way to approach Turkey is via one (or more) of the Greek islands. Not only is it visually the most rewarding, but by giving yourself a taste of Greece before moving on to Turkey you will be able to make cultural connections and distinctions later that can only enrich your experience of Turkey. Throughout the summer months there is a daily ferry service between Lesvos and Ayvalık, Chios and Çeşme, Samos and Kuşadası, Kos and Bodrum, Rhodes and Marmaris. The ferries continue to operate, though less frequently, in the off-season. Fares are all in the vicinity of $25 one way.

From further afield, and for considerably more money, Turkish Maritime Lines have car-passenger ferries in the summer from Venice and Ancona, Italy, to Izmir. Fares range from about $250 to $450 per person without a car; with car add about $175. Also during the summer Sealink British ferries operate, weekly, and more expensively, between Venice and Istanbul (and then Kuşadası). The fares, which include all meals, range from £175 ($315) for a cabin shared with others to £425 ($765) for a stateroom shared with one other.

USEFUL ADDRESSES

Consular Information

For general information contact one of the Turkish Tourism offices.

IN USA:
New York: 821 United Nations Plaza, N.Y., N.Y. 10017 ((212) 687-2194; telex 426428.
Washington: 2012 Massachusetts Avenue, NW, Washington, DC 20036 ((202) 429-9844 (833-8411; telex 251544.

IN BRITAIN:
London: 170-173 Piccadilly, London W1V 9DD ((01) 408-2021 or 355-4207; telex 895-4905 TTIOF G.

Charter Flights and Tour Operators

For information about air travel on scheduled carriers contact your travel agent or the local offices of the international airlines. For information about charter flights get in touch with one of the tour operators.

IN AMERICA I WOULD RECOMMEND:
Am-Jet/Amtravel, Suite 2008, 501 Fifth Avenue, New York, NY 10017. ((212) 697-5332.
Exprinter International, Suite 510, 500 Fifth Avenue, New York, NY 10110. ((212) 719-1200, outside New York ((800) 221-1666.
Globe Travel, 507 Fifth Avenue, New York, NY 10017. ((212) 682-8687.
Isram, 630 Third Avenue, New York, NY 10017. ((212) 477-2352, outside New York (800) 223-7460.
Sunbeam Travel, Suite 904, 274 Madison Avenue, New York, NY 10016. ((212) 725-8835, outside New York (800) 247-6659.
Trafalgar Tours, 21 East 26th Street, New York, NY 10010. ((212) 689-8977, outside New York (800) 854-0103.
Travel Magic, 555 Fifth Avenue, New York, NY 10017. ((212) 972-3036, outside New York (800) 543-0003.

IN BRITAIN:
Aegean Turkish Holidays, 53A Salisbury Road, London NW6 6NJ. ((01) 372-6902.
Blue Spot Travel, 28 Maddox Street, London W1R 9PF. ((01) 408-0094, (409-3034.
Bosphorus Holidays, Silver House, 33 Beak Street, London W1R 3LD. ((01) 437-7316.
Deltasun Holidays, 5-8 Paddington Street, London W1M 3RR. ((01) 935-9535 (486-1648.

Falcon Holidays, 33 Notting Hill Gate, London W11 3JQ. ((01) 221-6298.

Golden Horn Travel, Golden House, 29 Great Pulteney Street, London W1R 3DD. ((01) 434-1962.

Samson Travel, 127 Kingsland High Street, London E8 2PB. ((01) 240-2687.

Savile Travel, 32 Maddox Street, London W1R 9PF. ((01) 499-5101.

Simply Turkey, 480 Chiswick High Road, London W4 5TT. ((01) 747-1011.

Steepwest Holidays, 449 Oxford Street, London W1R 1DA. ((01) 629-2879.

Sunmed Holidays, Groundstar House, London Road, Crawley RH10 2TB. ((0293) 519151.

Sunquest Holidays, Aldine House, 9-15 Aldine Street, London W12 8AW. ((01) 749-9933.

Turkish Villas, 35 Hanover Gardens, London SE11 5TN. ((01) 735-6037.

(For special requests I have found the following to be particularly helpful: Bülent Özer at Samson Travel, Ali Barchman at Savile Travel, Erkan Kılıç at Sunquest Holidays, and Jean Nicholson at Turkish Villas.)

SPECIALIST TOURS OF TURKEY

For information about specialist tours of Turkey you should contact one of the following.

IN AMERICA:

Archeological Tours, Suite 1202, 30 East 42nd Street, New York, NY 10017. ((212) 986-3054.

Hürtürk Travel and Tours, Suite 501, 18 West 56th Street, New York, NY 10016. ((212) 586-2901.

Pacha Tours International, 20 East 49th Street, New York, NY 10017. ((212) 355-5141, outside New York (800) 727-4288.

Persepolis Travel, 501 Fifth Avenue, New York, NY 10017. ((212) 972-1333, outside New York (800) 221-5444.

Polo Travel, 271 Madison Avenue, New York, NY. ((212) 532-7177, outside New York (800) 223-1140.

Triaena Travel & Tourism, Suite 605, 850 Seventh Avenue, New York, NY 10019. ((212) 245-3700, outside New York ((800) 223-1273.

IN BRITAIN:

Aquasport Tours Ltd., 181 Edward Street, Birmingham BN2 2JB. ((0273) 685824 (685187.

Birdwatching & Wildlife, 8 The Grange, Elmdon Park, Soli-hull, West Midlands BN2 9EL. ((021) 742-5420 (705-5535.

Cygnus Wildlife Holidays Ltd., 96 Fore Street, Kingsbridge, Devon TQ7 1PY. ((0548) 6178.

Hann Overland, 286-270 Vauxhall Bridge Road, London SW1V 1EJ. ((01) 834-7337.

HF Holiday Ltd., 142-144 Great North Way, London NW4 1EG. ((01) 203-0433.

Inter-Church Travel Ltd., 45 Berkeley Street, London W1A 1EB. ((01) 734-0942.

Intra Travel Ltd., 5 Cheval Place, London SW7 1EW. ((01) 225-3266.

Serenissima Travel Ltd., 21 Dorset Square, London NW1 5PG. ((01) 730-9841.

Swan Hellenic Art Treasures Tours, 77 New Oxford Street, London WC1A 1PP. ((01) 831-1616.

MOTORING INFORMATION

In **America,** contact the **American Automobile Association,** 1000 AAA Drive, Heathrow FL, (32746-5063, and in **Britain** the Automobile Association, Fanum House, 5 New Coventry Street, London W1V 8HT, ((01) 930-2462.

SEA TRAVEL TO TURKEY

In **America**, the **Air Marine Travel Service,** 501 Madison Avenue, New York, NY 10022, ((212) 371-1300, and in **Britain**:

Turkish Maritime Lines, c/o Sunquest Holidays, Aldine, House, 9-15 Aldine Street, London W12 8AW, ((01) 749-9933. **Sealink Travel Centre,** Victoria Station, London SW1. ((01) 834-8122.

TRAVEL DOCUMENTS

American, British, Canadian, Australian, and Irish citizens—and citizens of most European and Caribbean countries—need only a valid passport to enter Turkey. You can then stay for up to three months, and if you want to stay longer all you have to do is pop over to one of the Greek islands for a day at the end of three months.

If you are a student, be sure to have an International Student Identity Card with you so that you will qualify for free admission to museums and for discounts on travel and accommodation inside Turkey.

CUSTOMS

In theory you are allowed to bring, in addition to your personal effects, 400 cigarettes or 50 cigars, seven bottles of liquor (of which no more than three can be of the same brand), five bottles of perfume, and one kilogram (2.2 lb) of coffee or tea. In practice customs officials seldom bother to open tourists' luggage, and if they do the inspection is likely to be *pro forma*. Indeed, Turkish customs officials tend to be much more interested in you when you leave the country than when you enter, as there is a strict prohibition on the export of antiquities. Moreover, you are not meant to take out souvenirs with an aggregate value of more than $1,000 or carpets worth more than $3,000, and in both instances you may be required to produce proof of purchase and currency exchange slips. With older carpets you may also need a document from the shopkeeper or from a local museum certifying that the carpet is not an antiquity.

WHEN TO GO

Generally speaking, the best time to visit Turkey is in those months that bracket the summer: April-May and September-October. That way you avoid both the hottest weather and the biggest crowds. Also, in the late spring the countryside is at its loveliest, ablaze with wildflowers, while in the early autumn the coastal waters are still delightfully warm.

The following chart will give you an idea of the average temperatures (Centigrade) you can expect from April to October in seven cities across Turkey. To convert to Fahrenheit double the figure given and add 30.

City	April	May	June	July	Aug	Sept	Oct
ANTALYA							
air	16	20	25	28	28	25	20
water	18	21	24	27	28	27	25
DIYARBAKIR							
air	14	19	30	31	31	25	17
ERZURUM							
air	5	10	15	19	20	15	9
ISTANBUL							
air	12	16	21	23	24	20	16
water	9	14	19	22	23	21	17
IZMIR							
air	16	20	25	28	27	23	18
water	15	20	24	26	26	24	21
TRABZON							
air	12	16	20	23	23	20	16
water	12	14	20	24	25	24	20

City	April	May	June	July	Aug	Sept	Oct
ANKARA							
air	11	16	20	23	23	18	13

WHAT TO TAKE

One could do worse than begin with the old maxim that wherever you go, you should always take half the clothes and twice the money that you think you will need. If you go to Turkey in the warmer months, you will certainly need very little in the way of clothing. As the country is a leading producer of high-quality, low-priced cotton, woollen, and leather goods, it makes much more sense to pack only essential items of clothing — perhaps with a small plastic bottle of liquid detergent for emergencies — and then fill in any gaps in your wardrobe while you are there. Besides, you will want space in your suitcase for all the clothes bargains you find.

On the other hand, there are a number of items widely available in Turkey that I would still suggest that you take with you. These fall into two categories. In the first category, Things That Are Easy To Get Except When You Really Need Them, I would put toilet paper (yes, just in case), tissues, tampons, soap, hand towel, disposable razors, earplugs, tea bags, mosquito repellent, corkscrew. In the second category, Things That Are Easy To Get But Are Absurdly Expensive, I would include suntan lotion, camera film, instant coffee, and books in English.

The Rumeli Hisari, the giant fortress on the Bosphorus that Mehmet the Conqueror built to cut off supplies to the Byzantines prior to the siege of Constantinople in 1453.

Then there are those things that are difficult, if not impossible, to get, but which could make all the difference to your comfort and well-being at some stage of your visit: an all-purpose sink plug, a miniature flashlight, a battery-powered shaver, cigars, a first-aid kit with disposable syringes, a small sewing kit, stain remover, an insulated refrigerator bag, a gadget for heating cups of water, and, above all, a Swiss Army knife. Remember, however, that although a Swiss Army knife is actually an ingeniously miniaturized tool kit, it will be seen as a potential weapon if

you try to board an airplane in Turkey with it on your person or in your hand luggage, and it will be confiscated. I lost one of mine that way.

GETTING AROUND

BY AIR

If you have a lot of ground to cover, it's best to do it from the air. Flying in Turkey is quite cheap and relatively hassle-free so long as you get to the airport in good time, because of the security procedures. Airport security may sometimes seem unnecessarily strict — there are guard posts on the roads leading to the airports, and there are X-ray machines for all luggage inside the airports, and your belongings and you will be politely searched before being allowed to leave the terminal, and you will have to identify your luggage out on the tarmac before it is loaded on to

A *dolmuş* (collective taxi) at the Galata Quarter.

the aircraft — but at the same time it's nice to know that because of this terrorists don't waste their time trying to hijack or place bombs on planes flying from Turkish airports.

Turkish Airlines (THY) has a route network covering most of the country. From the two main hubs, Istanbul and Ankara, there are flights to Adana, Antalya, Bursa, Dalaman, Diyarbakır, Elâzığ Erzurum, Gaziantep, Izmir, Kayseri, Malatya, Merzifon, Samsun, Trabzon, and Van. Few internal flights will cost more than $100, and there are discounts available to students and family groups.

BY TRAIN

Not much point, really, unless you are looking specifically for a Turkish rail experience — which means, at its best, traveling great distances in a more or less straight line at about the same speed as a bus for about the same amount of money. Unless, that is, you take a sleeping compartment in one of the night express trains between Ankara and Istanbul (the *Ankara Ekspresi* or the *Anadolu Ekspresi*), which are not at all expensive and can be great fun. All trains are operated by Turkish Railways (TCDD).

BY BUS

Bus service in Turkey, because it is provided by competing private coach companies, ranges from fairly comfortable to very comfortable and from surprisingly inexpensive to unbelievably cheap. In other words, I recommend it. The buses are all big Mercedes, and they all depart from the central bus terminal, or *otogar*, in each town or city, where agents for the various companies will be all too happy to escort you to a bus headed for your destination. Look around before buying a ticket; there may be an earlier bus going. Better still, buy your ticket a day or more in advance so you can be certain not only of getting the bus you want but the seat you want. As all tickets are sold with a seat assignment, and as it is important in the summer to get a seat on the side of the bus away from the sun, and behind one of the roof vents if the bus isn't air-conditioned, the earlier you buy your ticket the better.

By DOLMUS

For shorter journeys between towns and villages, or along routes not covered by the buses, you can always travel by *dolmuş*. The word itself is the past participle of the Turkish verb "to fill", which gives you a rough idea of when a *dolmuş* departs — when it is full. However, as a *dolmuş* is quite small — it may be a van, a minibus, or even a jeep — it fills quite quickly, especially in or near resort areas, and in villages in the early morning or late afternoon, and there is always another one along very soon, so there is seldom much of a wait. Moreover, they have a knack of being there when you need them — at the beach, in a nearby square — and they will drop you off anywhere you like en route.

By TAXI

Taxis are cheap and plentiful and their fares are regulated. However, for out-of-town journeys taxi drivers are often permitted to charge more than the amount which appears on the meter. For this reason, and for the equally good reason that you can often negotiate a much lower fare, you should always agree the fare in advance.

By THUMB

Actually, when trying to hitch a ride, the thumb doesn't come into it. To signal your desire for a lift you hold out your hand, palm downwards, and make a gentle patting motion. Hitch-hiking over short distances is quite common in Turkey, among Turks as well as among the more impecunious visitors. You should nonetheless, as a matter of courtesy, offer to pay for any ride you are given, secure in the knowledge that the offer will almost certainly be turned down.

Hitchhiking over long distances or by women traveling alone is inadvisable — in the first instance because the buses are comfortable and cheap and certainly more reliable; in the second instance because it's simply not a good idea anywhere.

By CAR

Although this is my own favorite means of getting around, and I have a battered and rebellious old Volkswagen to prove it, I am disinclined to recommend it for visitors. For one thing, car rentals in Turkey are cruelly expensive — much more expensive than in America or Britain. For another thing, driving in Turkey, unless you have lightning reflexes coupled with a serene and forgiving nature, can be both hazardous to your health and destructive of any affectionate relationships you might formerly have had with other people in the car with you. I know.

GENERAL INFORMATION

Wherever you are likely to go in Turkey you will find a Tourist Information office ready and willing (and usually able) to help. For enquiries that you think might be beyond the scope of a local tourist office or travel agent contact the Ministry of Tourism (Turizm Bakanlığı) at Gazi Mustafa Kemal Bulvarı 33, Demirtepe, Ankara (℃ 230-1911), or one of the Istanbul offices — in Atatürk Airport (℃ 573-7399), the Hilton Hotel (℃ 140-6300 or 133-0592), Sultanahmet Square (℃ 522-4903), or at Meşrutiyet Caddesi 57/6-7, Galatasaray (℃ 145-6593).

EMBASSIES AND CONSULATES

American Embassy: Atatürk Bulvari 110, Kavaklıdere, Ankara. ℃ 126-5470.
American Consulates: Meşrutiyet Caddesi 104, Tepebaşı, Istanbul. ℃ 143-6200. Atatürk Caddesi 92, Izmir. ℃ 13 13 69.
Australian Embassy: Nene Hatun Caddesi 83, Gaziosmanpaşa, Ankara. ℃ 127-5318.,
British Embassy: Şehit Ersan Caddesi 46/A, Çankaya, Ankara. ℃ 127-4310.
British Consulates: Meşrutiyet Caddesi 34, Tepebaşı, Istanbul. ℃ 144-7540. Necatibey Bulvari 19/4, Izmir. ℃ 14 54 70.
Canadian Embassy: Nene Hatun Caddesi 75, Gaziosmanpaşa, Ankara. ℃ 136-1275.
Canadian Honorary Consul General: Mr Yavuz Kivef, Büyükdere Caddesi, Ben-

gün Han 107, Kat. 3, Gayrettepe, Istanbul. (172-5174.

HEALTH

Unless you are planning to visit the more remote parts of eastern Turkey, for which tetanus, typhoid, and hepatitis shots might be a good idea, I think most inoculations are a waste of time. But that is just my personal opinion. Others would have you get all of the above shots plus vaccinations against cholera, polio, and yellow fever, with malaria tablets thrown in for good measure. As no inoculations are actually required to visit Turkey, your best course is to ask your doctor's advice in the matter and then follow it, or just get as many or as few shots as you need to make you feel safe and happy.

The same goes for health insurance. Get as much or as little as needed to make you feel comfortable. But remember, if you do get health insurance you want to make sure (as with car insurance) that it covers both European and Asian Turkey.

For all minor aches and pains you should go along to the nearest pharmacy (*eczane*). Turkish pharmacists are very competent diagnosticians and, what's more, they have a much wider range of drugs that they are permitted to sell you without a prescription than do their American and West European counterparts. In the case of more serious complaints, you will find well-trained doctors and dentists in almost every town, many of whom, especially in the big cities and resort areas, speak English.

In **emergencies** you should go to the nearest hospital (*hastane*) or Red Crescent clinic, taking your own disposable syringes with you if you have them. The level of care may not be quite what you would expect to find in some other countries, but it is adequate. And it is very inexpensive.

In addition to the excellent Hacettepe medical center attached to the university in Ankara ((324-2240), there are a number of foreign hospitals in Turkey. In Istanbul:
American Hospital, Güzelbahçe Sokak 20, Nişantaşı. (131-4050.
French Hospital, Taşkışla Caddesi 3, Taksim. (148-4756.

German Hospital, Sıraselviler Caddesi 119, Taksim. (143-8100.

There are also American hospitals in Ankara (Balgat Amerikan Tes., (33 70 80) and Izmir (9 Eylül Üniversitesi Yani, (13 20 46).

The International Association for Medical Assistance to Travelers (IAMAT) publishes a free list of English-speaking doctors who have had postgraduate training in North America or Britain. The list is available from IAMAT, 417 Center Street, Lewiston, New York 14092, ((716) 754-4883. In Europe write to IAMAT at Gotthardstrasse 17, 6300 Zug, Switzerland, and in Australia at St. Vincent's Hospital, Victoria Parade, Melbourne 3065.

MONEY

At this writing the Turkish lira is in free-fall, so there is no point trying to give equivalents in other currencies. In any event, as inflation is going up at roughly the same rate as the lira is going down, prices for the visitor remain fairly constant. It does mean, however, that the smaller-denomination coins are rapidly disappearing while larger-denomination bank notes are now being printed (1988 saw the introduction of the 20,000 lira note, then already worth less than $16).

In theory, therefore, you should wait as long as possible to cash your travelers' checks, to take advantage of the increasingly favorable exchange rates, and you should get your Turkish liras in the largest possible notes to avoid having to carry around huge wads of cash. In practice, however, I would urge you to do the opposite, for the following reasons. Unless you continually monitor your cash outlays, there is a good chance that you will run out of cash at precisely the moment when only cash will do to pay for something. Moreover, there is even a chance — I am not joking — that the nearby banks will have run out of cash at the same time you do. I have twice been told in a bank that I would have to come back later after the next shipment of bank notes arrived. This is because the banks consistently underestimate the surging demand for cash as tourism spreads. Which suggests a further reason for keeping plenty of spare cash:

the surging, demanding tourists who can make visits to the bank a purgatorial experience. Considering, too, that theft is rare in Turkey, there is really no good reason for not having enough cash to cover most contingencies.

As for having cash in small denominations, this is recommended because Turkey could well go down in history as The Country That Couldn't Make Change. However insignificant the transaction, or however grand the shop, the idea of coming up with exact change, or even inexact change if it

though you may have to wait a day or so to collect your cash. To get Turkish liras in exchange for notes or travelers' checks or Eurocheques or a Visa charge you will need your passport, and you will want to keep the currency exchange slip you are given so that you can change the liras back when you leave.

ACCOMMODATION

As all tourist accommodation in Turkey is

amounts to more than a dollar, is profoundly disconcerting to most Turkish shopkeepers, especially early in the day. If you don't mind waiting (and waiting and waiting) in shops while the proprietor's offspring goes scampering off to find change, or if you don't mind being given sweets, chewing gum, boxes of matches, etc. in lieu of change, then by all means carry only the larger notes. But life will be much easier if you also carry the smaller ones.

Banking hours are 8:30 am to noon and 1:30 pm to 5 pm. All banks, or almost all, will be delighted to change money for you. The exchange rates will be posted daily inside or outside each bank. Many banks will also give you money on your Visa card,

regulated either by the Ministry of Tourism or by the local authorities, and as room prices are usually posted in the reception area and in the rooms themselves, you can generally count on getting exactly what you pay for. However, it is important to know in advance what you are getting.

For this reason, except in the luxury hotels you should always ask to see the rooms, regardless of how the lobby is appointed. The manager or desk clerk will invariably be willing to show you a room, and in some cases will even be eager. In addition to checking for general cleanliness, make a point of

The bar at the Pera Palas, the hotel built specially for passengers off the Orient Express.

checking the hot water and the lights. Also try to gauge the overall noise level in the rooms; in most Turkish hotels the quieter (and cheaper!) rooms are at the back, away from the street.

It is important, too, to ascertain whether the hot water is constant or available only at certain times and in certain circumstances. Simply asking if a place has hot water will not help. The answer will always be Yes, but this could mean "Yes, in principle" or "Yes, in the mornings and evenings" or "Yes, if the furnace is working" or "Yes, if the sun has been shining." And even when you have determined what the hot water situation is, there is no guarantee that it won't change. Except in the fancier hotels, it is not at all uncommon for the hot water — and the cold water too, for that matter — to disappear without warning for several hours. Which is why, once you are in your room, if you are planning a bath or a shower later and there is plenty of hot water now, it's not a bad idea to wash now rather than later. You can always wash again later if there is hot water, but if there isn't it won't be catastrophic.

By the way, before complaining to the management about the lack of hot water, be sure to try both taps. Frequently, whatever the markings indicate, the hot and cold taps are reversed.

Electricity, too, has been known to go off suddenly for no reason. Don't worry. In a few minutes or hours it will suddenly come back on for the same reason.

Surprisingly, perhaps, given the general excellence of Turkish cooking, hotel restaurants tend to be disappointing. Obviously if breakfast is included in the tariff it makes sense to eat in the hotel, or if you are in a one-hotel town in the east it's probable that the one hotel will serve the best food. But by and large hotel meals in Turkey are expensive and boring.

Music-lovers should be aware that almost every hotel in Turkey comes equipped with a device that, as I discovered by accident one night, has a useful function other than that for which it was designed. The device is a cheap, two-piece metal ashtray.

If you have a portable radio or cassette player, and if you place it on its back and put one of these ashtrays upside down over the speaker, you will be amazed at the enhanced resonance of the sounds that come out.

Two final words about your hotel bill. Firstly, if the posted prices are a bit steep for your budget, it will do no harm, when you first enquire about a room, to look rather downcast and to engage in a bit of anguished debate with yourself or a traveling companion. If the place has plenty of vacancies, it is quite likely that the prices will come down for you. Secondly, if you are planning to pay your bill with a credit card, confirm in advance that they will take your card — *even if there are signs saying your card is welcome.* Sometimes these signs refer only to tour groups or to high-season bookings; other times they don't refer to anything but the owner's keenness to put colorful stickers on his door.

EATING OUT

The first thing you should know about Turkish cafés and restaurants is that, wherever you are, there is bound to be one nearby. The second thing you should know is that, whatever the time, it's probably open. For not only are Turkish towns and cities packed with places to eat, but most of them are open from early morning until late at night. Nor will you incur disapproving glances if you choose to eat at odd times. As the author Frederic Raphael once observed, "It is never too late for lunch in Turkey until it is not too early for dinner."

Add to this the fact that the food is wonderfully delicious and wonderfully cheap, and you will readily understand why Turkey is regarded as just this side of Paradise by gourmets and gourmands alike.

For breakfast, even if you have already paid for it where you are staying, I would urge you to go out and try one of the cafés or restaurants serving breakfast (*kahvaltı*). Here you are much more likely to get an authentic Turkish breakfast of fresh warm bread, butter, honey, white sheep's cheese, black olives, and tea or Turkish coffee. When breakfast is included in the price of your

A *simit* seller in Birecik.

room, it tends to consist of not-quite-so-fresh bread, butter, packaged jam, a wedge of processed cheese, possibly olives, and tea or weak instant coffee. Tasty, but not the real thing.

For lunch, by which I mean anything before it is not too early for dinner, you have an infinite array of choices. If you want to munch on the trot, there are street vendors selling *simit* (bagel-like bread rings covered with sesame seeds), nuts, dried fruits, sweet pastries, *börek* (hot, cigar-shaped pastry rolls usually stuffed with white cheese), sandwiches, and ice cream. And just about anywhere you can get cold beer and soft drinks.

If you want to sit down, but not for long, drop into one of the little cafés specializing in *pide* (a sort of Turkish pizza: flat bread topped with ground lamb or cheese or eggs or whatever you like) or *döner kebap* (a roll of lamb leg sliced from a revolving vertical spit and served either with a bit of flat bread and salad or, if you prefer, as a sandwich).

If you want something more elaborate, but still cheap and quick, go into one of the cafeteria-like restaurants where pre-cooked dishes are displayed on a steam table for you to select whatever takes your fancy. Beer and wine, however, are seldom available.

Finally, if you want a longer, more langorous lunch, go into any proper restaurant and begin by selecting your appetizers *(meze)* from a glass case full of vegetable dishes, exotic salads, purées, *börek*, and other treats. If you are wise, you will then go back to your table and enjoy what you have already ordered before you contemplate ordering your next course. You may find, as I frequently do, that you have no room left for a next course. Or you may find that your taste for something has changed during the first course. In any case, since Turkish waiters sometimes appear to be trying to break the sound barrier in getting your food to you, you don't want to be rushed into tackling your next course before you are ready for it. For your main course, you will choose from another glass case. It will have, at a minimum, several different types of fish and several different preparations of lamb — ground into meatballs *(köfte)*, skewered in lumps *(şiş kebap)*, or carved into lamb chops. Depending on the restaurant, there may be

endless variations on these two themes, and they will probably all be delicious, but I would resist the temptation to go for a steak if they have it. The Turks understand fish and lamb; they don't understand beef.

And, in common with all peoples east of Europe and the Mediterranean, they don't understand wine. They understand how to make it, and in fact produce some delightfully drinkable wines which sell for a fraction of the price of their European equivalents. But they still aren't sure what wine is *for*, and will even sometimes serve it after the meal. So you should order your wine before you order your food, and ask for it to be served now (*şimdi*), to avoid having to ask for it later. Bottles of cold water will automatically be put on your table when you sit down.

When the time comes for dessert, if you have a sweet tooth you won't believe your luck. Most Turkish desserts are incredibly sweet, having been drenched in honey or syrup and baked. Try one.

Dinner will either be a condensed or expanded version of one of your lunch options, depending on the size of your appetite and your wallet. A service charge will usually be included in your bill, but even if it is you will be expected to leave a tip.

EATING IN

It is worth bearing in mind that you can eat extraordinarily well, and extraordinarily cheaply, without ever setting foot in a restaurant. All you need is a sharp bread knife, a cutting board, and a few utensils, all of which you can pick up in a local market for next to nothing, and a Swiss Army knife, which you will have to bring with you. With these you can make a wide variety of delicious meals, to be eaten indoors or outdoors, using the wonderful, freshly-baked bread available everywhere and the abundance of fresh fruits and vegetables and cheeses and nuts and olives — all at a cost you will find difficult to believe. (Indeed, the price of bread is kept artificially low by government controls, to help protect the poor from the ravages of inflation.)

If you want to supplement this diet with hot food, there are street vendors selling *çöp* şiş, small pieces of lamb on little wooden skewers, *lahmacun* (ground lamb with chopped onion and tomato sauce on flat bread), and various grilled sandwiches. Or if you are seized with a sudden taste for home non-cooking, in most places you can easily buy mustard, mayonnaise, pickles, ketchup, jam, peanut butter, frankfurters, cold meats, and so on.

If you are planning to spend the day at a remote beach away from any shops and restaurants, may I suggest as a special treat that you take with you some fish which you can buy fresh from the fishermen every morning in the coastal towns. When you get to the beach the fish can be placed in the water to stay fresh until you are ready to eat them. Later you gather enough small wood to make a decent fire, and then when it has burnt down you toss the fish into the hot ashes. Leave them a few minutes, turn them over, leave them a few more minutes, remove them, blackened, from the ashes, squeeze a bit of lemon over them, and prepare to enjoy a memorable meal. If you like fish, and have never had them cooked this way, please try it just once.

For drinks to accompany your do-it-yourself meal, there is plastic-bottled spring water on sale in every grocery, as well as canned soft drinks, and milk and fruit juices in sealed cardboard containers. There is also the excellent Turkish lager, Efes Pilsen, and some quite decent Turkish wines, such as Kavaklıdere, Dikmen, and Villa Doluca (but NOT Doluca without the Villa before it).

SHOPPING

Whenever I am traveling, or visiting a place for a limited period of time, I subscribe to two cardinal principles of shopping:
(1) If you like it, buy it.
(2) Now, not later.

I know this goes against the grain of all the sage advice you will have received to take your time, think it over, not be hurried, sleep on it, shop around, compare prices, examine carefully, get an expert opinion, carry out tests, haggle endlessly, etc. etc. But if you value your taste and your time, all this is unnecessary.

I am not saying that you should hurl yourself into the first souvenir shop you see and go into a buying frenzy. Nor am I saying that you shouldn't have a good look round at what's available and use your bargaining skills accordingly. All I am saying is that when you are shopping for items to bring home with you, and you see something you really like, and it is affordable, it makes more sense to buy it there and then than it does to spend hours or even days looking for a finer example, or a better bargain. Even if you find one, you will have wasted precious time that you could have spent in more rewarding pursuits. And if in the end you fail to find something better, as is usually the case, you may have lost more than time: the object that originally caught your eye may well be gone by then.

Now, having said that, let me tell you what I would buy in Turkey and how I would buy it. To begin with, haggling over price is a perfectly acceptable, even expected, means of making a purchase. It is as much a social as a mercantile ritual, and the merchant will often prolong it by offering you cups of tea or coffee. But there are rules. You should never, for example, make an offer that is insultingly low — say, less than 60 percent of the asking price — and you should never make an offer at all unless you are definitely prepared to buy. Bargaining may be a ritual in Turkey, but it is not a game — you are still dealing with people who are trying to make a living for their families. The best way to bargain is to decide what the item is worth to you — as you would if you were bidding at an auction — and then leave if the price is too high. At that stage, if the shopkeeper is prepared to come down further, he will. If he isn't, you are still free to change your mind later and come back.

Secondly, you should be prepared for a paradoxical fact of shopping life in Turkey: because comparison-shopping is easy, decision-making is hard. I will explain. In almost every Turkish town of any size, but especially in the towns frequented by tourists, all the shops selling one particular type of merchandise tend to be grouped together, so that you will find one entire street, or even a whole area, crammed with nothing but shops selling leather goods, or jewelry, or carpets, or whatever. This means that you can see at a glance, or a few glances anyway, just about

the entire range of what is for sale. But it also means that you have to develop a kind of tunnel vision to avoid being dazzled and ultimately overwhelmed by the sheer number of items before you. So when you look at something, you have to forget that there are hundreds if not thousands of similar items nearby clamoring for your attention; and you have to remember that however many things you see like it when you buy it, you won't see anything like it when you get home.

This last point is crucial. I cannot count the number of times visiting friends have reluctantly let me bully them into buying things they thought they liked, but weren't too sure given the choices, only to bless me later for helping them to find something magnificently unique.

So much for how to shop; now let's consider for what. At or near the top of every serious shopper's list of things to get in Turkey are, of course, carpets and *kilims* (flat-woven tapestries used as rugs, bedspreads, or wall hangings). As these can represent a sizable investment, there are a few things you should know, if you don't already. If the shop is dark or artificially lit, take the carpet out and check the colors in daylight. Wet a handkerchief or cloth and give the carpet a little rub — if any color comes off, the carpet was treated with inferior synthetic dyes. If the knots on the back of the carpet are even and uniform, or if they come loose when you tug at them, it is not a handmade piece. As the finest wool is from the winter fleece and is much softer than the wool shorn in autumn, give the carpet a good feel to see if it is really soft. If it passes these minor tests and the single major one — do you want it? — then buy it. Thanks to the vast areas of the country given over to the growing of cotton, and the vast numbers of sheep given over to Allah every year at the sacrifice holiday, clothing made of cotton or leather is bound to be a bargain. It is. If you know what you need and have room in your luggage, you can outfit yourself for the next year on what you would spend in a month at home.

As gifts I would recommend anything made of onyx or alabaster, especially if you are visiting Cappadocia, though not if you have reason to worry about your weight allowance on the trip home. Lighter, but more fragile, are the gorgeous, hand-made ceramic plates,

tiles, bowls, and vases you will find on sale in most towns. With copperware the problem is not weight or fragility, but size. Still, you should find space in your bag for at least one of the many beautiful copper items, all made by hand, that you will see shining temptingly at you. Wooden boxes inlaid with mother-of-pearl, and delicately painted boxes carved out of camel bone, are also a joy to come upon when you unpack. But perhaps the best bargain of all in terms of value for money (and weight and strength and size) is the jewelry. Whether antique or modern, gold or silver, ornamented

with precious or semi-precious stones, fashioned into rings, bracelets, brooches, pendants, earrings or necklaces, there is jewelry to be found in Turkey that will make you or someone you love very happy for a very long time.

ETIQUETTE

Turkey is no different from any other place in that politeness is appreciated, rudeness

Doing what they do best. OPPOSITE TOP: carpets for sale in Side; BOTTOM: Colorful knitted socks are one of the sartorial joys of Turkey. These are on display in a shop in Sivas, east of Ankara. ABOVE: A shopkeeper — one of thousands — in the Grand Bazaar in Istanbul.

isn't. What is perhaps different is that even justified annoyance or impatience is often construed as rudeness, especially if accompanied by a raised voice or a pointed finger. But as long as your behavior is determined by the ordinary respect and consideration that any guest owes his host, you will be touched by the warmth of the welcome you will receive.

In most situations, common sense will dictate what is proper and what isn't. When you see all the people taking off their shoes before entering a mosque, you need hardly be told that this is the thing to do. Likewise, when you see that every woman puts on a headscarf before going into a mosque, you will rightly surmise that a headscarf is *de rigueur* for women.

Other situations are less clear-cut, and in any case are constantly changing. Topless sunbathing, for instance, was unheard of only a few years ago, but is now quite common on the Aegean and Mediterranean beaches. However, before whipping off your top it would be prudent to look around you to see how many others have shed theirs. This is not entirely a matter of offending local sensibilities. If you are the only one to be thus exposed, you might consider whether the benefits of an even tan outweigh the tiresomeness of being stared at by Turkish youths who will pass by, and pass by again, and again, for the sole purpose of staring. If that doesn't particularly bother you, you will be happy to know that you are unlikely to bother anyone else, because the Turks tend to classify all sunbathing under The Funny Ways of Foreigners. They can't imagine why anyone would want to risk looking like an Arab.

Sunbathing bottomless is another matter. Going bottomless anywhere that you can be seen by the public is an extremely bad idea. A lady friend of mine once scandalized the women in a Turkish bath by innocently taking off all her clothes.

To revert briefly to the subject of staring and being stared at, you will have to get used to the idea of being stared at in the less cosmopolitan parts of the country, especially by the children. Although it can be unsettling at first, it represents nothing more than eager curiosity, and is not considered rude.

On the other hand, it is considered rude to object to being stared at.

I am often asked if there is any problem with unmarried couples checking into hotels together. No, there isn't. Although the Turks are mostly serious Muslims and take marriage very seriously, they are also very tolerant and are thus disposed to include extramarital cohabitation among The Funny Ways of Foreigners. There have been a few reports of unmarried couples being harassed in hotels in the east, but in every case I know of, one of the couple was Turkish and the couple had been admitted to the hotel on the condition that they slept in separate rooms, which condition they accepted and then ignored. In other words, they asked for it.

You may be surprised, incidentally, by the way the Turks are quick to address you by your first name. This is not, rest assured, the instant familiarity of the insurance salesman. It comes from the fact that although it is now more than half a century since Atatürk insisted that his compatriots take surnames, most Turks are still more comfortable dealing with first names. Otherwise, you will find that Turks respond more readily to formality than to informality. You will, in short, win more friends with a little dignified courtesy than with a lot of backslapping bonhomie.

DRIVING

First, the good news. Turkish roads are generally good, the traffic on them is generally light, gasoline is very cheap compared to Europe, service stations are still *service* stations, and there are so many of them that you would have to work at running out of fuel, the traffic police are friendly and helpful, even when you've done something wrong, and Turkish mechanics are among the world's most resourceful, as evidenced by the fact that species of cars long thought to be extinct — Packards, De Sotos, Studebakers — can still be seen on the roads.

Now for the bad news. Turkish drivers are, arguably, the worst in the world; one only has to look at the appalling statistics for road accidents and deaths in Turkey to realize that. If that doesn't convince you, go out for a drive. You will soon find yourself being overtaken on either side; you will find that as you approach the crest of a hill two or even three vehicles are hurtling towards you; you will find that as you round a bend the road turns into a parking lot for goats; you will find that at any moment you may come upon a dog or a donkey or a sheep or a cow or a camel ambling across the road, or even, in the case of dogs, sleeping in the middle of it.

Although there are almost as many animals as cars on the roads at any given time, it is worst in the early morning and early evening, when unfortunately the light is poorest, as those are the rush hours for livestock as well as humans — if one can so misuse the word "rush". After nightfall most of the beasts you will see on or near the road will be motionless.

At night, also, Turkish drivers like to fiddle with their headlights, flashing them back and forth from high to low beam regardless of the circumstances. And some drivers don't have headlights to play with: I was once confronted on a steep hill by a tiny, flickering light coming at me at high speed, which I assumed to be a motorbike but which turned out to be, as it whooshed past, an elderly truck with its driver hanging out the window holding a flashlight.

It is worth mentioning, too, that day can turn to night in a split second if you happen to come upon a tunnel in Turkey. There aren't many, and they are signposted in advance, but you should still be prepared for the darkest experience of your life, even with your headlights on.

So much for the country roads; the cities are worse. Quite apart from the fact that you have far more incompetent drivers concentrated in a much smaller space, you have the deafening, distracting phenomenon of drivers who consider their horns to be not a means of alerting others but a means of conversation. Thus a series of blasts on the horn may mean anything from "Good morning, Kemal" to "Would you like to have tea with me?" to "Watch out for that dog!" In fact, one amusing way to spend a few minutes is to stand on any busy street corner and try to guess what the horns are saying to each other.

A less amusing way to pass the time is to try to guess what street you are driving on, or what street you have just passed, because

Turkish towns and cities are remarkably free of anything resembling street signs. Similarly, parking spaces are almost non-existent anywhere you would like to be, although as a visitor you do have the option of collecting parking tickets that you may later choose to ignore. What you cannot ignore, anywhere in Turkey but especially in the towns and cities, is that Turkish pedestrians have a knack of waiting until the last possible moment before crossing the road in front of your car. Indeed, after a while it is hard to avoid the suspicion that somewhere in the genealogy of many Turks there lurks a chicken.

Now, if you are still planning to drive in Turkey, you will need a valid driving license and an International Driving Permit, which you can get from your automobile club before you leave home. This latter is not strictly necessary, but it can come in handy as identification and it means you don't have to carry (and risk losing) your regular license. If you have an accident in Turkey you must report it at once to the local police. And if you have any questions or problems, you should contact the Turkish Touring and Automobile Club at Halaskargazi Caddesi 364, Şişli, Istanbul (℃ 140-7127), or at Topkapı Gate, Istanbul (℃ 146-7090). They are very helpful and efficient.

PUBLIC HOLIDAYS AND FESTIVALS

HOLIDAYS

1 JANUARY: New Year's Day.
23 APRIL: National Independence Day and Children's Day.
19 MAY: Youth and Sports Day, commemorating Atatürk's birthday.
30 AUGUST: Victory Day.
29 OCTOBER: Republic Day.

FESTIVALS

JANUARY
Camel wrestling in Selçuk, Aydın, and Denizli.

FEBRUARY
Kel Aynak Festival in Birecik.

MARCH
Traditional Troubadours Festival in Erzurum.

APRIL
Mid-April: Traditional "Powergum" Festival in Manisa, near Izmir.
Late April: Atatürk University Folklore and Music Festival in Erzurum.
Late April-early May: Tulip Festival in Istanbul.

MAY
First week: International Ephesus Festival

Second week: Music and Art Festival in Marmara; Kirkpınar Greased Wrestling Competition in Edirne.
Third week: Tea and Tourism Festival in Rize.
Late June to mid-July: International Istanbul Culture and Arts Festival.

JULY
First week: Tourism Festival in Amasra.
Second week: Nasreddin Hoca Celebrations in Akşehir; International Folklore and Music Festival in Bursa; Tourism and

of Culture and Art in Selçuk; Yunus Emre Culture and Arts Week in Eskişehir; Spring Festivals in Sinop, Iznik, and Bursa.
Mid-May: International Music and Folklore Festival in Silifke; Aksu Culture and Art Festival in Giresun.
Last week: Pergamon Festival in Bergama.

JUNE
Sound and light shows begin at the Blue Mosque in Istanbul.
First week: International Mediterranean Festival in Izmir; Rose Festival in Konya.

Culture Festival in Van.
Mid-July: Ceramics Festival in Kütahya; Apricot Festival in Malatya; International Folk Dance Festival in Samsun.
Last week: Water Sports, Music and Folklore Festival in Foça, near Izmir.

AUGUST
Sound and light shows begin at Atatürk's Mausoleum in Ankara.
15 August: Mass celebrating the Assumption of the Virgin at the House of the Virgin Mary near Ephesus.
Mid-August: Festival of Troy in Çanakkale.
Late August-early September: Izmir International Fair.

The folkloric dancers treat themselves to the lamb roasting after entertaining others.

SEPTEMBER

First week: Bodrum Culture and Art Festival, Kırşehir Ahi Evran Crafts and Folklore Festival in Kırşehir; Tourism Festival in Kuşadası.

Second week: Çorum Hittite Festival in Çorum, near Ankara.

Mid-September: Cappadocia Grape Harvest Festival in Ürgüp and Göreme; Arts and Culture Festival in Adana.

Last week: Whirling Dervishes perform in Konya; Culinary contest in Konya; Watermelon Festival in Diyarbakır.

Late September-early October: Textile and Fashion Fair in Mersin; Mediterranean Song Contest in Antalya.

OCTOBER

First week: Golden Orange Film and Arts Festival in Antalya.

Mid-October: Suhut Karadilli Wrestling Festival near Afyon.

Last week: Turkish Troubadours Week in Konya.

DECEMBER

Camel wrestling all month in Aydın province.

First week: St. Nicholas Festival in Demre, near Kaş.

Mid-December: The Mevlana Festival, featuring Whirling Dervishes, in Konya.

Religious Festivals

Ramazan, the Holy Month, consists of thirty days of strict fasting (which includes no drinking or smoking) from sunrise to sunset. However, the feasting by night eases the pain of the fasting by day. Ramazan falls at a slightly different time every year; in 1992 it will be during March.

Şeker Bayramı is the three-day festival (and official public holiday) that marks the end of Ramazan. It is a joyful time during which vast amounts of sweets are consumed by grateful children.

Kurban Bayramı is the most important period in both the religious and the secular calendar. It comes two months and ten days after Şeker Bayramı and lasts for four days, though shops and banks may be closed for longer. It could be called the Muslim Christmas, except that a sheep rather than a turkey is sacrificed, and the celebrants tend to remember better the sacred meaning of the event being commemorated. It is a bad time for traveling or looking for accommodation, just like Christmas, and a good time for lying low. Just like Christmas.

MAIL

Post offices are easily identifiable by their yellow-and-black PTT signs. (Mailboxes are yellow, too.) The PTT's are always centrally located, and almost always open. The major ones are open from eight in the morning until midnight six days a week (9 am to 7 pm Sundays), while even the smallest ones are open from 8:30 am to 5:30 pm weekdays.

If you are planning to send mail, it is wise to go to a post office early in the morning at the beginning of your visit and get all the stamps you think you will need (and a few more). That way you can make sure you have the right postage — postal rates rise with inflation frequently — and you can avoid the hassle of squeezing through a mob of tourists in a post office at some later stage.

If you are planning to receive mail, and you don't have a definite address in advance, you should have it addressed to you at: Poste Restante, Merkez Postanesi, (Town or City), Turkey.

You will need some form of identification to collect your mail, and you may have to pay a nominal charge for the service (a few pennies at most), and the postal clerk may act as if you have asked him/her to perform brain surgery while blindfolded, but the service is reliable. I have friends who have written to me c/o Poste Restante in Turkey, where it was faithfully kept for several months. When I had failed to collect the mail it was opened — because there was no return address on the envelope — and was sent back at the PTT's expense. That's nice.

TELEPHONES

By far the cheapest and easiest way to make telephone calls is to make friends first and then pay them to let you use their telephones. The next easiest, but far from cheapest, way is to place calls through your hotel. Absent these two options, you will have to go to a post office and buy telephone tokens *(jetons)* which you can then use either at the pay phones in the post office itself or at one of the modern, yellow push-button phones you will see dotted around most major towns and cities.

The advantages of making your call from the post office are that you can ask the man from whom you buy your tokens to place the call for you, and you can determine the rate you want to pay for the call. The rates depend upon the speed with which the call goes through: the *normal* rate is generally very cheap and the service is very slow, for *acele* ("rush") service you get twice the speed for twice the price, and with *yıldırım* ("lightning") service your call goes through about four times faster for about four times the price.

The advantage of using one of the yellow, automatic public phones is that while your call will be charged at *yıldırım* rate, it usually *will* go through at "lightning" speed. Moreover, you can make the call at any time that suits you, usually without having to stand around long waiting for somebody else to get off the phone. And the instructions for using the phone will either be posted in English or will be illustrated by a series of easy-to-follow drawings. The only caveat with regard to using these telephones is that if you are planning to make an international call do make sure that you have plenty of large *jetons* with you before you start or the call may be over before you're finished.

To make a long-distance call inside Turkey, you dial 9 first, wait for the tone to change, then dial the city code and number. For international calls, you dial 99, then the country code, the city code (omitting any zeroes at the beginning of the city code), and the number you are calling.

HELPFUL NUMBERS

Information — 011
Long-distance information — 061
International information — 062
Long-distance operator — 031

Long-distance "quick service" operator — 091
International operator   528-2303

COUNTRY CODES

USA and Canada 1	France 33
United Kingdom 44	Greece 30
Ireland 353	Holland 31
Australia 61	Italy 39
New Zealand 64	Norway 47
Austria 43	Sweden 41
Belgium 32	Switzerland 46
Denmark 45	West Germany 49

TURKISH CITY CODES

Adana 71	Giresun 0511
Adıyaman 8781	Hopa 0571
Ağrı 0271	Iskenderun 881
Aksaray 4811	Istanbul 1
Alanya 3231	Izmir 51
Amasya 3781	Izmit 211
Ankara 4	Iznik 2527
Antakya 891	Kâhta 8795
Antalya 311	Kalkan 3215
Artvin 0581	Kars 0211
Aydın 631	Kaş 3266
Ayvalık 6631	Kayseri 351
Balıkesir 661	Kemer 3214
Bergama 541	Konya 331
Bitez 6143	Kuşadası 6361
Bitlis 8491	Malatya 821
Bodrum 6141	Manavgat 3211
Bursa 241	Manisa 5511
Çanakkale 1961	Mardin 8411
Çeşme 5492	Marmaris 6121
Çorum 469	Mersin 741
Dalaman 6119	Milas 6131
Datça 6145	Muğla 6111
Denizli 621	Nevşehir 4851
Diyarbakır 831	Ordu 371
Dogubayazır 0278	Pamukkale 6218
Edirne 1811	Rize 054
Edremit 6711	Samsun 361
Erzincan 023	Şanlıurfa 8711
Erzurum 011	Selçuk 5451
Eskişehir 221	Side 3213
Fethiye 6151	Sile 1992
Finike 3225	Silifke 7591
Foça 5431	Sinop 3761
Gaziantep 851	Sivas 477

Tarsus 761	Uludağ 2418
Taşucu 7593	Ünye 3731
Tatvan 8497	Ürgüp 4868
Trabzon 031	Van 0611

BASICS

TIME

Turkish time is two hours ahead of Greenwich Mean Time, except in the summer when clocks are put forward one hour.

you will have other things to worry about anyway. The reason it is safe, however, is that it is heavily chlorinated — which means that it doesn't taste all that good. You will be much better off keeping with you one or more of the plastic bottles of spring water that you can buy anywhere. Even your steam iron, if you travel with one, will be happier with the spring water.

One note of caution: In the smaller, scruffier restaurants it is not a good idea to order a drink with ice in it.

However, as most of Europe and America also switches to summer time, Turkey remains one hour ahead of western Europe, two hours ahead of the British Isles, seven hours ahead of New York, ten ahead of Los Angeles, and so forth.

ELECTRICITY

Turkish current is 220 volts, although it is not always up to full strength. The outlets take European-style plugs with two round prongs.

WATER

It's safe to drink, except perhaps in the farthest reaches of the southeast, where

WEIGHTS AND MEASURES

Turkey, like most of the world, uses the metric system. But if you are used to thinking in feet and inches and pounds and ounces etc., it won't be much help to you to be told the precise formulae for converting from one system to another, as you would still require a calculator to get the conversion exactly right. In any case, you can get the equivalents, and the means of arriving at them, from any dictionary. So, instead, I have come up with a few rough-and-ready

The open market at the Ulu Mosque, Şanlıurfa.

conversions that can be managed instantly with a minimum of calculation. (In these conversions the highly non-technical term "a bit" represents one-tenth of whatever it is next to.) Thus: a meter is a yard and a bit, a kilometer is a half-mile and a bit, a kilogram is two pounds and a bit, while a liter is a bit more than an American quart and a bit less than a British quart.

If you want to know approximately how hot (or cold) it is in degrees Fahrenheit, double the figure you are given in Celsius and add 30. So if it is 20 °C, for example, it is roughly 70 °F.

CRIME

It does exist, of course, but seldom in the form to which you are likely to be accustomed — stealing, whether by burglary, robbery, or mugging. This is because almost all Turks are Muslims, and the most shameful crime among Muslims is theft. Even in prison, thieves are ostracized and spat upon by the other prisoners. Therefore, if you do encounter crime in Turkey, it will probably be at the hands of another tourist.

Maintenance of law and order is the responsibility of the *jandarma*, who are special soldiers in the army, recognizable by their dark green fatigues and red armbands. They may look menacing at first, especially with the automatic weapons they often carry, but if you approach them you will find them eager to be helpful — and probably eager to bum a cigarette off you as well. The police

you see wearing snappy green uniforms and white caps are the traffic police and are, in my experience at least, unfailingly polite.

RADIO AND TELEVISION

All broadcasting in Turkey comes from Turkish Radio and Television (TRT). The radio channels feature a wide selection of music, both Turkish and foreign. The TRT Third Program broadcasts in English, French, and German in the mornings on short-wave frequencies between 88 and 99 MHz. For news and other programs in English you can tune into the BBC World Service, which has broadcasts on different frequencies beamed from the BBC relay station on Cyprus. And, if you're so desperate that you're willing to put up with programming for the brain-damaged, you can receive the Voice of America loud and clear from its transmitter on Rhodes.

For sheer entertainment value, however, there is nothing that can quite compare with the English-language broadcasts of Radio Moscow and, even better, Radio Tirana broadcasting from Albania. Radio Moscow serves up lumps of poorly disguised propaganda swimming in a thick parody — even down to the accents — of the worst of American broadcasting. Thus you get "happy talk" newscasts ("Good morning, Sergei"… "Good morning, Natasha, what a pretty dress you are wearing"…"You're just saying that, Sergei"… "No, Natasha, I really mean it"… "What news do you have for us this morning, Sergei?"…) and you get wonderful little human interest stories with which you can play Spot The Message. One of my favorites was a feature on the Lost and Found office of the Moscow subway, in which I learned that ordinary Muscovites are forever losing gold watches and fancy umbrellas and beautiful raincoats and bulging wallets and portable radios and expensive cameras and such like. Spot the message. And thanks to Radio Tirana I have been privileged to hear the latest thoughts of the President of the Presidium of the People's Assembly of the People's Socialist Republic of Albania, Comrade Fillintheblank, who is always having thoughts on something or sending fraternal greetings to someone. Great stuff.

The *Ulu Cami* (grand mosque) near the bazaar in Diyarbakir, probably the oldest mosque in Turkey.

Television in Turkey, I'm afraid, is less rewarding, although there is a certain amount of fun to be had from watching *Cheers, Three's Company, The Cosby Show, Dr. Who,* and *Yes, Prime Minister* dubbed into Turkish. Similarly, it is amusing — though ultimately frustrating — to see familiar movies with unfamiliar dialogue. Sadly, the literacy rate in Turkey is still so low that if foreign movies were shown with subtitles they would be incomprehensible to perhaps half the audience. However, along the Aegean coast you can generally receive Greek television, which constantly screens subtitled American and British movies.

The main news is broadcast at 8 pm every evening and consists of about half an hour of national and local news followed by international news. TRT 2, the second channel, broadcasts the news in English at 10:30 pm. Sport on television consists mostly of football (soccer). Every Saturday afternoon during the season TRT broadcasts one live match with a small inset showing another match simultaneously, usually followed by the second half of yet another live match, and in the evening they show the highlights of all the day's First Division matches.

NEWSPAPERS AND MAGAZINES

English-language newspapers are easy to come by in all the major cities and resort areas. Most English dailies are on sale, as are *USA Today,* the *Wall Street Journal,* and the *International Herald Tribune.* But they are all very expensive, and reach the newsstands at least a day late. Fortunately, though, there is available a cheap and up-to-date alternative in English, the *Turkish Daily News.* Although it naturally gives priority to Turkish news, it provides more than adequate coverage of world news with stories taken from the Associated Press and Reuters wires. And while its layout shows the regrettable influences of both the *Herald Tribune* and *USA Today,* it is quite readable — even indispensable if you want regular cultural and entertainment listings as well as the latest sports news and scores from America and Britain.

All of this would be reason enough to buy the paper, but what sets the *Turkish Daily News* apart is that it is also possibly the world's funniest paper. This is due in part to the wonderfully eccentric selection of stories the editors choose to print — I have seen items about looming famines in Africa alongside the problems facing blind masseurs — and it is partly due to the paper's stable of untamed headline writers. Not only are they capable of composing headlines that sometimes wildly contradict the stories the headlines adorn, but in the sports pages one finds headlines that must be among the most bloodthirsty in contemporary journalism. As far as the TDN headline writers are concerned, no team ever simply loses a game. No, however close the contest, however slim the margin of victory, the losing team is always *smashed, trampled, mauled, walloped, conquered, destroyed, thumped,* or — my favorite — *creamed.*

Note: When buying any newspaper, Turkish or foreign, be sure to check the date on it. Turkish newsagents don't always distinguish between today's news and yesterday's, or last week's, or last month's — so you could find yourself paying the same price to read about recent history as to read about current affairs.

Time, Newsweek, The Economist, and most of the major European magazines are available — but, again, at a steep price. Much better to get *Dateline,* an English-language weekly paper published by *Hürriyet* in Istanbul, which is superbly edited and very well written.

TOILETS

They may take some getting used to. At the bottom of the line, so to speak, are the squatters — sunken porcelain rectangles with a hole in the middle over which you squat. If you have been in France you will have seen them before; if you are French you may even like them. Although there will be water for washing yourself, there is unlikely to be any toilet paper, which is one good reason why you should always carry tissues or toilet paper with you. If there is a wastepaper basket placed near the toilet, that is where you should put your used paper. Seriously. Otherwise you could cause a real problem with the plumbing.

Most Turkish toilets, however, are of the familiar Western variety, often with an added feature: a bit of copper tubing strategically positioned at the rear of the bowl to facilitate the rinsing of the bottom. I personally think it is a marvelous invention, but if you are not aware of its function, and you turn the knob beside the toilet thinking that you are about to flush, you may suddenly discover exactly how high you can leap from a sitting position.

In emergencies, you will find the public toilets in or near places frequented by tourists, in bus and train stations, and in every mosque.

TURKISH BATHS

The Turkish bath, or *hamam*, has been a feature of life in Turkey since medieval times. Unlike in the West, where its main purpose is to make you feel better, in Turkey its main purpose has always been to make you cleaner. Indeed, because the spread of public bath houses was in response to the Muslim emphasis on cleanliness, they could almost be considered secular adjuncts to the Islamic faith.

There are separate baths for men and women, or different days for bathing in towns with only one *hamam*. On entering the *hamam* you are given a towel to wrap around you, and after leaving your clothes in a cubicle you go into a warm, marble room where there is a large heated stone. Here you sit and sweat for a while, and then a bath attendant comes and soaps you and gives you a good scrubbing and a rubdown. Whether you then consider yourself to have been vigorously caressed or brutally mauled, you will definitely emerge from the experience clean and refreshed.

Many Turkish baths are also of great architectural interest. Of these the two most stunning are the 300-year-old Cagaloğlu Hamamı on Hilaliahmer Caddesi near the Blue Mosque and, also in Istanbul, the Galatasaray Hamamı on Suterazisi Sokak off Istiklâl Caddesi.

OPPOSITE TOP: The entrance to the 300-year-old Turkish bath in Cagaloğlu, near the Blue Mosque in Istanbul. BOTTOM: The interior of the Yenikaplica Turkish bath in Bursa.

WOMEN ALONE

Although one sometimes hears worrying stories about single women being harassed in Turkey, I personally know of no such instances. Nonetheless, common sense dictates that in a country unused to the idea of women traveling alone, or even walking around alone, where the men expect their women to be demure and inconspicuous, it is not a terribly good idea for women on their own to dress or act in a manner likely to attract unwelcome attention. But this is true anywhere. When in Rome, etc... Still, if you are worried that you might inadvertently provoke unwanted interest, your two best forms of protection are a dignified demeanor (which includes a refusal to respond in any way to approaches) and a wedding ring. Turkish men are loath to risk offending an unseen husband.

In the unlikely event that you are persistently pursued against your will, and against all the signals that I have suggested, you should feel free, as a last resort, to make as big a fuss as you like. The *jandarma* take a dim view of oafs who molest women, especially respectable foreign women, so they will be firmly on your side. And the oafs know this.

TIPPING

Although a service charge is automatically included in almost every restaurant bill, you should nonetheless leave the waiter a tip of around 10 percent, as it is common in Turkey for the restaurant proprietor to help himself to the service charge.

In hotels, the porter who shows you to your room and carries your luggage should be tipped about a dollar, while the chambermaid should receive about 50¢ a day. At the hairdressers, you should tip about 20 percent to the person who cuts your hair (remember that haircuts are very cheap in Turkey) and perhaps half that to anyone else who renders you a service.

Turkish taxi drivers have traditionally not expected tips but with the tourist boom that is begining to change. You will still not be expected to add anything on to a prear-

ranged fare or to a *dolmuş* fare, but you may want to round off a metered fare so as to incorporate a small gratuity. This will not only make the taxi driver happy but it means that you won't have to wait while he struggles to make change.

Tipping in Turkish baths is slightly more complicated, because you can pay different fees for different services provided by different people. As a general rule, though, you should add about one-third of the total charge and then distribute this among the staff who served you as you leave.

have already mentioned — taps running out of water, wires running out of electricity, banks running out of cash, shopkeepers running out of change, toilets running out of toilet paper, animals and pedestrians running out in front of your car, etc. — so you no longer have any excuse for being surprised by them. But there are still a few potential surprises that you may later be thankful you anticipated.

One is that Turkish towns off the beaten track, or even on it, can shut down in the evening with breathtaking suddenness. More than once I have arrived in a (fairly remote)

SURPRISES

Most of the surprises you will encounter in Turkey will be big, happy ones. This is because, no matter how favorably predisposed you may be towards the country and its people, it is almost impossible not to be surprised over and over again by the beauty of the place, the warmth of the people, the gastronomic glories of the cuisine, and so on. And there will be many little happy surprises, such as the discovery on arrival by ferry from one of the Greek islands that the duty-free shop in the harbor is opened for *arriving* passengers.

Then there are those surprises of the other kind. The most unsettling of these I

place bustling with activity at 7 pm, only to find a ghost town when I emerged from my hotel an hour later. So if you arrive somewhere needing to get something, get it before you unpack and have your shower.

Nor should you expect a shop to have something you need simply because all logic (and maybe even a sign) says it must. For example, Turkey is a leading producer of tobacco, and every known Turkish male acts as if it is his sacred duty to smoke as much as he can, and the state has a profitable monopoly on the manufacture of cigars, and there are tobacconists everywhere in Turkey, so it follows that cigars are everywhere in Turkey. Yes? Well, it follows — but the fact is that cigars can be extremely hard to find outside the biggest cities. So if you like cigars as much as I do, and you suddenly get lucky and find a shop that stocks them, buy up the shop.

The only truly nasty little surprise I can think of is the experience of opening a bottle that has an aluminum screw-off top. I don't know why it is, but I have found in my travels that the hotter the country, and therefore the greater the demand for bottled drinks, the poorer the bottletop technology. Thus, in simmering summertime Turkey, if you're not careful you could end up drinking the blood you shed trying to unscrew a self-destruct-

legally to prolong your stay is to spend a day or so visiting one of the nearby Greek islands. When you re-enter Turkey, the clock starts all over again. I know people who have lived in Turkey (and in Greece, too, for that matter) for more than twenty years without going through any formalities other than four short trips a year.

If, however, you plan to stay in a part of Turkey where the occasional over-and-back excursion is not feasible or convenient, you should apply for a residence visa. For this you will need to fill out a short application

ing, finger-lacerating top from a bottle.

And there will be other little surprises to make your visit more memorable than it might otherwise have been. Not for nothing does the Ottoman Bank have as its advertising slogan, "Surprise-free Banking."

Still, as I said, the big surprises should all be happy ones. So if you go expecting a lot of nasty little surprises, then I would be willing to bet that you are in for the biggest, happiest surprise of all.

STAYING ON

Should you decide to stay on in Turkey for more than three months, the easiest way

form and submit it together with your passport, a passport-sized photograph, a banker's statement about your finances, a document giving details of your assets and/or other sources of income, and a short statement giving your reasons for wanting to stay in Turkey. This can be done at government offices anywhere in the country, but is best done in advance at a Turkish consulate general abroad.

If you want to to go the whole hog and buy property in Turkey, you should first

OPPOSITE: Under Atatürk's watchful eye, bidders attend a carpet auction in Istanbul. ABOVE: Where there's smoke there isn't always fire: post-prandial puffing in an Istanbul restaurant.

consult a Turkish lawyer who is familiar with the laws governing foreign ownership of property in Turkey. In fact you will find the restrictions are both eminently reasonable and flexible, and are mostly designed to prevent high-rise horrors and over-development from ruining the coastline, and in rural areas to prevent wealthy foreigners from ruining the property market for less prosperous local people. Generally speaking, if you want to buy freehold property in Turkey you will have to do so within a large town or municipal area, and you can expect to pay about 12 percent on top of the purchase price to cover taxes, transfer costs, and other fees. For leaseholds, which customarily run for 99 years, you will only have to spend about two percent extra for stamp and notary fees and land registry charges. Whichever way, buying freehold or leasehold, it will be a bargain.

TURKISH FOR TRAVELERS

The travel writer Paul Theroux tells of once coming across an Irish dialect so melodic, and so utterly incomprehensible, that a local man acknowledged that a stranger struggling to make sense of it would probably feel "like a dog listening to music". A similar experience awaits most people hearing Turkish spoken for the first time. It is easy on the ear, thanks to the Turkish system of "vowel harmony" which prevents discordant syllables from bumping into each other, and hard on the brain, thanks to a grammatical structure which is completely unlike that of English or any of the other Indo-European languages.

It is, however, not as impenetrable as it might at first sight appear. For one thing, unlike English, it is supremely logical, and it obeys its own rules almost without exception. For another thing, it is strictly phonetic and therefore is pronounced exactly the way you would expect it to be from the spelling, once you have learned the sounds represented by the letters of the Turkish alphabet. These sounds I have given below. What I haven't given is a guide to the complexities of Turkish grammar. There simply isn't enough space to do more than rough justice to such a subtle and highly-inflected lan-

guage. Those wishing to go beyond the basic terms and expressions to a more sophisticated grasp of the language should get a Turkish primer; by far the best available is *Colloquial Turkish* by Yusuf Mardin, published by Routledge & Kegan Paul.

PRONUNCIATION

There are three crucial things to remember about Turkish pronunciation. Firstly, with the exception of *i*, every letter has only one correct sound; get the letters right and you've got the words right. Secondly, with the exception of *ğ* every single letter is pronounced; there are no diphthongs. Thirdly, all syllables should be pronounced with approximately equal stress; where a word is accented the accent will be very light indeed and will almost always fall on the last syllable.

The vowels *a* and *e* are pronounced like their English counterparts in *cart* and *red*, while *o* is the same as in the English *boat*, and *u* is the same as in *put*. The other vowels:

i short as in *sit*, though sometimes with a long "e" sound, as in *ski*, usually at the end of words

ı undotted, a soft "uh" sound, like the "er" in *waiter*

ö as in German, like the "ur" in *further*

ü as in German, or the *u* in the French *tu*, like the "ew" in *dew*

Most of the consonants are pronounced as they are in English, with the following exceptions and additions:

c pronounced like the English "j" in *jam* (this will be the hardest single pronunciation for you to remember)

ç "ch" as in *chat*

g always hard, as in *good*

ğ not pronounced; its only function is to lengthen slightly the preceding vowel

h always pronounced as in *hard*

j as in French, like the "s" sound in *pleasure*

s always unvoiced, as in *send*; never like the "s" in *pleasure*

ş "sh" as in *show*

VOCABULARY

Numbers
0 *sıfır*
1 *bir*

2   iki
3   üç
4   dört
5   beş
6   altı
7   yedi
8   sekiz
9   dokuz
10   on
11   on bir
12   on iki
13   on üç
14   on dört
20   yirmi
21   yirmi bir
30   otuz
40   kırk
50   elli
60   altmış
70   yetmiş
80   seksen
90   doksan
100   yüz
200   iki yüz
1,000   bin
2,000   iki bin
10,000   on bin
100,000   yüz bin
1,000,000   milyon

One half is *yarım*, except when it follows a number, when it is *buçuk*. Thus, one-half kilo is *yarım kilo* but 1-1/2 is *bir buçuk*.

Calendar
Sunday   *Pazar*
Monday   *Pazartesi*
Tuesday   *Salı*
Wednesday   *Çarşambe*
Thursday   *Perşembe*
Friday   *Cuma*
Saturday   *Cumartesi*

January   *Ocak*
February   *Şubat*
March   *Mart*
April   *Nisan*
May   *Mayıs*
June   *Haziran*
July   *Temmuz*
August   *Ağustos*
September   *Eylül*
October   *Ekim*
November   *Kasım*

December   *Aralık*

spring   *ilkbahar*
summer   *yaz*
autumn   *sonbahar*
winter   *kış*

day   *gün*
week   *hafta*
month   *ay*
season   *mevsim*
year   *sene, yıl*

Clock
hour, time   *saat* (in front of a number it means "o'clock"; thus "nine o'clock" is *saat dokuz*
now   *şimdi*
later   *sonra*
morning   *sabah*
noon   *öğle*
evening   *akşam*
night   *gece*
today   *bugün*
yesterday   *dün*
tomorrow   *yarın*
what time is it?   *saat kaç?*

Key words and phrases
yes   *evet*
no   *hayır*
none   *yok* (an emphatic, all-purpose negative)
much, very   *çok*
please   *lütfen*
thank you   *teşekkür ederim*
...very much   *çok teşekkür ederim*
thanks   *teşekkürler, mersi*
you're welcome   *bir şey değil*
hello   *merhaba*
good morning   *günaydın*
good evening   *iyi akşamlar*
good night   *iyi geceler*
goodbye   *Allaha ısmarladık* (said by person leaving)   *güle güle* (said by person staying)
welcome   *hoş geldiniz* (to which the person welcomed should reply *hoş bulduk*)
excuse me   *affedersınız*
good   *iyi* (pronounced eee)
lovely, beautiful   *güzel* (an all-purpose compliment)
very lovely   *çok güzel*
how lovely   *ne güzel*

there is *var*
is there…? …*var mı?*
how? *nasıl?*
how are you? *nasılsınız*
how many? *kaçtane?*
what? *ne?*
what is this? *bu nedir?*
what is that *o nedir?*
what is your name? *adınız nedir?*
when? *ne zaman?*
who? *kim?*
why? *niçin, neden?*
which one? *hangisi?*
where is…? …*nerede?*
how much is it? *ne kadar?*
this much *bu kadar*
I want… …*istiyorum*
I understand *anlıyorum*
I don't understand *anlamıyorum*
I know *biliyorum*
I don't know *bilmiyorum*
I don't speak Turkish *Türkçe bilmiyorum*
this *bu*
that *şu*
here *burada*
there *şurada*
this one *bunu*
that one *şunu*
near *yakın*
far *uzak*
left *sol*
right *sağ*
hot *sıcak*
cold *soğuk*
big *büyük*
small *küçük*
open *açık*
closed *kapalı*
new *yeni*
old *eski*
cheap *ucuz*
expensive *pahalı*
money *para*

Places and things
airport *havaalanı*
bakery *fırın*
bank *banka*
barber *berber*
bay *körfez*
beach *plaj*
boarding house *pansiyon*
bookshop *kitapçı*

bus station *otogar*
butcher *kasap*
cake shop *pastane*
carpet shop *halı dükkanı*
castle *kale*
cigarettes *sigara*
cigars *puro*
city *şehir*
dry cleaner *kuru temizleyici*
fish shop *balıkçı*
florist *çiçekçi*
fountain *çeşme*
greengrocer *manav*
grocer *bakkal*
harbor *liman*
hairdressing salon *kuaför*
hotel *otel*
island *ada*
jewelry shop *kuyumcu*
lake *göl*
leather shop *deri dükkanı*
marina *yat limanı*
market *çarsı*
mosque *cami*
mountain *dağ*
museum *müze*
palace *saray*
pharmacy *eczane*
photographic shop *fotoğrafçı*
police station *karakol*
post office *postane*
restaurant *lokanta*
school *lise*
sea *deniz*
small street *sokak*
square *meydan*
street *caddesi*
theater *tiyatro*
toilet *tuvalet*
town center *şehir merkezi*
train station *gar*
Turkish bath *hamam*
village *köy*

On the road
highways *karayolları*
map *harita*
car *otomobil*
bus *otobüs*
gasoline *benzin*
regular *normal*
super *süper*
oil *yağ*

service station *benzin istasyonu, petrol ofisi*
engine *motor*
tire *lâstik*
battery *akü*
headlight *far*
brakes *frenler*
spark plugs *bujiler*
speed *hız*
accident *kaza*
CAUTION *DIKKAT*
SLOW *YAVAŞ*
STOP *DUR*

In the hotel
room *oda*
single room *tek yataklı*
double room (twin beds) *çift yataklı*
double bed *iki kişilik yatak*
bath *banyo*
room with bath *banyolu oda*
shower *duş*
room with shower *duşlu oda*
hot water *sıcak su*
soap *sabun*
towel *havlu*
toilet paper *tuvalet kağıdı*
laundry *çamaşır*
key *anahtar*

In the post office (PTT)
stamp *pul*
letter *mektup*
envelope *zarf*
postcard *kartpostal*
parcel *koli*
air mail *uçak ile*
special delivery *ekspres*
registered *kayıtlı*
money order *havale*
telephone token *jeton*

In emergencies
hospital *hastane*
doctor *doktor*
nurse *hemşire*
dentist *diş hekimi*
sick, ill *hasta*
pain, ache *ağrı*
fever *ateş*
allergic to *alerjisi olmak*
toothache *diş ağrısı*
help *imdat*
first aid *ilk yardım*

In restaurants
meal *yemek*
breakfast *kahvaltı*
lunch *öğle yemeği*
dinner *akşam yemeği*
menu *yemek listesi*
waiter *garson*
bill, check *hesap*
plate *tabak*
glass *bardak*
knife *bıçak*
fork *çatal*
spoon *kaşık*

napkin *peçete*
salt *tuz*
pepper *biber*
sugar *şeker*
bread *ekmek*
butter *tereyağ*
water *su*
mineral water *maden suyu*
lemonade *limonata*
fruit juice *meyva suyu*
milk *süt*
ice *buz*
coffee *kahve*
Turkish coffee *Türk kahvesi*
unsweetened *sade*
slightly sweetened *orta*
sweet *şekerli*

tea *çay*
beer *bira*
wine *şarap*
red wine *kırmızı şarap*
white wine *beyaz şarap*
gin *cin*
vodka *votka*
whisky *viski*
cheers *şerefe*
bon appetit *afiyet olsun*
appetizers *meze*
cheese *peynir*
olives *zeytin*
pickles *turşu*
soup *çorba*
broth (mutton) *et suyu*
tomato soup *domates çorbası*
fish soup *balık çorbası*
red lentil soup *mercimek çorbası*
vegetable soup *sebze çorbası*
chicken soup *tavuk çorbası*
salad *salata*
Russian salad *Rus salatası, Amerikan salatası!*
mixed vegetable salad *çoban salatası*
mashed eggplant salad *patlıcan salatası*
green salad *yeşil salata*
meat *et*
beef *sığır*
lamb *kuzu*
mutton *koyun*
veal *dana*
chicken *tavuk*
roast chicken *piliç*
turkey *hindi*
liver *ciğer*
kidney *böbrek*
beef steak *biftek*
rare *az pişmiş*
well done *iyi pişmiş*
lamb cutlet *kuzu pirzolası*
fish *balık*
anchovy *hamsi*
sardine *sardalya*
mussels *midye*
trout *alabalık*
red mullet *barbunya*
gray mullet *kefal*
turbot *kalkan*
bonito *palamut*
Aegean tuna *trança*
plaice *pisi*
sea bass *levrek*
swordfish *kılıç*

crab *yengeç*
lobster *ıstakoz*
squid *kalamar*
vegetables *sebze*
eggplant *patlıcan*
artichokes *enginar*
beans *fasulye*
peas *bezelye*
spinach *ıspanak*
carrots *havuç*
cabbage *lahana*
tomatoes *domates*
potatoes *patates*
onions *soğan*
rice *pilav*
fruit *meyva*
apple *elma*
orange *portakal*
peach *şeftali*
pear *armut*
pomegranate *nar*
watermelon *karpuz*
strawberries *çilek*
raspberries *ahududu*
banana *muz*
grapes *üzüm*
dessert *tatlı*
ice cream *dondurma*
pastry *pasta*
cake *kek*
cheesecake *peynir tatlısı*
chocolate pudding *krem şokola*
rice pudding *sütlaç*
Turkish Delight *lokum*

In case you get lucky
I love you *seni seviyorum*
...very much *seni çok seviyorum*

Recommended Reading

AKURGAL, EKREM. *Ancient Civilizations and Ruins of Turkey.* Tirk Tarih Kurumu, Ankara 1983.

ASLANAPA, OKTAY. *Turkish Art and Architecture.* Faber and Faber, London 1971.

BARBER, NOEL. *The Sultans.* Simon and Schuster, New York 1973.

BEAN, GEORGE. *Aegean Turkey* (1966), *Turkey's Southern Shore* (1968), Turkey Beyond the Maeander (1971), and *Lycia* (1978). Ernest Benn, London.

BROSNAHAN, TOM. *Turkey: A Travel Survival Kit.* Lonely PLanet Publications, Berkeley, California 1988.

EREN, NESET. *The Delights of Turkish Cooking.* Redhouse Press, Istanbul 1988.

GOODWIN, GODFREY. *A History of Ottoman Architecture.* Thames and Hudson, London 1971.

HERODOTUS. *The Histories.* Tr. Aubrey de Slincourt. Penguin, 1985.

HILLS, DENNIS. *My Travels in Turkey.* Allen and Unwin, London 1964.

HOTHAM, DAVID. *The Turks.* John Murray, London 1972.

KINROSS, LORD. *Atatürk: The Rebirth of a Nation.* Weidenfeld and Nicolson, London 1964; *The Ottoman Centuries,* Jonathan Cape, London 1977.

LEWIS, BERNARD. The *Emergence of Modern Turkey.* Oxford University Press 1968.

LEWIS, RAPHAELA. *Everyday Life in Ottoman Turkey.* Batsford, London 1971.

MANGO, ANDREW. *Turkey.* Thames and Hudson, London 1968.

MARDIN, YUSUF. *Colloquial Turkish.* Routledge and Kegan Paul, London 1976.

MICHAUD, ROLAND AND SABRINA. *Turkey.* Thames and Hudson, London 1968.

PETERS, F. E. *The Harvest of Hellenism.* Simon and Schuster, New York 1970.

RICE, TAMARA TALBOT. *The Seljuks in Asia Minor.* Thames and Hudson, London 1961.

STIRLING, PAUL. *Turkish Village.* Weidenfeld and Nicolson, London 1965.

SUMNER-BOYD, HILARY, and JOHN FREELY. *Strolling Through Istanbul.* Associated Book Publishers, London 1987.

WILLIAMS, GWYNN. *Eastarn Turkey: A Guide and History.* Faber and Faber, London 1972.

XENOPHON. *The Persian Expedition.* Tr. Rex Warner. Penguin, 1967.

Photo Credits

Quick Reference A–Z Guide to Places and Topics of Interest with Listed Accommodation, Restaurants and Useful Telephone Numbers

Illustrated Blueprints to Travel Enjoyment

INSIDER'S GUIDES

The Guides That Lead